Destined to Serve

From the Queen City to Daejeon
and the Presidency of a Korean University

John E. Endicott

Destined to Serve
From the Queen City to Daejeon
And the Presidency of a Korean University

ISBN: 9781713359425

Photo Credits
All photos are from the author's private collection, except those on pages 152 (bottom), 158 (bottom), 160 (bottom), 161 (bottom), 245, 251, and 252 which are courtesy of the Woosong Education Foundation and page 253 (bottom), which is courtesy of the USO.

Also by the Author:

Japan's Nuclear Option: Political, Technical, and Strategic Factors
The Politics of East Asia: China, Japan and Korea, with William R. Heaton
U.S. Foreign Policy: History, Process, and Policy, with Daniel S. Papp and Loch Johnson
Regional Security Policy, with Patrick Garrity and Richard Goetze

Cover Design by Robert Williams

Edited by Jeffrey Miller

The views and opinions expressed in this book are those of the author and do not reflect those of the United States government and its various agencies or Woosong University.

DEDICATION

For Mitchie and Dad

TABLE OF CONTENTS

Part IV: The Woosong-SolBridge-Endicott College Years

Introduction

At the outset, I would like to make it very clear, that most of what has been accomplished in the 83 years I have been lucky to be on this planet was largely the result of having the incredible luck to meet Mitsuyo Kobayashi in 1958 and convincing her to become my wife. But there are others as without their involvement, I would not be writing this at all—Mom and Dad, for example. My sister was also so very important to this narrative and it will be my pleasure to introduce her as well. They, of course, are my American family and will be first to be introduced; there is another key figure who can best be described as my Korean mentor, the Chairman of the Woosong Education Foundation, Dr. Kim Sung-kyung, who crafted the opportunities of the past thirteen years here at Woosong University. You will have to wait until later in this story to meet him; please be patient.

First, a bit about my father, Charles Lafayette Endicott, who was born on December 25, 1901, on the plains of Kansas in a one-room cabin near the city of Pittsburg, down in the southeast corner of Kansas. His father was a farmer, who in the early years of the 20th Century took up the opportunity to homestead 160 acres in northern New Mexico. My father was very young at the time, perhaps five or six years old. They went as a family—taking a railroad flatbed for the first portion of the trip and then going from the rail line by covered wagon to find their future.

Somewhere in the panhandle of New Mexico—now I am remembering to the best of my ability—they came across a beautiful green valley and immediately fell in love with the location. Granddad, Lewis Endicott, registered his claim to 160 acres and started the

1

process of improving the land. (If he did "improve the land" by building a house and live there five years, the total 160 acres would be his.) Since the land was prairie, there were few trees, requiring the house be made out of sod—the first five or so inches of soil on the surface. Blocks were cut from the ground and a hole, perhaps four feet deep was dug the size of a large room—big enough for a kitchen and one bed. The sod blocks or bricks were then assembled around the hole and a house went up. Because wood was so scarce in such an area, my grandfather would have used the wood in the wagon to build his roof, doorframe, door, and perhaps one window. In any event, it afforded only a small shelter from the cold winters and very hot summers.

My father told the story that the first time they used the fireplace to warm the sod house, all the insects living happily in the sod believed it was spring and started coming out into the room. His job was to take care of the living wall decorations. He never mentioned if they became part of a protein-loaded soup or not. In any case, times were very tough for all at that time for the lovely green valley had become scorched from the lack of rain. That rain did not come eventually causing the death of one child and all their cattle. After two years it was time to return to Kansas and leave New Mexico behind—forever.

So, my father really grew up in Kansas on a dairy farm near Pittsburg. He suffered an eye injury as a young boy as they were harvesting feed for the cattle. That kept him out of World War I and of course, World War II. After high school, he went to Pittsburg State University which was a teaching college for two years, and began teaching himself in high schools in various parts of the state. Before doing that however, he sat down with his father who wanted him to take over the farm. It must have been an interesting conversation as Granddad really wanted him to stay. My father finally offered a deal. "Buy a tractor and I'll stay."

As my father told the story, Granddad looked at my father long and hard, and didn't say a word until..."and what am I to do with my mules?"

The mules, it seemed, were very high up on Granddad's order of priorities. He hated horses and talked about the time one got out of the corral and came upon fresh apples placed on the ground to dry. Well, he used to say, "That stupid horse ate 'like a horse' filled up his belly and then went over and took a drink. Ka blewey! That horse was dead. No siree, a mule would never do that—they are smart and they have been my friends."

That was the beginning of Dad's teaching career. He went off teaching to earn money and then returning to State to finish his teaching degree in Industrial Arts—things like wood shop, electric shop, and industrial drawing (blue prints, etc.) were his main fields, and he loved classroom teaching. He turned down several opportunities to be a principal in a high school as that would have taken him out of the classroom where his heart was.

As I write this introduction, it has been 33 years since my father, passed away, and I have had some time to understand what he did for me, especially, even though he impacted so many other people as a teacher and a deacon in the Price Hill Baptist Church in Cincinnati. As I look back, perhaps my almost 30 years in the Air Force was a tribute to Dad who did not serve in either World War I or World War II. I know that hurt him significantly, as it came up in conversations on many occasions. I think because of that we went to many activities that involved the military. But it was the air arm that really interested my father, and we would drive to Lunken Airport in Cincinnati when we still had a car—just prior to the beginning of World War II and watch airplanes take off from an overlook near the end of the runway. Then, of course, Alice, my sister, only wanted to fly for her birthday in 1941, and Dad and "Sitty" (my sister's nickname) took me along. I was four and would turn five in August. Then in that same year, he sent my mother, Sitty and me to Kansas by TWA, another trip by air while I was still a young lad.

Then came the war, and Dad, in his school woodworking shop at Olyer Junior High School, made aircraft models used by pilots for aircraft recognition in the war. Any models cracked or not acceptable found their way into my eager hands. After the war, we walked from our home in Price Hill to the new Kentucky based airport for Cincinnati. That was a hike that involved crossing the river by ferry and trudging up and down the hills that make the Ohio River Valley at the bend in Cincinnati, appear like the Rhine Valley in Germany. Once to the airport, it was looking up at planes flying overhead or displays on special days. Gradually, I was becoming an airplane enthusiast, and my dad was largely my coach.

Then he went to Japan for a year in 1946 and came home with tales and melted glass from the bombing in Hiroshima. (I don't know how many times I held that glass in my hands and looked at it. Be careful if you shake hands with the author!) He also was given the rank of Captain for the work he did in Japan, and he looked great in a uniform. In 1950 when I was 13, he treated me as a man and gave me the right to take part in a family decision to go to England as the war in Korea had engulfed the peninsula. Mom and I both voted in favor of the family going to England, so Dad could accept the Fulbright he had been awarded. It turned out to be the most meaningful year I have ever lived. (Can you imagine that as a result, I saw Churchill debate Attlee, have Churchill pass my table by two feet or so, take part in the opening of the Festival of Britain, and compete at the White City Stadium representing Paddington Technical College High School.) Can't get any more meaningful than that!

Years later, when I met my wife to be in Japan, he took a positive stance that I can never forget. And during my 28 years in the Air Force, he was standing by the phone to listen to my adventures and give advice when asked.

Whenever asked who the most important man in my life was, I answer "my father." You can see I still, after 33 years, miss him very much.

Part I
The Early Years

ONE

The Cincinnati Kid

With apologies to the 1963 novel and 1965 film, this story has nothing to do with poker nor does it star Steve McQueen or have supporting actors like Edward G. Robinson, Ann Margret, or Karl Malden—all favorites of mine. This is the story of my life, and in 1965, I was not in a comfortable movie theater in Cincinnati; instead, I was in Vietnam, spending half of that year assigned to the Military Assistance Group in Nha Trang, Central Vietnam and the other half with the 522nd VNAF Fighter Squadron in Saigon, now Ho Chi Minh City. Something in that last sentence tells you about the ultimate fate of my time in Vietnam, but not at all about the totality of the experience—the impact it would have on me. However, I'm jumping ahead of where I wish to begin this story—almost thirty years to be exact—and my ever favorite city, Cincinnati.

* * *

I was born in August 1936, and so I was told, about nine-thirty in the morning. "Just in time for Sunday school," as my mom would always say. Growing up in The Great Depression, times were still very tough in the old Queen City (the nickname given to the city, which, one hundred years earlier, was symbolic of the country's westward expansion; perhaps, given the fact that amidst the wildness of the times, Cincinnati was seen as "cultured" and refined). The depression was still very much with us and my birth receipt (literally a "receipt" given at the hospital when a child was born indicating payment for delivery costs; not the same as a birth certificate)—although I never saw it—had a stamp in big bold letters, "Depression Baby." What this receipt announced was that the Endicott Family was entitled to a one hundred dollar "rebate," if that is the right word, and, in 1936, that one hundred dollars was mighty nice to have in those times. The money was supposedly an incentive to have children as folks were just not having children in the late thirties and 1936 had just about the lowest birthrate in those dark days.

Looking back, the low birthrate was actually beneficial, as the competition was really not keen and jobs for our age group just always seemed available. (Not so in places like South Korea where today's low birthrate has created many social and economic problems). Of course, one could not be too choosy. Growing up, I delivered newspapers for the Thursday advertiser <i>Price Hill Journal</i>, worked as a clerk in Duwel's Hardware Store, ushered in the Westwood Movie Theater, and finally, when going to college, worked at one of the Hamilton County Parks, in the summer as an assistant greens' keeper in the morning and a "roustabout" in the afternoons. (A "roustabout" did anything that needed to be done from harvesting bales of hay for the riding horses, painting signage for the park, cleaning out septic tanks, and emptying the trash after major holidays like the 4th of July and Labor Day.) What I remember most vividly about that job was cutting the greens every other day at six in the morning. That was the best time of the day for me—especially those mornings when the red foxes that lived near the greens would come out to greet me—jumping around and having a great time, but staying a comfortable ten feet away. On the days we didn't have to cut the greens, we still had to wipe the dew off them which meant I still had a chance to meet my four-legged friends. That job was a lot of fun, that's for sure.

But again, I find myself jumping far too much ahead in this story. As a youngster in Cincinnati, I was able to enjoy life lying in front of the fireplace and listening to FDR, giving one of his Fireside Chats. Of course, I don't recall any specifics, save for once when he was discussing a coming Christmas (I have always been attentive about Christmas), and he wanted to say something about how we should spend our money. Across the airwaves, FDR's calm and steady voice gave Americans something they needed to hear. In those days, hardly anyone had much money to spend on presents, but our president did have some advice. He said something like, "When you do buy your presents, buy socks in one store, shirts in another, and pants in a third. That way you could give everyone a bit of your business."

Growing up during this time was not easy, but folks seemed to get by the best they could. Remember, and this may come as a shock to younger readers, television was still in its infancy having only just been invented (1927), and radio was our main form of entertainment (going to the movies was a close second). In fact, people would gather around the radio and listen to the news and other radio programs the same way that folks today gather around the television. Radios were a lot bigger then. I still remember the one we had in our house (it was a Zenith and about the size of a television console). Newspapers were the main source of information, and my family took two: one with morning delivery and another delivered in the late afternoon. My favorite was the *Cincinnati Times-Star,* and admittedly my preference was based on the comics included. There's something to be said about sitting down with a newspaper over the breakfast table or in the evening after supper. I must admit that I still love reading the comic sections of today's newspapers and can't wait for the Sunday e-mail edition (*Atlanta Journal and Constitution*) that arrives around 9:00 PM on Sunday night, Korean time.

Every night at dinner we would tune in to Lowell Thomas and his delivery of the day's news. He was a classic newspaper reporter who had traveled extensively and clearly had his finger on the pulse of the nation. By the late 1930s and early 1940s, he had become one of the foremost American newscasters. My initial love for politics and international affairs I am sure was helped along by this gentleman's deep melodic voice. Truly, he covered the important news well. I never had to worry about passing the current events tests that often came our way as I got into the upper grades of Carson Elementary School.

One of my earliest memories of this time, at least one of a political nature that still stands out in my mind, was changing the way we saluted the American flag before the outbreak of World War II. Europe in early 1940 had just witnessed the 1939 invasion of Poland by Nazi Germany. The universal salute to hail the leader of Germany, Adolf Hitler, was an outstretched arm with the palm of the hand facing downward. It had come synonymous with the political furor happening in Germany itself and the events generally that had drastically impacted all of Europe. We also used an outstretched arm when we saluted the flag, but with our palms facing upward—until pressure mounted in the U.S. to change our salute to the flag.

One morning, as we prepared to salute the flag and say the Pledge of Allegiance, my teacher, Ms. Buhrer, informed us that there would be a change. She noted how we all loved our flag and our country and that putting our hands over our hearts would show how we loved America, even more. So from that day on, we saluted the flag and said the pledge with our hands over our heart. It was a far cry from what was happening across the Atlantic. Something we would find out soon enough with the attack on Pearl Harbor and America's entry into the war.

The strongest memories that I have of those early days were memories of war and things related to war. You might not believe it, but I do have memories of Pearl Harbor. I was five at the time, so it's not really that hard for me to remember those dark days. Without question, life as we knew it changed forever from that day on. Whereas today younger generations might use the 9-11 tragedy as a benchmark, for my generation, it was the attack on Pearl Harbor. One of these memories I have at this time predates December 1941, but it is connected to the upcoming war with Germany and Japan. It was the day my dad took me to the Cincinnati Reds baseball game during the 1941 World Series, which was all the more special because it was our first time to attend a ballgame together. To this day, I clearly remember the red, white, and blue bunting hung all around the stadium. There was another memory from that day that had nothing to do with baseball, which foreshadowed what was about to happen. My dad bought me the last metal toy that I had until the war was over. Back then, most toys were made of metal or die-cast aluminum; once America found itself in the war, many of those toys were no longer manufactured with the metal being needed for the war effort. Believe it or not, the toy my father bought for me was an aluminum Graff Zeppelin with Nazi markings on the tail! Well, it was before the war, and it was Cincinnati—at that time a very German city.

(My father, who was an industrial arts teacher at the time, really wanted to serve, but in 1941, he was too old for the war. He had one eye that was pretty bad due to an accident harvesting hay when he was a boy in Kansas, which also would have made him 4-F—meaning that he couldn't serve. Sometimes I think my decision to join the Air Force was in part for my father to serve vicariously through my service.)

Once America entered the war, one of the first lines I can remember lining up in was to get our Ration Books. During the war, ration books were used to apportion all sorts of things from gasoline, tires, sugar, meat, and so forth. We had ration books, and soon we had War Bond Books (which were used to "finance" the cost of the war). After the war started, as a way to take extra money out of circulation and make everybody feel a part of the war effort, major war bond drives took place. In the case of school children, we brought our dimes once a week—I believe it was Monday each week—and individually we went up to the teacher's desk and gave our dime. She, in turn, would give us a stamp which we put into our small war bond books. Once you got several pages filled up, you could put one book aside and start a new one. Each book was worth twenty dollars, but you had to wait some time before cashing them in. (I still have mine. Guess it might be time to cash them in!)

The war affected people's daily lives in many small ways with sacrifices and other adjustments to our daily routines. Our family life was quite impacted during the winter of 1941 shortly after Pearl Harbor when my father forgot to do one of the most essential steps in preparing for an Ohio winter—put anti-freeze in the car. He just forgot. (It wasn't as bad as a friend I had later, who, when his father told him to "put the anti-freeze in the car," put it on the floor in the back seat—resulting in a cracked (engine) block several days later.) My father just was too busy. He taught junior high students during the day and adults at night at Olyer School at the base of Price Hill. He usually got home late and was just dead tired. One morning after a particularly hard freeze—we had frost on the windows inside the house when we awoke in those days—he went to start the car and broke the block.

I can still hear him now talking to one of the Sieve Brothers who owned the Plymouth Car Dealership on the phone and rejecting—with words that I truly did not understand at the time—the $60.00 offered for our 1934 Plymouth sedan. Well, we did not have to worry about gas and tire rationing, but our life changed fundamentally as we turned to a wartime experience with streetcars and primitive buses. (I really don't have anything against buses as such, but in the 1940s, they were underpowered and in the summer could only get three-quarters of the way up the hills before overheating and spouting steam like a geyser. Many a day we would suffer such a calamity and have to walk to the streetcar routes several blocks away. What I didn't understand in those days was even the beer trucks would suffer the same fate. Thus, we frequently saw powerful horses pulling beer wagons up the hills in and around Cincinnati. Now that was serious.)

The way that the outbreak of the war affected people in Cincinnati was much the same, I assume, all over the Midwest. However, the impact of the war had some "special moments" as our city had been settled by many Germans over the years. Our neighbors were the Helmer's, McSurley's, Meyer's, Reineck's, Schlichtee's, and Schwartz's and just about everyone spoke German to their grandparents. In fact, on hot summer nights, everyone sat outside on the porch and sipped iced tea or ate homemade lime or lemon sherbets. Before America's entry into the war, we sometimes could clearly hear Hitler's booming/shrill voice coming from our neighbors' radios. In those early days before December, there was much support for Germany and the economic recovery that had occurred, so the German *Bund* (in English, association) was pretty active in the city. When war broke out, the German leadership of the city was interned in the top seven floors of the best hotel in Cincinnati—the Carew Tower. They were held for some time but released soon after. In any event, it was a far cry from what was happening on the West Coast where Japanese were being placed in "relocation camps" to begin a hardship that resulted from several factors, not excluding racism.[1]

In our own case, we benefited from living on a street that abutted a large undeveloped field. Actually, the Elsesser Family of German origin, who were major investors in Cincinnati and owners of hotels and restaurants, at one time owned the entire city block and had donated the property to the immediate west of their block for the construction of St. William Catholic Church. When war broke out, the Elsesser's opened this big undeveloped field for all the families

---

[1] For the historians reading this book, please note that I made quite an effort to verify this story, but could not find a reliable source. So, please be advised that it was what we believed at the time, but it may not have actually happened. Wars and rumors go hand in hand.

surrounding it to have their own Victory Garden. It was wonderful! Each family had a plot about 300-400 feet square, and these plots became the source of wonderful fresh vegetables to be eaten and canned throughout the summer and fall. We grew green onions, tomatoes, lettuce, radishes, potatoes, pole beans, and bush beans, and I learned to love the land for what it could do for those who nurtured it.

My father, who left the farm at age twenty, had a religious attachment to the garden. As we placed onion sets in the ground, at times, he would gently pick up the soil and say, "This can take care of you, if you take care of it." Actually, my father had a homesteading experience with his father as a very young boy, going from Kansas to New Mexico and claiming 160 acres of land in a lush green valley in the Pan Handle of New Mexico. After building a sod house (a house made from blocks or bricks of "sod" cut from the earth; the long prairie grass roots were what kept the sod "together") and spending two winters waiting for the rain, they finally returned to Kansas less one baby girl and all their cattle. When I talk to students especially in China, I point out that America's streets were never paved with gold and only one generation away was my father in a one-room cabin in Kansas waking up with snow on the covers. To his dying days in the cold of winter, he would often look outside at night and weep. While there might not have been any streets of gold, America would one day earn its "place in the sun" by working its way to prosperity.

Another way our lives changed during the war was the termination of the rites of spring rituals that had been performed by young children for many, many years, I'm sure. In this, I am referring to the welcoming of spring that was part of our school's activities in May of each year. Traditions such as dancing around the May Pole were stopped at least at Carson Elementary School soon after the war began (the last time I remembered participating in this annual ritual was in 1942). I can remember the boys would surround the pole interspersed with girls, and we would each have one of two colored ribbons streaming from the top of the twenty or so foot tall pole. The music started, and the boys went in one direction and the girls in the opposite. The music I remember was "Pop Goes the Weasel," but I am sure similar upbeat songs would have sufficed. We wore short pants and the girls pretty flowing skirts as we went streaming by each other to the applause of our parents standing or sitting on the sidelines. As most happy things came to an end with the war, I remember only once participating in the school May Day festivities.

As the war ground on, some degree of civility was lost to the cause of national defense. Metal of any shape or size was a valued commodity, and scrap drives for the war were periodically staged. However, there was one that stands out in my mind as an indicator as to how we can change in times of war. All during the war, we received our news by reading the newspaper, going to the local movie house (The Sunset Theater), and watching a feature film preceded by previews of coming attractions, cartoons, and a newsreel—usually *Pathe News of the World*. However, on Saturdays, there were special showings for kids that added a serial or an adventure story told in segments, one for each Saturday. One that I remember was *Don Winslow of the Coast Guard*. He was always saving the nation at the last moment from devious plots and schemes hatched by the enemy— Japanese or German subversives. There were many, and all stressed the national crisis we were witnessing. One week, the papers and radio announced a special scrap drive at our nearby Sunset Theater. It was really special as one pound of metal scrap would get you free admittance.

My family had just finished some work on our coal-burning furnace, and we had some especially heavy parts that would guarantee a free movie. Off we went. Actually, I put my contribution in my red wagon and pulled it the three blocks up the road to the intersection of Sunset and Glenway Avenues. As I approached, I will never in my life forget the writing on the marquee that greeted all: "Today: Bring a Pound of Scrap; Kill a Dirty Jap!" As much as it pains me to recall this event, it represented the hysteria which gripped the nation following the attack on Pearl Harbor. After the war, of course, things would change dramatically, and we same residents of Price Hill were leaders in the rebuilding of relations between America and Japan.

One interesting thing happened after the war, which became indicative of the role that America would soon play in Europe and Asia. While we had contributed to the war effort in earnest by buying War Bonds, when we returned to school after Labor Day in 1945 (at this point, I was in the 5th grade and still at Carson Elementary School with Mr. Jacob as our Principal), the contributions to the war bond effort continued. However, at some point in that first year after the war was over, as we all expected to give our dime to the teacher we were met with a startling announcement: "Class, since the war is over, we will no longer collect dimes for war bonds. Instead, please bring in contributions of pencils, pens (no ballpoint pens as yet) writing paper, and easy books (primary readers) written in English for beginners. We will make a package to send to our sister school in Japan."

This I believe was a conscious effort on the part of some individuals who wanted to do things differently after World War II that we hadn't done after World War I. We didn't want to fail in our responsibility. I would like to think that this was indicative of how America evolved and matured as a more benevolent world leader after World War II. Even when my father went to Japan from 1946 to 1947 to teach GIs industrial skills, it was part of this international civic and social responsibility (something that we can be proud of at SolBridge). Without question, as the movement for the United Nations gained momentum, we became activists for peace. My red wagon that had carried scrap to defeat the Japanese now became a "float" in parades calling for support for the United Nations.

Especially in the fifth grade, I can recall many a lecture by Ms. Butler about the need for the United Nations—as we read our weekly current affairs newspaper that was published nationally—so we would not repeat our mistake with the League of Nations. It might sound a bit "over the top," but at least one student, me, was caught up in the need for some international organization. Convinced almost daily as we ate dinner listening to Lowell Thomas on the radio—America was still needed beyond our shores.

This kind of advice, I should add, was not always received with enthusiasm by my parents. They were, it is probably the best way to put this, Taft Republicans. Cincinnati was the home of the Taft Family, and President William Howard Taft was the champion of a family that had a long history of involvement and leadership in and around Cincinnati and Ohio. Senator Robert A. Taft of Ohio, also a Cincinnati boy, was a "true conservative." Certainly, after the war had begun, he responded with support for the war effort, however, how long would this have to continue? Support for China was a given, as Generalissimo Chang Kai Shek and his lovely wife were defending the Christian family values of a "new China" against the Godless communist armies springing up all over China. That was one thing, but maybe that was enough. He was not isolationist, but proactively cautious about our involvement overseas.

After Japan surrendered, my father responded to a call from the Army for industrial arts teachers to go to Japan to teach GIs (the term used to describe the ordinary American soldier that came from the term "Government Issue"). I will never forget the call. For some reason, it came late at night. Maybe it was "late" as I was already in bed, but dad took the call. It was from Washington, and on the same phone that he had cussed Sieve Dodge and Plymouth Autos, he excitedly learned his application to go to Japan had been accepted.

(I have been waiting all my life for that kind of call, but actually, if I think for a moment I did receive it but turned it down. Talk about a tease—I was offered the Japan portfolio in the International Security Affairs [ISA] section of the Pentagon in 1977 but turned it down so Charlene our daughter could graduate from high school. Had we accepted that our life would have gone in a completely different direction—do we ever know?)

Having accepted the Army position in Japan left me, the senior (only) male in the Endicott family in Cincinnati. Mom, my sister, Alice, and I were now in Cincinnati, and Dad was off to Japan. I was ten at the time, so it didn't make for a very big male of the household, but certain jobs around the house now fell to me. The one that immediately comes to mind was the stoking of the coal and wood-burning furnace that heated the entire house. We lived in a two-story home that had a full basement. The basement was used to wash clothes on Monday— that was the traditional day to wash your clothes—and to store food that was "canned" at home and used throughout the winter: peaches from our trees, tomatoes from our garden, cucumbers that we turned into sweet pickles, and grape jam made from Concord grapes. It was also where we stored sacks of potatoes that we usually bought in a hundred pound lots or grew in our garden. The most important function as far as my stoking of the furnace was concerned was the massive furnace with pipes leading to each room above (looking somewhat like an octopus) and the coal bin—a room set aside especially for the storage of coal that was usually delivered one or two tons at a time. Coal was always dumped on the street in front of your house, and it was my job to get it into the coal bin as rapidly as possible so not to become troublesome for traffic—including buses—that used St. William Avenue.

Thus, one of the main jobs I had was "superintendent in charge of heat." There were three main times of the day when I had to attend to the fire in the furnace: upon waking up in the morning; after coming home from school; and just before taking a bath and going to bed. The house with that system stayed cozy and warm until about two o'clock in the morning. Then the fire died out, and there was no more heat until the fire was rekindled in the morning. Did it get cold? In the depth of winter, one would get out of bed in the morning and look through frost and ice that had built up on the inside of the windows overnight. That's how cold it got. So, getting the fire started was critical in beginning the day. I don't want to claim sole responsibility for that job as my sister helped out as well as Mom, but I certainly remember that aspect of missing my father.

Dad, in Japan, really enjoyed his work and built up a very credible training facility to teach GIs how to build houses. He liked it so much that he applied for a second year to bring his family to join him in Tokyo. The Federal Government was just fine with that, but the Cincinnati Public School System said: "One year is enough. Stay if you wish, but lose your tenure with our system." That, of course, played out over many months until my father decided to return home. In the meantime, as a fifth-grader, I learned a valuable lesson in strategic planning. Knowing that I would leave Carson and go to Japan, I was not worried at all about sixth grade. Admittedly, my attention to studies dropped off considerably. When the word came that indeed I would be facing Carson teachers for the sixth grade, it was too late. I had collected more Ds—the grade just above the dreaded failing F—than ever in my academic life. Thus, when Dad returned, and I returned to Carson, it was with my banners not flying too high. I really learned a wonderful lesson from that experience, which I hope my young readers will never repeat.

One of the immediate positive aspects of my father's return was the installation of a gas furnace and hearing his tales of things Japanese. As a teacher, my father was always willing to share his experiences with anyone so interested. Often I would accompany him as he spoke to men's groups all around Cincinnati. In fact, I still have his slide show that went with his lecture. I could probably give that lecture today but still would rather hear it from Dad.

In a sense, if I try to assign moments in my life when lifelong interests were generated, these talks about Japan would rank very high. Pearl Harbor got my attention and of course, the entire war effort, but my father spending a year and learning to love the defeated enemy taught me so much about our fellow men. One thing is for certain, it definitely opened my eyes and helped me to view the world differently.

One thing that hadn't worked out for me was now that my father had returned, I had to stick it out at Carson Elementary School. I got through the sixth grade, and then I turned my attention to becoming the Captain of the School Patrol. It might not sound like such a big deal now, but when one is in the sixth grade, it certainly was! I was in command of the entire group of students who manned the various intersections to make sure our enthusiastic drivers actually stopped at the crosswalks and obeyed the law. It was the first of many "command" roles that I would have in life and one which reminded me that many valuable "life" lessons are learned in elementary school. It was a revelation that so many people did not respect the law or the safety of the children heading to school every day on foot. Perhaps I took my "command" a bit too seriously, as I understand that upon moving on to Western Hills High School (with a Junior High embedded), they discontinued the unit. I formed some great friendships during that year, and my best friend Robert "Bob" Marmer and I worked together. (As an ophthalmologist many years later, he actually saved my life, but that's another tease for later revelation.)

As I began the seventh grade at Western Hills High, I experienced another one of life's indoctrinations, this time, my first introduction to organized bullying. It was actually a ritual where the senior boys terrorized the underclass boys with all sorts of harassment that included putting us on top of drinking fountains and turning on the water, which might pale in comparison to some of the bullying today, but were terrorizing just the same. We learned how to spot roving seniors looking for prey, and soon, we were handling the challenges as if they did not exist. (This, of course, helped me greatly in understanding hostile intent body language. That has been useful throughout my life.)

Western Hills High School was a very big high school and very beautiful. It had a great music program, football, and baseball teams, and now has the claim to fame of being the school that baseball legend Pete Rose attended (he graduated in 1960). I am much older than Pete, but later, as a quirk of fate, his wife looked at the house we owned in Cincinnati as my wife was preparing to join me in Japan after my one-year tour in Vietnam. Whatever the reason, we did not rent to the Roses, but when Mitchie (my wife) told me that the Roses' almost rented our house, it thrilled me.

Thus, you can see, I am a baseball "nut." I love baseball and all during this time at Western Hills—as well as before—I probably spent as much time playing baseball as I should have spent studying. As most young boys growing up in America's Midwest, I was fascinated with baseball. During summer vacation, I was probably on the baseball diamond eight to ten hours a day. My dream at the time was to become a famous baseball player, and upon retiring from baseball, go into politics. I can remember telling the neighbors on St. William Avenue that line, as I was really hoping to realize it. Although politics may have taken a backseat to my love for baseball, my political leanings were toward the right, the same as my parents. We discussed politics every night around the dinner table. We read the newspapers, often together, and we listened to Lowell Thomas on the radio together. I can remember when Thomas Dewey defeated the Cincinnati favorite, Robert Taft (known as Mr. Republican) for the nomination for president—actually several times, in 1944 and 1948. We were devastated that a New York liberal had eliminated the Taft challenge, but I was even more distraught when Dewey had been trounced by first, FDR and then by the Vice President who became President on the death of FDR, Harry S. Truman. My parents both coming from Kansas had been watching Truman advance in Missouri politics ending up as a senator in Congress and then being picked as FDR's running mate in 1944. Shall I say they were "somewhat" critical of the man from Independence, Missouri, and were aghast at his elevation to the presidency after the death of FDR on April 12, 1945.

With my main interests alternating between baseball and politics and general Asian affairs after my father returned from Japan, the news of the North Korean attack on South Korea took us all by intense surprise. However, on the home front, another war raged. While it did not distract us from what was happening on the Korean peninsula, there were other "battles" that needed to be fought. In a sense, however, it came at a period when the family as a whole was somewhat "distracted" by the surprise marriage of my sister on her 18th birthday to her high school sweetheart. Alice married in Indiana, right next to Ohio, as marriage without parents' permission was possible upon reaching 18 there. "Sitty" became Mrs. Mills, and the nation went to war. Now I can write this with a smile, but back then our home was not as hot as it was along the 38th Parallel, but at times came pretty close.

It was right around this time, when a major opportunity for my father precipitated the marriage, as he had applied for one of the first Fulbright Exchange opportunities and won. Going to London for a year was not at the top of this couples' desires at the moment, and taking this bold step of marriage basically announced that she would remain in Cincinnati with Harold, and we would begin an adventure in London as a family of three.

The attack by the North, however, put everything on hold. Many in the United States, even the world, believed the attack by the North was only the prelude to a major attempt by the Soviet Union to invade Western Europe. Since China had just fallen in October 1949 into Communist hands, the communist threat was real, and many of our friends thought it foolhardy to go to Europe when the world was at the very edge of World War III. It was at this time that I received my first opportunity to be treated as an adult.

With all the talk about the possibility of South Korea becoming the catalyst for a new world war, my father decided to call a family meeting. Basically, one evening after dinner, Dad turned to the chance to go to London and the possibilities of being there when World War III broke out. He turned to Mom, and myself and said, "What do you think? Should we go or stay in Cincinnati?" And then he added, "I don't want to make this decision alone."

Mom responded first and thought it would be a wonderful chance to visit the land that both she and Dad had roots. Mom was a Campbell, with Inverness as a family starting point, and Dad, an Endicott, had kin who came from the midlands in England, possibly Dorset.

At this point, Dad turned to me and asked for my opinion. I was actually being asked to take part in a major family decision; I really felt he was saying to this 13-year-old boy, "Son, I really want your opinion." I really don't think I had any clear objective in wanting to go other than to take part in what could be a great adventure. It was something no one else did in those days (at least in Cincinnati), and I let Mom and Dad know that I was very much excited about the trip. For the first time in my life, I had been given a full vote in the family council and voted for going.

And, as you will see, it was the first of many defining moments in my life.

TWO

A Year in London

We arrived in Southampton via the SS *Washington*, in late August 1950; it was a beautiful passenger liner belonging to the United States Lines that had been built in the 1930s, served as a liner to Britain, France, and Germany, was turned into a troop ship during the war, and returned to cross-Atlantic service as a one-class ship after the war was over. It was fantastic for me as a young 14-year-old. With only one class, I could roam the entire ship, from stem to stern without being stopped by a ship steward telling me to get back to my assigned space. (I say this, as coming home a year later, we traveled on the *Queen Elizabeth* that very much had distinct zones for first, cabin, and "last" or tourist class travelers.)

In those days, there were no such things as roller bags. We used footlockers and steamer trunks that were massive. These were loaded and were not handled by one person. We were told, in advance, that England was still in the midst of food rationing, so you had better bring as much as you could. Thus, our steamer trunk was filled with Spam, powdered milk and eggs (try making an omelet with powdered eggs!), sugar, and other essential staples.

Our gear was put on the train for us, and we headed off for London—Paddington Station—and our destination on Oak Lane in the Hampstead Heath area of London. We did not realize it at the time, but that was a very selective area of London and not far from our home was that of Sir Hugh Gaitskell, the Chancellor of the Exchequer. Please do not be fooled or misled by my use of "home." Our home was actually the third floor (second floor in English usage) flat above the quarters of a very successful doctor from Harvey Street. We were to supply additional funding for the owners of the house who were, like all other inhabitants of the British Isles at that time, trying to get through the austerity period of British life. Rationing was severe, and life generally was dark, as London was trying to recover from the vast areas of destroyed houses and buildings. In parts of London, especially in the area near St. Paul's Cathedral, all that greeted one's eyes were cellars. The rubble was gone, but the construction or should I say reconstruction was just beginning.

When one thinks of the weather in London, they might conjure up an image of a grey, rainy, chilly day (sorry, London), and that's exactly what the weather was like as we reached our residence in the late afternoon. Although I was excited to be in London, one of the first things I did after I arrived was to search for a newspaper. You see, it was August and the baseball season back in America was coming to an end. I did not know what had happened to the Cincinnati Reds and had to find out. So, while moving in with our heavy trunks and other luggage, I asked our landlady where I could buy a newspaper with the latest baseball scores. The surprised look on her face was precious. After all, we're talking about a country where cricket, football (not the American kind), snooker and possibly racing rule…but baseball?

"Only an international newsstand would have such information, and that would be at Finchley Road Underground Station some distance away," she said, after getting over the initial shock of my question.

That was just fine for me. "Just give me directions," I said.

So, there I was, recently arrived in London, and I had already embarked on my first adventure. I think you already know what happened. I raced pell-mell to the underground station, bought the newspaper, turned to go home, and realized with a pain that I can still feel today, that I did not know my address, telephone number, landlady's name…nothing! Oh, how we learn in life, and I had just received a Ph.D. in paying attention!

It must have taken almost two hours to complete the matrix that I designed to retrace my initial steps. Mom and Dad were worried sick, as you can probably imagine (and so was I!), but upon returning I just said it took a long time. They were relieved, but I never told them how much I was too.

The first thing the next day was to "settle" me into a proper "school." I use the exact words that Mrs. Ford used. She was our guide and helpmate from the English Speaking Union, an organization very much involved in the exchange program which had brought my father to London. She would indeed be showing up throughout our year in England and was always a force for positive good. Mrs. Ford had taken the liberty of enrolling me in the London Polytechnic High School, and together with my father and Mrs. Ford, we went to meet the Head Master.

Although his name has slipped my memory over the years, what I do remember about the headmaster was that he reminded me of Henry the VIII. His advice and subsequent guidance made my year in England truly memorable. When the four of us sat down, the Headmaster asked some basic questions like, "How much Latin have you had?" "How much algebra?" and "What foreign languages do you speak?" And when it came to answering these questions, I could only respond—the same way that any schoolboy in the U.S. could respond—"We start that this year."

The headmaster smiled and looked at me. "John, for your own good, I am going to call a friend of mine and see what we can do."

His friend turned out to be the Headmaster of the Paddington Technical College High School in Paddington, a rather rough area of London at that time full of socialists, communists, and folks of the working class. Next to my father, however, he is treasured in my heart more than any other man. Headmaster John A. Hullett welcomed me that same afternoon and told me about the standards that I would have to meet and clothes I would have to wear as a student at his school. After my father and I left, we were abandoned by Mrs. Ford maybe because the area was a little too exciting for her. Mr. Hullett, however, called an emergency meeting of all the 200 boys of the school (I only learned of this as I was preparing to leave some ten months later) and laid down the law. Knowing the science to which bullying has been developed by British schoolboys, he announced that a Yank, John Endicott, was going to join the school and be assigned to Faraday House—one of four houses all students were assigned to—(just watch a Harry Potter movie again to get an idea of what it was like). "If anyone touches John, you will have me to deal with!" Truly it was the beginning of a relationship where his steady hand made sure that I would be exposed to all that is great and wonderful about Britain and its people.

(In a sense, he set the standard that I still try to reach for SolBridge and Woosong. When I left England in 1951, Mr. Hullett said, "Now, John, be an ambassador and tell your American friends all about Britain." I try to have all our students who come from over 60 nations of the world, return as ambassadors for South Korea, and, if possible, have a good feeling about the United States as well.)

While I settled into my new life in London, my father also settled into his life for the next year as an exchange teacher. Although the name of the school where my father taught industrial arts has slipped my memory, his English counterpart went to Cincinnati and Olyer Junior High School. One amusing back story to my father's year in London was that he had come from an industrial arts program with all these modern bandsaws, drill presses and the like, but that was not the case at this school where things were done the old-fashioned, traditional way. I have often wondered what my father's English counterpart felt when he saw what was waiting for him at Olyer!

Recalling my school year in London could easily become a book ala *Tom Brown's School Days* or *Goodbye Mr. Chips,* and I could get lost telling you about that unbelievable year in London. What stands out most in my mind though are learning to adapt to another culture which in many ways laid the groundwork for my professional career—in the military and out. It was an eye-opening experience, to say the least.

I'll never forget my first day at school for Morning Prayers when all the boys were lined up in the gym for announcements. The teacher in charge of the session was having a fit and shouting at some poor lad in the front rows. Not understanding a word he was saying—after all the English do not speak "American"—I turned to the fellow next to me and said, "Gee, he's really mad at someone." Upon which the boy responded, "He's mad at you, bloke! Get your hands out of your pockets!" This shook me to the core as I realized it was going to be a lot different than Western Hills High. Like Dorothy in the *Wizard of Oz,* "Toto, we're not in Kansas anymore."

This was only the beginning. As the year unfurled, I was given two coveted tickets to the Strangers' gallery in the House of Commons, the

British Parliament. I was able to see Winston Churchill and Clement Atlee in debate and came only feet away from the former Prime Minister when invited to eat in the Commons cafeteria. I was introduced to cricket and became the wicketkeeper for Faraday House, and played soccer as a defensive right back. (I was eternally grateful for that position as I only had to patrol one half of the football field or pitch, I never have liked to run that much.) During the fall encampment, the entire school went camping in a campground near Winchester and visited the hallowed grounds walked by King Arthur. We also went on board the HMS *Victory* at Portsmouth the ship used by Admiral Nelson in the historic Battle of Trafalgar off Spain. I was at the camp over Guy Fawkes Night and joined in the revelry as a giant bonfire was lit, and firecrackers exploded marking the failure of an attempt to blow up Parliament in 1605.

My pride in being an American developed to a new and higher pitch being the only representative of my country among 200 very outspoken British kids. One thing that happened to me as an American living overseas, I found myself more interested in keeping up with the political scene back home. When the Blair House was attacked—the temporary White House because the White House was undergoing needed repairs—I wrote a letter to President Harry S. Truman congratulating him on his narrow escape. I received a nice letter from the U.S. Ambassador in England saying thanks, but the president has more important things to do at the moment than answer your letter. Only later did I realize that my letter had been "intercepted" by the U.S. embassy.

While on the topic of politics, there was no student government apparatus at Paddington Technical College High School, so I lobbied with one of my favorite teachers—Mr. Bayless from Cambridge—to allow our form (class) to have a student government with limited powers. They let me run free, and we had all sorts of exciting debates and ultimately an election. I couldn't understand why my British opponent won, and he was an avowed communist at that! (Somewhere I have some of the posters from that heralded Election Day, but I think it best they remain as memories.)

As 1950 neared an end, my memories included going with my father to a dinner at the Guild Hall in London—I believe recently recovered from the devastating damage from the war. The hall was beautiful, and as we emerged, we found the ground perfectly covered with a fresh layer of snow. It was a scene right out of Dickens. As we walked toward the subway station, the snow cracked below our feet, and somewhere I knew we would find Bob Cratchit's house.

Another one of my fondest memories of London was one of the most delightful evenings of our entire year. It was Christmas Eve, and our third-floor flat had a living-dining room that featured a small fireplace lodged in an alcove flanked by an overstuffed sofa and a similarly overstuffed Queen Ann high-back chair. Out away from the alcove and in the middle of the room was a good-sized circular dining table where we ate just about every meal of the day, as the kitchen was too narrow—just allowing for a small refrigerator, stove and oven with geyser (an instant hot water heater mounted on the wall) and shelving space for storage. There one would find the now dwindling supply of powdered milk, eggs, and spam and the necessary china and cutlery.

That night, however, in the middle of the table was our Christmas tree. It stood about three feet tall, but on the table had a more majestic appearance. Mom and I had gone to Woolworth's to buy Christmas decorations for the tree several days earlier. One kind of decoration stood out as truly exceptional: four-inch candles with the necessary candle holders. That afternoon we had placed all the decorations around the tree, and in the evening light from the fireplace, it looked wonderful. But now we were to turn "wonderful" into "brilliant" when we would light the thirty or so candles that we had earlier placed in strategic locations to minimize any chance of fire.

One-by-one we carefully lit the candles and slowly the light from the fireplace was supplemented by a bright glow—a radiance, that I have never seen again—from the candles glowing and flickering on the tree. Truly a Christmas tree lit by actual candles is enchanting and a time when the word "awesome" is appropriate to describe what it looked like. Dad, Mom, and I stood back when all the candles were lit—near a bucket of water, in case the tree suddenly caught on fire—and allowed the scene to become part of our lifelong memories. Then, as fast as we could, we put out each candle knowing that any mischance at this moment could cost us not only our third-floor flat but the entire house. (I don't recall if the landlord downstairs had a similar encounter, as we were not invited down until Boxing Day on December 26. Boxing Day, for those Americans who already have an image of Joe

Louis taking on Max Schmeling, is the day one remembers all the individuals who made your year a little bit nicer: mailmen, dustbin [garbage] collectors, and folks upstairs who paid a handsome rent each month.) All and all, the memories of that Christmas in England formed one of the grandest memories of the entire year. But soon it was over and back to the regular school routine began.

In December 1950, I should say, at any time in the winter that we experienced a temperature inversion in London in 1950, and conditions were right for fog, we entered into a world that seemed to come from a parallel universe. Except, our twin city was dark, foggy, and by four in the afternoon, visibility was becoming difficult. Because of the fog and it was cold, we soon experienced a deadly smog. Smog, in this case, was the result of the already existing fog mixing with the smoke coming from every household in London that was burning soft coal for heat and cooking. The major conversion to natural gas and central heating had not begun, and it would take the even more serious events of December 1952 to trigger a shift in London's heating methods when as many as 6,000 people died that month from the yellowish-black concoction that rolled over London like a dark and sinister blanket as the late afternoon approached.[2]

From a school boy's perspective, it was eerie indeed. As the skies became darker, we could see this smog start to flow underneath the bottom of the door to our classroom. At the same time, this yellow vapor began inching its way through the keyhole to start filling up the room. Soon, the guys in the back of the classroom could not see the teacher, let alone the blackboard. It was really awful, but we continued until four in the afternoon when the class was dismissed. Then the real fun began. Reaching the bus stop area to wait for my double-decker bus to Finchley Road, it became obvious that getting home was going to take some time. My bus arrived with the conductor, who normally rode inside the bus to collect tickets, walking three or so paces in front of the bus carrying an old-fashioned lantern to guide the driver who was gripping the steering wheel and craning his neck to see the lantern. Onto the bus I went and made the journey at a walking pace. It took

---

[2] Robert Lacey, *The Crown,* Crown Archetype, London, 2017, pp. 93-96. Many good examples of the scope of the smog are given. Certainly, even when we complain of Beijing's smog today, it comes nowhere near to the "deadly smog of London in the 1950s."

at least four hours "walking" to Hampstead on a bus. That was some heavy fog.

Now I am sure some of my readers are about this time saying, "sure, John, that really happened," but it did. However, it would take another episode in the winter of 1952, when an even more severe repeat of my experience drove the government to act and finally passed the Clean Air Act of 1956.[3] Just how bad was it? One movie theater announced by a poster "Screen visibility nil." The movie screen could only be seen from the first several rows of the theater. At the Royal Festival Hall, site of the Festival of Britain, patrons heard the music, but could not see the stage. How long that performance went on is not clear; it would have been dangerous to all performers singers and musicians who use the power of their lungs to sing or play their instruments—anyway not much fun for the customers either. The airport shut down. By all accounts, it was 1950 all over again, but longer and more deadly.

Outside the school activities, our year in England was filled with endless trips to museums and historical places. My father, bless him, believed that weekends were to be used and used they were. One weekend I "ran into" Jeremy Bentham in the London University Museum. He was just sitting there in a booth that looked somewhat like a London telephone box. He was very much dead. The famous philosopher of utilitarianism had willed his estate to University College London with the stipulation that he would attend the annual board of directors meeting. So, at that time, he would be rolled out to sit at the table even though he had been dead for more than 100 years. Interesting folk, these Englishmen! We also went to Scotland, where my mothers' relatives came from, (and found out that Campbells are not necessarily loved in all corners of Scotland), and then on to Ireland, Wales, and so many, many towns and byways now only found in the *Doomsday Book* I am sure. (*The Doomsday Book* was the "great survey" of England and Wales by King William the Conqueror in 1086).

As spring arrived, so did the annual spring athletic competition between the four houses of the school. I competed in the discus throw and the 100-yard dash. To my surprise, I did so well that I represented Paddington Tech at the London Athletic Games held several weeks

[3] *Ibid.*

later at the White City Stadium—a mammoth venue that was my high point in school-related sports (forever). Well, I did not win, but my mom said she heard some spectators talking about the great form of the Yank as he valiantly tried to do his best for America. Strangely, I still have the brochure associated with that day, so you see, it really was the highpoint in my sports career—though I recall my cricket and football (soccer) experiences with greater fondness and satisfaction.

Another event that I experienced around this time that was also weather-related was the annual Oxford-Cambridge boat race held on the Thames River. Thanks to the English Speaking Union, I was able to join my parents on a river craft that followed the boats from a safe distance. The river was high from a flood tide and very rough from winds making the river very choppy. Of course, it was cold, but we followed in relative comfort. After a start, which Oxford won, it was clear that the boats were having trouble. Fairly soon, the Oxford crew took on water, and their boat sank. That was it. A "no row" was called invalidating the race, which was of course canceled. A second attempt to have the race was announced for the morning of March 26—the Monday after Easter that year. Mom and Dad had had enough of the race and permitted me to retrace my steps and attend once again. This time there was no comfortable boat for a first-hand view, so I found a spot on a bridge and watched Cambridge win by one of its largest margins in race history—up to that time at least. The rematch happened on a calm river, but this time it was raining. I do not remember if I had to miss school that day or if the London County Schools, for some reason, had the day off. Whatever the condition, I am so happy I have that memory and that Cambridge won. Our House Proctor of Faraday House was Mr. Bayless, and he had graduated from Cambridge, Hurray!

There is one more memory of springtime in England, which is as beautiful as can be as the spring rains guaranteed a dazzling array of flowers and beautiful grass. Most people take grass for granted, but British grass is exceptionally lovely. It was a combination of flowers and grass, mixed with white gloves and pageantry that I did not get to see. My parents were invited to one of the Queen's spring garden parties. I can recall expressly *not* being invited. The Queen, Elizabeth, and mother of the current Queen was the hostess, and my parents, as an honored Fulbright exchange teacher and wife, were invited. Well,

Mom bought a pair of elbow-length white gloves, met the Queen, and never wore them again. She put them away carefully, and I think they now reside under the watchful eye of my sister, Alice.

My last memory of Paddington Technical College High School was Honors' Night when all the four houses that had competed all year were recognized for their accomplishments. It was right out of Harry Potter, or should I say the reverse? The Headmaster handed out the prizes for individual achievements and the winning House was also honored. In the end, not because I deserved anything, for sure, I had just had the most fabulous experience a young lad could ever have, but Mr. Hullett called my name to the cheers of my wonderful classmates. He gave me a book of photos of England's countryside as it existed in the 1940s and 1950s. It still has a place of honor in my library in my home in Atlanta; sometimes when it is very late, and the fireplace is glowing, I take it out, and I am back in 1950 again. That year made me a lifelong advocate of overseas educational experiences. Today, it forms the bedrock of our Woosong and SolBridge mission.

We returned from England on the *Queen Elizabeth* setting sail in August 1951, and, as I mentioned previously, this ship besides being posh, was posh for only certain passengers—those in First or Cabin Class. I soon found that the freedom possessed on the SS *Washington* was not part of this trip, but I found a chum in Tourist Class and had a great time. The highlight for me was the evening of my fifteenth birthday. The chef made a birthday cake, and the eight folks eating at our table had a wonderful time. On the 13th, we were back in New York and took the Chesapeake and Ohio Railway to Cincinnati's Union Station and returned home.

THREE

Onward and Upward

Returning to Cincinnati in mid-August gave me time to adjust to Ohio once again and arrange the transfer of my courses to Western Hills High where I had left just a year prior. I soon learned that educational professionals are very wary of transferring credits from one school to another. (If I do say—today we have made revolutionary advances in the ability to assess and transfer (accept) credits from one international school to another—perhaps I helped in establishing certain precedents.) Actually, the principal and staff were very understanding with everything I had done except French. They looked at my "marks" as the British called them, and in essence, said, "No way!" In truth, they were correct as I only received a 20 in a system were 50 was at least passing. It was the end of my French career, and I went back to my much more familiar German and got on with becoming just another student at my school.

I was now in the 10th grade and was not the same old John anymore. I had learned study habits, picked up the ability to prioritize, and acquired many Soft skills that would stand me well. I also had picked up a bit of a different accent, and kids I had not known before kept asking where I came from. What ultimately happened, as if the Fates themselves had spoken: I finally had become a serious student and focused on the courses necessary for getting into a university. Without question, the year I spent in London, was a year well-spent

30

regarding this new-found devotion to my studies. I also became active in the school Marching Band and Orchestra playing French horn—mainly at the third chair level—nowhere near my sister's ability, but she was now already a mother and was concentrating on her new family.

While I still loved baseball, a year of cricket and a year of British rationing took its impact. I was a good wicketkeeper for cricket, but no one was too interested in a "used" wicketkeeper when it came to baseball. Also, I was no longer the big kid in the class. In fact, I was the same size as when I left (still am except for some extra inches around the waist). A catcher in baseball had better be fairly large to defend the plate. My relative advantage had disappeared. One thing was clear: cut protein, and you don't get growth spurts. (I wonder if I can go back and sue the London City Council. Just kidding!) It was at this time that I reassessed my career plans and cut out baseball; I would have to become a famous politician on my own.

Relative to this last point, it was now 1952, and America was deep into uncovering anti-American activities, really communist-related activities, led by none other than the Senator from Wisconsin, the Honorable (and later, infamous) Joseph McCarthy, and a Republican.

I was taking an English communications course, and we were practicing debating each other on selected issues of the day. My teacher, in passing out the assignments gave me the pro or positive side in the debate over the activities of Senator McCarthy. In truth, at that time in my life, I was still a devoted Republican, still holding fast to Senator Robert Taft of Ohio, "Mr. Republican." I did not keep any secret of my political leanings, and I am sure (now) that my teacher, in giving me the defense of McCarthy, probably winked to herself as she did. Anyway, I was delighted to be given a chance to present the true defense of this great American and to do it in front of the class.

One thing that I have always believed is that each and every person grows intellectually at his or her own pace. This was when I made my "Giant Leap Forward." Eager to win this debate, I went to the Carnegie Library, which was about a 20 minutes' walk from my home every night and on the weekends of the two weeks I was given for prep. (After all, there was no Internet, and the library did not come to you like today on your smartphone, tablet, or computer. You couldn't just "Google" things back then. Well, here I go, showing my age again, but there's something to be said about going to your local library, smelling the old books, feeling the books and other periodicals in your hands. It's what Ray Bradbury wrote about in his classic dystopian novel, *Fahrenheit 451*.) With the help of a wonderful librarian, I incessantly worked to prepare my case. Only one problem; every day, the evidence mounted that this person was a classic "jerk!" (At eighty-three, I suppose I would choose a more diplomatic word, but at fifteen, it was perfect.)

On the day of the debate in front of all my friends, and those who were not, my cause collapsed into a collection of demagogic tricks, much the same of the person I was trying to defend. It was the worst defeat of my life, but actually marked the day that I declared my intellectual independence from my parents and from a blank and unquestioned belief in an ideology. So, was it a defeat? Not in the least; my teacher also said some very nice things about my delivery and my grasp of the issues. I have used her tender let-down techniques many times myself as a teacher but appreciated her sympathy all the same. In a sense, it marked my emergence as a truly "thinking" being, and set my strong advocacy in debate as one of the best means of education. It also explains why I say "yes" to every request from our debate coach as our SolBridge Debate Society (SDS) engages in debate throughout Asia.

What all of this meant was that I had become a serious student and was running with the rest in the race for college. I was no longer the happy-go-lucky kid but had taken a big step on early maturity. And I was about to take another important step.

To help out around the home in the 11th grade, I started working after school at Duwell Hardware. I knew a lot about tools and hardware generally because my father was an industrial arts teacher, but still fell for the "John, go get a left-handed wrench." With that, the old guys would just about die laughing, but I loved the work and the lessons that the plumbers and carpenters taught me. It also gave me a taste of the small "Mom and Pop" stores that still played a major role in merchandising in America at this time. The customer, believe me, was always right! I will never forget when my first paycheck came in: I went to Shillitoes the major department store in Cincinnati and bought my mom a Thanksgiving-themed dinner set. (I think it sits, now in a box carefully awaiting its emergence on some Thanksgiving dinner table. One question remains: will the new generations really appreciate that relic from the 1950s?)

When 1953 arrived, there was a big event for Ohio. It was the sesquicentennial (150th anniversary) of the state, and many events were scheduled to mark its arrival. My high school advisor called me one afternoon knowing my interest in history and politics and told me about a statewide contest on Ohio history. Each county would have county-wide examinations to pick one representative to travel to our first state university—Ohio University in Athens, Ohio. There, many events were scheduled as well as the final test to identify the one student most knowledgeable about our state.

Off I went to the Carnegie Library again and immersed myself in one history book about Ohio. (You can already figure out that it was not taught in the schools, or why would I have returned to Carnegie?) Well, just reading one book won me first place in Hamilton County. At that time, Hamilton County had over 500,000 in population, and I was first! Although I might have won, it was also a shame. It demonstrated the low level of awareness that people had about Ohio's history that existed at the time. (I am sure it is even worse today!) But certainly, I was not going to complain. On the appointed fall day I boarded a train (eight hours late—the twilight of the American railway system) and was off to Athens. I was greeted by the president of the university and taken to the gathering point for all contestants from each county in Ohio. It was my first ever ride in a Cadillac, which might have convinced me to become a university president one day!

Sadly, my "day in the sun" was short-lived. I suppose some students had read *two* books on Ohio history, and my role became one of congratulating the winners. This I did not mind, and today, this is something I tell all students who come to Woosong to compete, whether you win or lose, the fact that you competed contributes to your personal "experience portfolio." I always tell them to fill that portfolio as much as possible. The "take away" for me was the experience at Ohio University. It was a classic campus and still is, with beautiful buildings and gardens. I still hold it as one of the loveliest campuses I have ever seen, and that image stayed in my mind and played a role in selecting a university for our daughter some years later. (It was also where she met her husband. I guess university choices really do matter!)

It soon became "crunch time" for choosing a university for me. There was only one university that we considered as a family: the University of Cincinnati. We all held it in high regard, and it was the school where many members of the Cincinnati Tafts had gone to in the past. I applied and was accepted; in fact, I went to one orientation session in perhaps June of 1954 and had selected my major as Pre-law. (My love of politics was still glowing.)

One afternoon, I was called to my high school counselor, Mrs. Dorothy Heninger's office (I should be saying prayers daily on her behalf, but right now a belated "thank you" will have to do). She had been helping me ever since my return from London, and she saw a different boy from the person she met years ago. "John," she said. "I just received a request from Ohio State University for a recommendation for a "development scholarship." I had no idea what a development scholarship was, but she noted it was for a "late bloomer." For those unfamiliar with the term, which means a person whose talents or abilities are not obvious until a later age, it fit me exactly. Before going to England, I showed no tendencies requiring universities to take a second look at me. But from the 10th grade on, I had picked up steam, so to speak, and was now running a competitive race with the school's academic leaders. And now, here was one person who was about to turn my life around.

"John, I would like to submit your name," Mrs. Heninger said.

The scholarship was for tuition, and if grades were kept high, it could continue through the senior year. I told my parents, and we thought we would be able to handle it. Living expenses would be our own responsibilities as well as book and lab fees. After talking it over with my parents, it was clear, Ohio State it would be, and, indeed, Ohio State it was. I entered in the Fall Semester of 1954, lived in the Stadium Dorms with 21 other guys—no secrets in this open bay shower—it was a converted military barracks suspended from the inside of the Ohio State Stadium, but costs, which included meals, were low. I majored in Political Science with pre-law as a major focus, minored in Music and Russian language, and joined the Air Force ROTC as in those days all males had to select Army, Navy, or Air Force ROTC—no exceptions—for two years of training.

It was a great experience. I wanted to try a different language from German and chose Russian as it was the era of the great American-

Russian confrontation. I already knew the Sun Tzu dictum of "know your enemy," so I went headlong into the most difficult language I have ever tackled. I will forever be grateful to one of my dorm mates from the Ukraine. He drilled me on pronunciation, and I got through. Although our wonderful teacher Mrs. Epp often asked me why I had a Ukrainian accent, I could only smile.

Music and the French horn helped me immensely keeping an even keel with concerts, competitions, and road trips to bring Ohio State music to cities and towns all over Ohio. Air Force ROTC began taking more and more of my time, as after the first two years—required of everybody—Advanced ROTC was a different thing. It complemented my interests in history and political science, and I actually enjoyed everything but rappelling down mountains (maybe hills) during our summer camps. In my senior year, I was the Deputy Wing Commander making me second in command of the roughly 2000 cadets (Ohio State was large even in the 1950s). I ended receiving a Distinguished Graduate award which gave me the option of applying for the Regular Air Force as opposed to the Reserves.

Continuing my interest in politics, I ran for the Student Senate leading the university "independents"—students not affiliated with sororities or fraternities—and won, providing many opportunities to be involved in activities that were at the intersection of faculty and student life. As the only independent Senior Senator, I became involved in one issue that I campaigned about: the embargo on inviting political candidates to the campus. We fought that issue with the college administration and made an impact. Only several years after leaving campus, politicians were allowed to speak and interact with students—as it should be.

I did well in school graduating *Cum Laude* and *Phi Beta Kappa* and was asked to give the valedictorian speech at the March 1958 graduation. Immediately after graduation, with my mom and dad, I walked to the Air Force ROTC Building and was commissioned a 2nd Lieutenant in the Air Force Reserves. (About one year later, I was commissioned in the Regular Air Force.)

After graduation, I spent a little over two months working in the public park system of Hamilton County—Winton Woods to be exact. It was a huge public park with a golf course, lake, 90 riding horses, and trails and served as an excellent example of money spent on the people in general. The public could play on a decent golf course, and it only cost around $15 for eighteen holes. And the greens and fairway were great!

Actually, I had worked there during summers for most of my years at Ohio State, so it was a wonderful way to prepare for entering the Air Force. Why? Because every other day, I would have to cut the greens for the 20 golf greens that we maintained so 18 greens would always be playable. A special mower was used to cut greens as it cut the grass very short—as needed for a green. Once a green was cut, fairway wheels were attached to the mower and I literally ran behind the mower and got in shape. I am sure when I entered on active duty on May 23, 1958, I was in the best shape I have ever been in!

PHOTO GALLERY ONE

The "Cincinnati Kid" ready to take on the world!

Here I am at two years of age—ready for a Cincinnati winter.

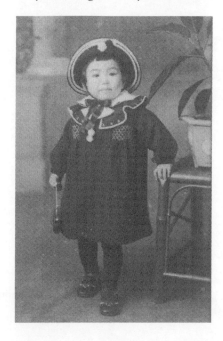

Mitchie at three years old getting ready for the 3-5-7 Ceremony in Tokyo, 1940.

My mother, Alice Willa Campbell shortly after her marriage to Charles Lafayette Endicott in May 1928.

My father, Charles Lafayette Endicott.

Here I am, on the left, at six years of age, with my good friend "Sonny" Schlichte. Long pants were still to come—knickers first, then long pants.

A TWA C-47 aircraft that my Mother, sister and I flew on to Kansas City in the summer of 1941. A wonderful experience.

The London taxi that took our family to our British home from the train station. Note the heavy steamer trunks on the roof—end of August 1950.

The entrance of Paddington Technical College which housed our high school. No longer a school, but still standing at last report. Really right out of Harry Potter.

A tentative young lad standing next to his mother in London, 1950.

Mom and son outside of Westminster Palace in the fall of 1950.

John E. Endicott

The Ohio State...
LANTERN

Published by the Ohio State University School of Journalism

VOL. LXXVII, NO. 105   COLUMBUS, OHIO, MONDAY, MARCH 10, 1958   Price Five Cents

Subject-ed to Thought
In the boiling of the development of the St. Lawrence Seaway just another example of letting others do our thinking for us? See editorial, page 5.

OSU Grants 500 Degrees Winter Term

Ohio State will confer approximately 500 degrees at its Winter Quarter commencement exercises at 3 p.m. Thursday, March 20, in the St. John Arena.

More than one-fourth of the class will be candidates for advanced degrees, including approximately 30 who are scheduled to receive Ph.D's.

Among the graduates will be students from Canada, Ceylon, Chile, Egypt, France, India, Iraq, Jordan, Nigeria, the Philippines, Thailand and Turkey.

Commencement speaker will be Dr. T. Keith Glennan, president of Case Institute of Technology, Cleveland, whose subject will be "The Challenge of Abundance."

President Novice G Fawcett will preside. The Rev. Horace B. Houf, minister to students of the Baptist-Disciple Student Fellowship, will deliver the invocation and benediction.

John E. Endicott, A-4, will give the response for his class following the recognition of graduates

John Endicott, A-4, Cincinnati, will be the response speaker for the March Commencement. Endicott, a political science major, is president of Stadium Club, treasurer of USA, a member of ROTC, Buckeye and Concert bands, Student Senate and Senior Class Cabinet. He is a member of Phi Eta Sigma, Pi Sigma Alpha, Kappa Kappa Phi, Upsilon Pi Upsilon Pi Upsilon and Scabbard and Blade honoraries.

Trustees Approve Carson For OSU Vice-Presidency

Gordon B. Carson, dean of the College of Engineering, today became vice-president of the University in charge of business and finance.

The appointment was approved Friday by the Board of Trustees upon recommendation of President Fawcett. Dr. Gordon relieves Jacob B. Taylor, who left the University last October. Other actions taken by the Trustees were:

1. Approval of three revisions in admission standards for the College of Law.

2. Approval of a construction project to enable the University to obtain emergency power from the Columbus and Southern Ohio Electric Co.

3. Approval of architectural photogrammetry research, the first in the United States.

4. Awarding of insurance contracts to two companies on basis of low bids.

5. Awarding of contracts totaling $392,070 for four projects.

6. Authorization of $180,000 expenditure for civilian military training expenses from the Ralph D. Mershon Fund.

7. Appointment of public accounting firm for annual audit of dormitory revenues.

8. Acceptance of a gift to establish "Oley Speaks Memorial Scholarship Fund."

Beginning Autumn Quarter, students will be required to have an undergraduate degree before entering the law school. They will also be required to take the Law School Admission Test. Prospective students will have to present evidence of moral fitness for the legal profession.

A utility tie-in between the University's power supply and that of the Columbus and Southern Ohio Co. will provide electricity in the event of an emergency, plus additional power to meet the increasing demands on campus.

Carson Says Post Offers Big Challenge

The Ohio State newspaper announcing details for the coming March 1958 Spring Graduation. I am shown as the response speaker for all graduates.

43

Part II
The Government Years:
1958-1989

FOUR

Into the Wild Blue Yonder

By the time I completed Air Force ROTC at Ohio State, I had changed the program I was in from Pre-flight to Administrative Officer. I really wanted to be a pilot, but in my third year of ROTC, the Air Force changed the time one had to stay in the Air Force after flight school from three to four years. I am sure the Air Force budget folks believed that four years was a better return on their investment than three years; however, at that point in my life, an additional year seemed like an eternity and a change to a promise that I thought should be honored. So, I stayed in the ROTC Program but had only a three-year commitment after graduation. I was assigned to the Intelligence Training School in Texas and began my service.

Upon graduation about six months later, I was assigned to Japan and began another phase of my life that has been as instrumental as that defining year in London.

· My arrival in Japan was less than auspicious. The flight which took me halfway around the world was a grueling series of flights from Cincinnati to California; California to Hawaii; Hawaii to Wake Island; and finally Wake Island to Tachikawa, Japan. In those days it was not unusual to look out the window and see streams of oil coming from the reciprocal engines as they groaned hour after hour to get to the destination. The point of no return was a really special place, as it meant that failure of one or two engines would not mean a return to the starting point but a crash landing in the ocean. Usually, on a military flight, once the point of no return was reached, it was announced, and anyone awake would burst into a massive cheer. Just to give you a feel for the time required, it was about eight hours to Hawaii, six hours to Wake (usually with an overnight stay in a dorm with dinner), and eight or so hours to Tokyo. Many a time, it was when we did not make a point of no return, and we all sat back in our seats and hoped that no other engines would quit or be feathered due to fire or some mechanical malfunction. Without question, folks my age marvel at the great reliability of today's aircraft and give thanks to all those gallant pilots who got us to this point.

The not-so auspicious circumstances of my arrival continued when the driver and jeep provided to take me to my assignment, Shiroi Air Station, took hours to find the place, and when we did, we were told it had already been shut down. "You had better go to Washington Heights," we were told, the new location for my intelligence unit. What luck! Instead of being at Shiroi Air Station way out in the "boonies," Washington Heights was a major housing area for the many dependents who were accompanying their military spouses. My quarters were located on the 4th floor of an Officers' Bachelors Quarters right in the middle of the housing area and only minutes away from one of the most renown shrines in Japan, Meiji Shrine, built in memory of Emperor Meiji—the first emperor to reign after the collapse of the Tokugawa *Bakufu* in 1868. In fact, the entire era of the restoration of imperial authority, the Meiji Era, bears his name.

One could say, the location was almost in the center of Tokyo. Only minutes away by subway was the Ginza, Kabuki Za (the famous Tokyo kabuki theater), and the very heart of the massive city of Tokyo. But as to any secrecy about the location of our office, there was none. As soon as I would get in a taxi and say, "Washington Heights," the driver would say, "Ah, American intelligence!" That is the way it was. Tokyo was still very much showing the residue of the bombings of World War II, and at night in the fall and winter, the significant usage of charcoal for cooking and heating ensured that practically every night the city would be cloaked in a blanket of soot making shirt collars very much of a one-day affair. Initially, I found myself drawn to study martial arts (judo) at the Kodokan—the home of judo for Japan, and the study of the Japanese language. I enrolled in the Naganuma School of Japanese and took long walks among the neighboring commercial areas practicing my Japanese with shop vendors. As a bachelor, I often dined in the Meiji Club or the Officers' Club, where on selected days one could eat a spaghetti dinner with wine for twenty-five cents! And the dollar was exchanged at 360 Yen per U.S. Dollar. As you can imagine, it was a life that a 23-year-old could easily enjoy.

On some weekends I would go to services at the Tokyo Union Church, which was an interdenominational church where services were held in English. I must level with you and assure you, that this was not something I did every weekend, as sponsored ski trips, pheasant hunting near Mt. Fuji, trips to see the Takarazuka Theater, and chances to hear the symphonic orchestras of Tokyo tended to make weekend space very competitive. But there was one Sunday that truly changed my life.

Let me give you a bit of background: When I left for Japan in the fall of 1958, my father took me aside and said, "By all means, please look up my missionary friend, Ms. Florence Wells and say, 'Hello.'" When Dad was in Japan, he had made one of his missions the aiding of an orphanage that aided children of mixed blood. One of the missionaries there was Ms. Wells, who was Methodist. (Now in those days, "sprinkling" Methodists did not spend much time with "Full emersion" Baptists. But given the nature of helping a recovering nation, some of the "restrictions" were reduced, and Dad and Florence became good friends.) This was the person I had promised to look up while in Tokyo. It turned out that at one of the coffee klatsches (a casual social gathering for coffee and conversation—a partial translation of the German word *kaffeeklatsch*) held after 4:00 services, we met.

Like a scene right out of a movie, an elderly gray-haired lady approached and said: "Hello, I'm Florence Wells." I was dumbfounded and replied, "I am Charlie Endicott's son, John!" What followed was an animated discussion as Ms. Wells related her tale of life in Japan and her new calling—no longer with the orphanage, but now as an English instructor at Jissen Woman's College which was nearby. At that point, she stopped short and turned around as a young lady was politely standing next to her side.

"May I introduce Ms. Mitsuyo Kobayashi who is one of my former students?" she said.

At this point dear readers, my life changed. First of all, she was strikingly beautiful! She was full of energy; ideas and opinions flowed like water from a sparkling stream. She knew as much about the world as I did—knew far more about literature, both Asian and Western—and she had gone to college when only 1-2 percent of Japanese women went to college. As a result, her English was far better than my Japanese (she had studied English since the seventh grade, whereas I had studied German). It was love at first sight. It may sound very corny, but I had made a list of attributes that I wanted in a partner. Even without going back to my room to find it, I knew that she was "full marks" as they say in England.

When we reached the point in the story of our lives when our next chapter was getting married—that was going to take some work. You see, this was 1958, and the United States was resplendent in anti-miscegenation laws——ones that prohibited marriage between different races. As a rule of thumb, just picture all the southern states and all the western states and realize different races could not get legally married. I was in the Air Force, so it was a serious issue. Even though we were madly in love with each other, we had to have permission from the Air Force before we could legally get married and I had security clearances which compounded the problem. We both filled out more forms than most folks fill out in a generation, maybe slightly exaggerated, but it was a huge ordeal. One of my steps was to go to the legal office and be "counseled." At the appointed time, I stood before the legal officer—a major if I remember correctly—who asked for my home state of record. That was very important, as all military once in the service are still governed by the particular laws of the state from which they come.

"Ohio, Sir," I said.

"God damn it! You can get married!"

You see, Ohio had no anti-miscegenation laws, and indeed it would be possible. I was delighted, but it was not over.

While technically it was legal to get married, I still needed Air Force approval. And, it turned out, that was not going to be easy. Out of the blue, I was informed that I was being re-assigned to our "mother unit" in Hawaii; in less than a week, I found myself on the beach in Waikiki. Sure, there was an official reason for my immediate transfer; who knows, it might have even been the military's way to let this boy "cool off." Nonetheless, relocating me to Hawaii was not all that bad. In fact, it actually resulted in the expedited handling of our official request to marry papers. Being a young fellow, I met most of the junior officers working in the personnel directorate that would handle such matters, and by the middle of August permission was granted by Pacific Air Force (PACAF) Headquarters.

My boss in Hawaii upon hearing the news mused that he needed some papers delivered to a photo analysis unit at Yokota Air Base, just outside of Tokyo. He turned to me and said: "John, do you mind being a courier for about a week?" Those wonderful words resulted in our marriage on August 25, 1959. It still was a complicated matter, but you should really know this story as I am sure many GIs in my same position endured similar trails.

Once we had the permission to marry from PACAF in Hawaii (the commanding unit for all Air Force units throughout the Pacific), we went to the Japanese Ward Office and were married in a Japanese civil wedding. We were given an official document and for a small fee, a very beautiful certificate in Japanese suitable for framing. At that moment, we were married according to Japanese law. Then we traveled to the U.S. Embassy Annex in the Taranamon District—fairly close to the main Embassy. There we waited and finally met with a consular official. After looking over the documents, he said, "Where is the 5th Air Force approval?" Patiently, I explained that PACAF was the senior organization in the entire Pacific, and if we had authority from Hawaii to marry, it was good throughout the region. "No!" was the answer. "My regulations say the 5th Air Force must approve and PACAF is not the 5th Air Force" Now we all know to deal with bureaucrats can be trying, but I had already overcome over six months of bureaucratic behavior and was ready to explode. Thankfully, I responded, "OK, if you don't believe me, would you believe the Air Attaché who has an office several floors above?" It was a deal and off I ran with Mitchie in hand to see the Attaché.

Some folks in this entire story warrant special recognition and to whom I should pray on their birthdays; this Lt. Colonel, whose name has slipped my memory, was one of those saints.

He asked the nature of the problem and upon hearing my plea and looking at the documents noted: "Yes, anything PACAF says is good enough for the 5th Air Force, or the 13th Air Force (the Philippines). Let me put that on paper."

After a few minutes, the Lt. Colonel handed us the letters asserting the authority of the documents, and we were off to return to our "friend" on the first floor.

After looking at the documents, the official asked us where our witnesses were. Oh, we need witnesses? Several folks in the office who were waiting on other matters just popped up and said, "We'll be witnesses." And that was that. Thus on August 25, 1959, we officially became husband and wife and had it recorded in the U.S. Embassy Annex in Tokyo. Of course, that did not mean that Mitchie and I could return to Hawaii on the next available flight; she would now have to have travel papers, and that would take time. It did mean that we could start that process and aim for October when we agreed would be a great time to marry in the church where we met and take a honeymoon throughout Japan.

My week in Japan was over, and I exited on "Cloud Nine," an expression that means I probably do not remember a thing about the flight. My thoughts were exclusive with the wonderful conclusion of our efforts to marry.

*   *   *

From August to October, I worked in our unit producing a weekly intelligence digest called *Fast Tracks*. In it, several of us worked summarizing and highlighting the major intelligence items of the week. It was always a hectic schedule as items came in that had to be assessed and articles written—similar to any newsroom in a newspaper or weekly journal. It was really a great experience, and when major issues occurred, we were called upon to personally report to the meeting of the 4-star commander of PACAF and his staff. That always took place in the big PACAF Headquarters building, which in 1941, was a barracks for soldiers. It was still pock-marked with bullet holes from

Japanese planes that had hit Hickam Air Base at the same time Ford Island was hit where so many ships were docked.

During the first week in October, I returned to Japan having requested 21-days leave to marry in the church and take a long honeymoon through historic parts of Japan. In early October, in the midst of a typhoon, Mitchie and I were married. We married in the Tokyo Union Church with the reception at the Officers' Club at Washington Heights. It was certainly a mixture of East and West. On the bride's side sat Mitchie's relatives and friends. On the left side sat my co-workers and many of the junior officers I had made friends with during the early stage of our courtship. I really wanted to walk down under raised sabers of my friends, but the minister, not too happy to see such a display of militarism in his church, vetoed that. Remember also it was a period in Japan when things military were not too well received. So, rather than do that on church property, we did it at the reception at the Officers' Club.

We had a marvelous reception resplendent in ice sculptures and great food. The only problem was that I made one of my greatest protocol mistakes and did not have a sit-down dinner. All the Japanese were waiting to be seated, and many Americans, as well. We just persevered and did all the toasting and speechmaking standing. Well, it was my first wedding—and the marriage has lasted—so I hope all will forgive. It was as nice as any wedding could have been, but it was short of what I have experienced since—especially in Asia. Perhaps, if my parents had come, Mom would have saved us before the event, but traveling by air in those days was not something a junior high school teacher could afford. So, we all stood, smiled, and toasted to an event that could have been grander, but will always be the grandest in my memories.

Now that we were a married couple, we settled in a basement apartment in Manoa Valley just behind the University of Hawaii. It cost all of $90.00 per month, but life in Hawaii was not exactly the place for a junior officer. We just got by; in fact, it was so expensive that I asked for and was given permission to work on the weekends as a night manager in a local beachfront hotel. It proved a great experience, and my boss invited us to use the rooftop suite on special occasions. One of those special occasions was New Year's Eve in Honolulu. If ever you wanted to experience a war zone without going to war, a night in Honolulu on New Year's Eve is a close second. (This experience gives me great credence with our Hotel Management College at Woosong even though this was eons ago.)

In Hawaii, our lives were enriched by friends from work, the local community, and businessmen and women who we met and shared the Hawaii experience. I say "experience" because it truly is something special. We had opportunities to meet and share our lives with people from all over Asia as well as the "Mainland," as the continental United States is called. We were nothing exceptional. Unlike Kyoto, when an old man fell off the curb because he could not stop staring at the foreigner and his young wife, we were in the midst of true diversity. (In a sense it became a model we meet and exceed at SolBridge International School of Business with 61 nations represented.) The highlight of our life in Hawaii was the visit of my parents shortly before the birth of our daughter, Charlene. Mom and Dad visited us in July just as we were told that we were now eligible for base housing at Radford Terrace in Naval Housing. We all celebrated the 4th of July together, which was just before our daughter, Charlene, was born. Charlene was born on the morning of August 20, 1960, one year after Hawaii became a state.

In a professional sense, my career in "human intelligence or collections intelligence" ended as the era was engrossed in what technical intelligence could do for the nation. It was clear, so they thought, that the days of gathering intelligence the old fashioned way, through people, had come to an end. We could end any dependence on human sources and rely on high tech answers such as the U-2 aircraft capable of providing all sorts of data, far inside the borders of any country we had questions about. Certainly, human intelligence had its problems with agents and double agents and operatives ending face down in the canals of Tokyo and results probably not satisfactory to the data mongers of the new Kennedy Era. Thus, our Intelligence Group was deactivated, and I found myself in the Targeting Directorate of PACAF Headquarters. Here I became trained as a Targeting Officer, learning how to recommend the right kind of munitions for any target, using the full range of weapons then available, both conventional and nuclear. (Remember, this was the era of the "dumb bomb" where kinetic energy, wind, and luck interacted—

sometimes requiring hundreds of sorties to destroy specific targets, especially if those targets were hard or reinforced.)

It was during this time—well into my tenure in the Targets Directorate—when I had an experience that has long stayed with me. It was a few days after the May 16, 1961 Coup in South Korea led by Lt. General Park Chung-hee and the Military Revolutionary Committee. All analysts in the intelligence community, as well as the policy community, were interested in what this new turn of events might produce for the delicate South Korean Republic. As I opened my mail and read the distribution for that morning, I came across a very small pamphlet that outlined the objectives of the coup. As I read it, I became increasingly interested in this manifesto that was clearly stating the objectives of the new government. It was clear and well written. (I only regret that I have no copy.) This was a major event, I thought, and I immediately wrote a summary saying how significant this was and distributed it to the approximately 50 analysts in the directorate, both military and civilian.

Well, someone, I am really not sure who took my work into the Colonel's office. I mean THE COLONEL'S OFFICE! Soon in a loud and booming voice, came the words of a gentleman who I deeply respect (he is well into his 90's and at last report still healthy), but then he was much younger, and his voice needed no microphone. "Endicott!" The colonel's voice boomed like a squadron of B-52's taking off. "Get into my office!"

I quickly learned that a 2nd Lieutenant newly assigned to the Targets' Directorate had no business sending what he might have thought about a particular event, especially a geopolitical one, to any of the esteemed analysts who were deeply engaged in this subject and did not need to be distracted by unauthenticated and unreliable information! Can I say now, who was right?

Since I had become a well-qualified targeting officer during the latter part of our assignment to Hawaii, my next assignment became a major topic of interest throughout the Targeting Directorate. In this event, I can only say that the guys in the mailroom had a little too much time on their hands. One day, when it was getting close to the time for receiving orders for a new assignment, I, indeed, received a fresh set of orders. Endicott goes to Minot, North Dakota! (Minot AFB, is one of the colder assignments that airmen and officers dreaded; and I am sure, still dread to this day!). The entire Directorate was abuzz as the young kid (I was still 25) would get a taste of the "real" Air Force. Well, as it turned out, I was the recipient of a well-played practical joke by the folks in the mailroom who had created a false set of orders good enough to fool even the Inspector General's Office. Finally, as the day neared its end, so did the joke. The youngest member of the mailroom came out with the real orders—to the center of all strategic thinking, SAC Headquarters in Omaha, Nebraska. I did not know how lucky I was, but everyone congratulated me and made up for a day of fun at my expense. Then again, maybe I wasn't so lucky after all: getting orders to Omaha instead of Minot was like jumping from the frying pan into the fire!

FIVE

Cold War Warrior

Leaving the comfort of sunny, tropical Hawaii behind (for now), I checked into SAC Headquarters and learned that I would be assigned as an augmentee to the Joint Strategic Target Planning Staff (JSTPS), the organization deep inside the bunkered underground that was responsible for making the SIOP—the Single Integrated Operations Plan—short for nuclear war plan. You have to remember, this was the height of the Cold War, and the Strategic Air Command was the tip of the spear—if not the whole darn spear and then some. Guess I really did jump from the frying pan into the fire!

While there were many things to do which were associated with mastering my duties as a targeting officer, Mitchie and I also had to get settled and find a house to turn into a home.

With not all that much time to find a place to live, we ended up following the path of other officers assigned to SAC. Many were buying houses in a new development across the river from Omaha, in Council Bluffs, Iowa. Houses there were reasonably priced, which was good news for a newly promoted 1st Lieutenant whose salary in 1963 was modest, to say the least. We were also a family of three now with the addition of our daughter, Charlene. I don't think you can imagine the price we paid—we considered it a lot and the monthly payment was all of $90.00. We took out a mortgage for a $13,000 house, and Mitchie immediately turned it into a home. As is the lot with most military wives, Mitchie was in charge of moving us in and making it as lovely as possible. I was on duty, and in those days, duty also included Saturday mornings when many "Honey do" missions are normally done. ("Honey do" is short for, "Honey, please do this or Honey, please do that.") So, in those days our wives were really busy. (Again it is appropriate to thank my wife for all those unpaid chores that she did without complaint. I hope all my military friends will go home after reading this and say, "Thanks for everything, Honey.")

Soon the summer turned into fall, and the pace of events began to pick up. 1961 had been a year of tension and stress between the United States and the Soviet Union. The Berlin Wall went up, and Fidel Castro withstood an American attempt to invade Cuba using CIA trained forces. It was the height of the Cold War, and both sides were seeking to enhance their positions related to each other. Unbeknown to the United States, the Soviets began efforts to have a nuclear presence in Cuba. Secretly, ships were fitted out with necessary support gear and left from the Crimea with a destination of Cuba.[4] Because of the fear of discovery by U.S. intelligence aircraft, the soldiers were kept below decks during the day and only allowed to go out on deck during the night. As the ships neared their destination, security became even tighter, and conditions became almost unbearable as the heat of the tropics increased day by day.

This story was related to me and about 1000 attendees at a conference held in Moscow in September 2012 to mark the 50th Anniversary of the Cuban Missile Crisis. I was asked to give my account from the underground at SAC Headquarters and Lt. General Yesin—then a Captain—was asked to provide the Soviet story. His story was one of extreme hardship, as their construction crews dealt with high heat, undergrowth consisting of very sharp needles, having to work only at night, and general failing health due to food, stress, and constant heat. Finally, as they neared or completed their work to set up the missile sites, American reconnaissance aircraft discovered the activity.

Of course, my activity was of a much different sort. Once the Soviet presence was discovered, SAC went into crisis mode to make sure all aspects of the war plan were in order. The tension reached a

---

[4] Much of the account of Soviet efforts was given to me by Lt. General Yesin a Captain at the time as part of a dual presentation that he and I gave in Moscow in September 2012 to mark the 50th Anniversary of the Cuban Missile Crisis.

high point when Soviet ships were approaching American naval forces ordered by President John F. Kennedy to embargo any nuclear-related equipment reaching Cuba. At one moment, our boss, a three-star (a Lt. General) came into the room in the underground bunker where several of us were working and said, "Men, we may have as little as twenty minutes before execution, why don't you call your wives and say good-bye." We all knew what that meant as our families were in regular houses on the surface of the ground and when under attack by nuclear weapons would be immediate casualties.

I called my wife and said something like, "What's for dinner?" It is still something she clearly remembers, as those on the surface were also watching TV and listening to radios, completely aware of the moment all feared. Happily, of course, when the ships turned around, and everyone could breathe easier, the situation could return to the diplomats, not the warriors.

As I told my story, I noticed that General Yesin was not happy. Actually, he was furious. However, and interestingly, his anger was not directed at me or the American enemy. He was angry at the role Nikita Khrushchev played and his decision to ignore the fact that Soviet forces actually had attained operational capabilities in early September. The Soviet leader wanted to announce this great feat on the coming anniversary of the Great Soviet Revolution, November 7, 1917. The only problem was, it came too late. He did not use the fact that nuclear weapons were ready for use on the beaches of Cuba and therefore lost the deterrence value of the success of his men earned at great sacrifice. Well, I am not sorry; he should have taken my class at the U.S. Air Force Academy where I taught Defense Policy, and would have realized deterrence is a result of actually knowing with high reliability what your opponent can do. For example, I am not deterred from a spirited conversation with a bigger fellow as long as I do not see the pistol under his jacket. However, once I take notice of the bulge and see the handle, I might become much more diplomatic. The United States was not deterred and was able in the end to work a deal that resulted in the removal of Soviet missiles from Cuba, and a later reciprocal action by the U.S. as it removed intermediate-range missiles from Turkey.

In the drawdown period after the crisis, we all began to focus on additional things in life. One was thinking about working on a Master's

Degree from a local university. After looking at the options in the Omaha/Council Bluffs area, I settled on the University of Omaha; at that time, a city-owned university of good reputation. Since no programs were available in Political Science, I opted for European History. After receiving permission from my boss, I began a program that involved two nights a week and Saturday. All the classes were at the university which took me across the river and west of the city of Omaha to where the university was located. It was not a tough drive but became treacherous when winter came with blinding snowstorms and "white-out" conditions. A whiteout is when the snow and wind come down so hard that you literally could not see past the hood of your car. Driving at 60 or 70 miles an hour and running into a blast of snow could put you in a line of traffic with 18-wheel trucks not being able to see a thing. Even sitting here writing about the ride across South Omaha Bridge with trucks behind me makes my hair (what little of it is left) stand on edge. Anyway, that is Omaha in the winter and life, luckily, did go on. Working and going to school at the same time is known to many of us. It is no fun, but it is the basis of future opportunity and thus is a privilege.

During these days of life on the great prairie of the Midwest, several events happened that changed our country and our way of life. On November 22, 1963, as Thanksgiving was approaching, our young president, John Fitzgerald Kennedy, was assassinated. Of course, SAC went on alert as in the early stages no one knew who was behind the event and many an eye was cast toward the Soviet Union. The humiliation of the Cuban Missile Crisis was only a year prior, and we all made ready for the worst-case scenario. In time, that view subsided, but the nation mourned unlike any other time in my life. I am sure the shock of Pearl Harbor gripped those affected in 1941 in a similar manner, but on that tragic day in November, our nation plummeted to a new low.

As hope springs eternal from a tragedy, early the next year, on May 29, 1964, joy was brought to our house with the birth of our son John. We now had two delightful children, Charlene approaching four years old and John.

While we had so much to celebrate, something was going on between SAC Headquarters and Air Force Headquarters in the Pentagon. The situation in Southeast Asia had heated up, and headquarters was looking for young officers to be assigned to Vietnam. My name came out on one of the very first lists, and SAC had responded that Endicott was not to be touched. He was far too much engaged in knowledge about and the peculiarities of the SIOP to ever be released for something as low order as Vietnam. I should point out, that up to this point what SAC said to the Pentagon usually had a significant weight that the SAC position or opinion won. All of a sudden, this was no longer to be the case. "Endicott is on the block and tell him so!" was the response from the Pentagon and a new era had begun.

Soon I received a message from Headquarters that offered me three options: go immediately; go in six months after preliminary training for an assignment in Vietnam; or go in approximately 12 months after preliminary training and six months of intensive Vietnamese language training. As far as I was concerned, the offer for language training was the only one that made sense. As an Asian specialist, which I hoped to be, I already had extensive Russian language training, my Japanese was getting better every day, but another Asian language would be a major asset.

After debating these three options, which reminded me of the TV game show, *Let's Make a Deal,* where contestants had to choose "prizes" behind three doors, I chose the third option and soon we, as a family, were headed off to Alexandra, Virginia, and FSI, the Foreign Service Institute, to study about Vietnam generally and the Vietnamese language specifically. For me, it was one of the toughest periods I have ever known. We had intensive language drills with native speakers for five hours a day, followed by another three hours of self-study using tapes. Then when you went home, you were expected to hit the tapes again. For anyone wanting to learn a new language, that is certainly the way. It was also a good way to become ill from all the stress and commitment that comes with total language immersion. For the next year, it represented the bulk of our life as a family, but it came with its own share of benefits. As we soon found out, living in Alexandra, Virginia was worth all the trouble because we were in the middle of much of America's history, current history as was being made in Washington, DC, and early history as could be seen by visiting Gadsby's Tavern or Mount Vernon, the fabled home of George Washington.

John E. Endicott

Gadsby's Tavern first opened in 1770 and Washington reportedly dined there with friends fairly often, and especially liked having his birthday celebrations there. This is not a book on travel, but if you do find yourself in the Washington, D.C. area, you might really enjoy stopping by for a drink or dinner in one of the places frequented by the Father of our Nation. Before moving on, however, I must relate the story of our visit to Mount Vernon—George Washington's home in northern Virginia—really not that far from Gadsby's. Charlene was just coming up on four years old as we toured the grounds, home and servants' quarters of this large estate. George Washington, after all, was the richest president in American history until Donald John Trump[5].

During our tour, we came to the tomb of both Washington and his wife, Martha. As the docent briefed those standing around the tomb, our daughter realized that our President was deceased and began to cry to the consternation of the others on tour. After further explanation to Charlene everyone was okay, but only when she began to cry did we realize that we had done an inadequate job of preparing for the excursion. Both Mitchie and I remember that moment as if it were yesterday and marvel at the innocence of youth, but also in the power of knowledge. I would think, as I remember Pearl Harbor, my first grasp of history, that Charlene's began with George Washington, or at least that visit one cloudy day to the monument holding his tomb.

By the end of April, my program for intensely studying Vietnamese was at its end. For anyone who has gone through such a program, it will not be news when I say it was my introduction to Purgatory. And during this training, during which my wife took courses in conversational French, the news came that the Defense Department could no longer support the sending of dependents with the advisors; Mitchie would have to stay in the United States. Flatly, the security situation had become so unstable that it just was not safe for families.

With that news, it was clear that we had to choose Plan B, or more correctly, create a Plan B. We decided that it would be best to send my young bride and two children close to my home in Cincinnati. Accordingly, we drove to Cincinnati and picked a new house in the Westwood section of town, not far from my parents and sisters' homes. After getting everyone settled, it was time for me to take off

---

[5] Kate Murphy, "Ten richest presidents before Trump takes top spot," *Yahoo News,* 8 January 2017.

for Vietnam. That day is easy to remember, May 24, because it was my mother's birthday. So having entered the Air Force on May 23, 1958, I took off for Vietnam on May 24, 1965. Leaving my family standing and waving from the greater Cincinnati Airport was pretty tough, as my long journey to Southeast Asia and war had begun.

Of course, such assignments are difficult for the military members involved, but let me make a case for the spouse and children left behind. Charlene was almost five, and John II was five days shy of one, and Mitchie and I had only been married for five years. While this is the story of my life and my adventures, Mitchie had ones of her own that included closing the home in Cincinnati before she moved to join me in my new assignment in Japan after I came back from Vietnam. That included traveling halfway around the world with two small children. As fine as the mentor system is within the military, medals should be made for wives who dauntlessly move with children in tow, luggage and all. But, I'm getting ahead of myself again. Now it's time to talk about a little place called Vietnam.

SIX

In Harm's Way

When I arrived in Saigon, I arrived armed with some fairly advanced knowledge of the Vietnamese language, and lucky was I, as the dialect that I studied was that of Southern Vietnam. (Most military officers were trained in that of the North, but my job was communicating with officers and men of the Vietnamese Air Force.) The first week was spent (and please do not worry, this is not going to be a week-by-week narrative) in Saigon getting intelligence and cultural briefings for our assignments "up north." Interestingly, during that week, I was ordered to assemble with a few other advisors at a football ground in Saigon. We arrived at the designated time and saw what appeared to be a helicopter overhead. (It could have been a fixed-wing aircraft—the years have clouded some of the details—but what I do remember is an individual leaping out of a perfectly good aircraft and come parachuting to the ground.)

That individual was our commander, General William Westmoreland, who seized upon this moment to make a dramatic entrance.

"Welcome to Vietnam, and you are lucky to be here. You are the chosen few!" Although that might not have been his actual words, the sentiments were the same.

We received his encouragement about the mission we were about to undertake and then returned to more pressing business—preparing for our departure to our duty stations. While most of the week was very Air Force-oriented, one special person had greeted me upon arrival, an officer who I worked with at SAC Headquarters. It was Major Eugene Schaffer, and he was one of the most interesting individuals I ever had the pleasure of working with. For a Major, he was very old, but he was fluent in French, had made a trip around the world before World War II, and was a man fascinated by all things Vietnamese. Luckily, he also had a classic French car, a black Citroën Traction Avant. I think you now get the picture. At a time (May 1965) when American military personnel were scrambling to put their hands on a jeep, with all its comfort and reliability, Gene had a car that fit in like he fit in with his fluency in French. For several days, he even invited me to his apartment, where we dined on meals prepared by his Vietnamese cook. Sitting on the balcony high above the city, our conversations were punctuated by the sounds of howitzers pouring shell after shell into the terrain surrounding Saigon, occasionally illuminating the countryside with starburst shells. Of course, in those days, it was clear that what we heard was "outgoing" and not "incoming." Time, unfortunately, would change that for the residents of Saigon.

My appointed city "up North" turned out to be Nha Trang, and my assignment was with the Military Assistance Advisory Group (MAAG) stationed there. As the Intelligence Officer assigned to the Group, my duties were clearly gathering information about events in and about the Nha Trang area. We had a compound with a wall, looking somewhat like a French Foreign Legion post in the movies of the 1940s. Every so often, I would be Officer-of-the-Day, but more correctly, Officer-of-the-Night. Responsibilities included regular checks on the guards who were posted all around the compound. It was always a good idea to make enough noise as you did your rounds so as not to wake them up in a start. With very effective automatic weapons in their laps, one did not want them to think a Viet Cong (our term for Vietnamese Communist Forces) raid was underway.

While a raid or attack never actually happened during my six months, sometimes we thought we were about to be attacked and would call in for artillery or air support on suspicious targets. One of my ancillary duties was to fly down to Cam Ranh Bay just south of Nha Trang and coordinate with South Korean Army units who had joined the war in mid-1965. These flights were the most dangerous as they were made in O-1 aircraft. Something straight out of the 1930s and 1940s, the O-1 was made largely of wood and some kind of fabric covering—nothing that could offer much protection. We sat on our seat parachutes which might have helped slow down a bullet, but the entire plane was as close to a motorized glider that you can get. Thanks to the good Lord, we never had any hostile fire on those flights. A far different experience from the A-1 flights that began when I joined the 522nd VNAF Fighter Squadron based in Saigon as an advisor.

I cannot stress enough the beauty of Nha Trang. It is located on the beach and offers some of the finest seafood dining in Asia. Generally speaking, the security situation in the area was as good as any in all of Vietnam at that time. It paled in comparison to the stories we heard about other duty stations. We even heard of bombs being placed in the old-style chain pull toilets of the day. The image conjured up was not too good, but the threat mattered little at times when the effects of tainted drinking water were taking effect, and the only refuge was a facility with a chain pull toilet.

The move to Saigon happened in time for me to mark Christmas in the capital city. Almost as soon as I had left, I received word that my roommate in Nha Trang had been gravely wounded in a night mission. He had come across a fallen tree as he drove his vehicle and attempted to remove the tree. However, the tree had been booby-trapped with an IED (improvised explosive device). The subsequent explosion critically injured him, and he died sometime later in hospital. That cast a pall over the move and the holiday season.

As much as the military attempts to make Christmas as pleasant as possible, frankly, it is an impossible job. Just hearing Bing Crosby singing his trademark song "I'm Dreaming of a White Christmas" with his rich, baritone voice sends everyone into immediate homesickness. The USO (United Services Organization) tried hard to bring a "little" home away from home holiday cheer for the troops, and I really give them all the credit they deserve, but anyone away from home at Christmas knows the feeling. It is just more acute as a soldier, sailor, airman, or marine, and especially so in a combat zone.

Of course in the mid-1960s there were no cell phones, no e-mail—things taken for granted nowadays—but we did have letters from home and the precious reel-to-reel tape recorders. The tape size was small, perhaps three inches across and it held about 15-20 minutes of recordings from home. You can only imagine how we must have felt to hear the "sounds" of home when we were halfway around the world. These cherished voices and sounds—kindergarten dances for Charlene and John II's first haircut from Bill the Barber (my barber as well as my father's barber)—brought us much joy and comfort. Late at night, alone in our quarters, we would listen and re-listen to the tapes. In a sense, because you could replay them, they were even better than the phone. Want to hear your daughter giggle again? Push the rewind button and listen again. Your son attempting to sing a song? Push the button. Listen again. My wife and I still have both the letters and tapes we sent, plus a tape machine that will still work. 1965 is only 54 years ago, but regarding technology, we have left it like the gramophone of the past. The Gramophone, you say? Go ahead and "Google" it. Another sign of the times!

My last six months in Vietnam were, as I said, with the 522nd VNAF Fighter Squadron. Their aircraft inventory was principally the A-1 aircraft or the Douglas Skyraider. It was huge for a fighter plane and had a great capability to protect soldiers in the field. Aircraft sent to assist ground forces could loiter for eight hours over the target area. Some missions were air patrol where A-1s would be circling and waiting for a request to come in. Others had specific objectives and were planned in advance. I flew with the more senior pilots some who had over 2000 missions flying since 1954, and the plane was actually an A-1G. That aircraft had the pilot and observer sitting next to each other—side-by-side. It also had a large compartment in the rear where we could put six or so crew members for when we deployed to other bases outside Saigon.

Most of the flights were standard air patrols and thus, could be expended wherever an emergency was happening. Sometimes the flights were eight hours in length as we circled in a large racetrack formation waiting for a call from a ground-support observer. When the call came in, the action was rapid and often dynamic. By that I mean, not just one-sided. Ground fire could be very worrisome, and sometimes, too accurate, as on one flight our oil line was severed, and after some hasty looking around for a place to land, we made a "dead stick" landing with the engine shut down and really no room for error.

Thanks to a very skilled pilot, we landed and were able to have the line repaired to fly again.

One source of many losses in this airplane was the lack of an ejection seat. I believe one was put in by 1970, but that did not help us in 1966. I lost another roommate from such a situation, as he was struck during a low profile run. Not able to gain altitude and climb out of the cockpit, we lost him as he attempted to make a crash landing. Another dear friend, a very young Vietnamese pilot, was asked at the last minute to put on an airshow for a Boy Scout Jamboree. Aiming to please the Commander of the South Vietnamese Air Force who had asked for the show, he took to the air and put on a fine demonstration until he decided to fly past the scouts upside down. I do not know what happened except he crashed in a fireball that I will never forget. Trying to please the boss sometimes is just not worth the cost.

One of the most exciting moments for me was flying with the Squadron Commander on a deployment out of Danang Air Base in northern central Vietnam. We were flying after participating in a strike, and the Commander looked up and saw several North Vietnamese MiGs. He dove as fast as he could and went so low that we were flying among the very tops of the trees and sometimes taking off several feet of timber. Of course, he was doing the flying, and I am exceedingly grateful as the mighty A-1 did a fine job of cutting timber and losing our pursuers. Of course, upon landing the crew chief and mechanics were all over the plane pulling branches and leaves from all sorts of locations using words that you only hear on the flight line. Anyway, I was as grateful as one can be in such circumstances. Major Toung, our Commander, looked at the gold Buddha around my neck that he had given me some weeks before and smiled. "You see, it is mighty powerful," he said, and we both thanked his mother for sending it from Laos to protect this young man from America.

Another exciting moment, which ended up being slightly more than a moment, was when individuals in the Vietnamese Army decided it was time to change the leadership of the government and get rid of the Air Force Brigadier who was also the Prime Minister. The day started like most days, I had breakfast with a pilot and his family who lived on base. Getting into the control room, I started to see a lot of commotion and pilots running to their planes and crew support teams running out to put rockets on the planes instead of bombs. These antitank rockets are very specific weapons and work best when used against armored vehicles because, in 1966, not many Viet Cong forces were running around in armored vehicles.

Soon I heard from my colleagues that all "foreign" troops were being denied access to Tan Son Nhut Air Base and the perimeter was being closed—no one in and no one out of the base. And in the words of one southern sports announcer for the Georgia Bulldogs' football games, it was time to "hunker down" and get ready for action.

It was right about this time when I got a call from U.S. Forces Headquarters, and they said: "What the hell is going on—you are our eyes on the scene;" or something not quite so dramatic. As it turned out, I was their man "inside" as it were, the "only" American inside the Operations Room of the 522nd VNAF Fighter Squadron. It soon became clear that ARVN tanks were trying to block the runways to prevent the A-1s loaded with armored piercing rockets from taking off. It was a coup attempt, and the Army was leading it.

Of course, the pilots of the 522nd out-smarted the tankers and took off using the taxiways instead of the runways. Into the air our squadron went, and it was clear that they were armed with the kind of firepower tanks and their inhabitants do not necessarily like. The planes made threatening moves toward the tanks as the two sides negotiated on the phones. Of course, the North was listening in and waiting to see the outcome (we never did have good ComSec—Communications Security—in Vietnam). Soon the tanks turned around and left the field; it was a clear indication that airpower—and Nguyen Cao Ky—had won the day.

It took several hours before the base was opened again, but the American forces did not appreciate that they had been denied access to the base. They called to see if I was okay, and all I could do was remark that I had been safe all along enjoying the unfolding drama that had taken place with one U.S. observer inside the Command Center. Later I received a Bronze Star for that moment, but oddly the excitement did not come from the enemy, but our friends. Well, Vietnam was complicated, and perhaps all those nuances were not understood even in Washington.

Another nuance came by living in the Cho Long District of Saigon in 1966; it was clear that Chinese-Vietnamese relations were not all positive. The Cho Long area was basically a "China Town," and I soon found out that the "average Vietnamese male," at least those on the flight line, did not particularly care for the Chinese, even though they might have lived in Vietnam for hundreds of years. Perhaps I should point out that the average Vietnamese Airman did not care for Chinese. How do I know? Well, whenever an A-1 was going through post-flight, the crews would turn the aircraft, so it faced Cho Long. In the process of clearing the 20mm machine guns every once in a while, pow! They would fire off a round still in the guns, and that was that. Not only did that endanger the Chinese, but Vietnamese who happened to be in the area as well as American servicemen who lived there. I hope my protestations were effective, but at this writing, I cannot say; I really don't know.

Looking back on the entire year that I was in Vietnam, has left me with very mixed feelings. I had many conversations with General Nguyen Cao Ky, and many of his senior lieutenants and grew to respect my Vietnamese colleagues who fought and flew daily. I remember vividly eating *pho bo*—beef noodle soup—one breakfast morning with a pilot and his family on base and having to go back that evening with the news that husband and father would never eat breakfast with them again. I also remember my American roommates that never went home. Likewise, my immediate American boss, who was a mentor and close colleague so enjoyed the call to arms that he extended at least twice and perhaps took a third year in Vietnam as "it was the only war available."

I, of course, did not take this latter path; I couldn't wait until I could be back with my family and asked for a "consecutive overseas tour" so we could return to Japan for Mitchie to be among her family once again. In May 1966, I left Vietnam for Japan and an eventual reunion with Mitchie and our two young children, Charlene and John II. As I left, the situation had stabilized considerably. South Korea had sent two divisions: the White Horse and Tiger Divisions, and the American presence had reached over 200,000. But the war was becoming unpopular at home. When I left for Vietnam in May of 1965, I had been given cookies and good wishes as I left for war; when I finally returned I dodged spit and the condemnations of fellow Americans who could see a "lifer" (a derogatory term used to describe someone who made a "career" out of the military) when they saw one.

The problem was, a lot of people didn't know what was actually going on over there and as a result, the war was sometimes misinterpreted. What is done is done. However, as I return to Vietnam and interact with Vietnamese in Vietnam and here at school in South Korea, I am constantly amazed at the forgiving attitude of these fine people. I made no secret that I was there and participated earnestly to stop the "aggression" from the North. Generally, they nod, smile, and change the subject.

(Years later, Mitchie and I, on one trip to Saigon (Ho Chi Minh City), stayed at the hotel I had stayed in when waiting to go "up country" when I first arrived in Vietnam. On the light table next to the bed was a book, much like the Gideon Bibles we see in the States. It was a history of Vietnam. Interested to see what was said about the late war, I quickly opened it to its coverage of the conflict. In a 700-page book, perhaps 2.5 lines were given over to the war. Something like "Between 1965 and 1975 the U.S. and Vietnam had severe differences. We now look to the future." That was how I remember the quote, but remember, it only catches the meaning of the entry. For all we did, the Vietnamese look to the future and see America as a friend in a new world of new opportunities and perhaps different, not necessarily new, enemies.)

As I left for Japan, and my next assignment at 5th Air Force Headquarters in Fuchu, Japan, I had no idea how events in Asia would unfold over the next three years. I was soon to find out. But first, we had one important task—move from Vietnam to Japan for me and move from Ohio to Japan for Mitchie, Charlene, and John II to reunite the family once again.

SEVEN

Cold War Showdown in Korea

The move to Japan by the Endicott Family was not one I particularly wish to write about. I was required to go to Japan and take up my duties in 5th Air Force Headquarters; my wife had to settle affairs, ship the housing goods, and travel with two young children from Cincinnati to Tachikawa, Japan on her own. I have a most understanding wife who will do and does anything to support our family, and I am most grateful to say, her husband. But the move to Japan was, shall I say, one of the most difficult for Mitchie ever. (It also did not help, when in Japan we had to move from one on-base house to another while I was on TDY or temporary duty back in the States.) The military wife is certainly part of the military team and now is generally recognized as such—but still no pay. All I need say is going roughly 7,000 miles with a one-year-old and a five-year-old takes all the managerial skills that one can have. (Mitchie, thanks again!)

The opportunity to return to Japan was wonderful. It allowed our children to meet their Japanese relatives and actually experience festivals, birthdays, weekend dinners, and just growing up together—experiences even I did not have with my cousins living in Kansas. They started to pick up the Japanese language at a rate only the young can enjoy, and soon they were playing with neighboring kids who lived just outside the boundary of Grant Heights, the family housing area where we lived, which also included a commissary, elementary school, and the Officers' Club.

In a sense, it was a really big deal when we had Japanese visitors. Their names had to be sent in advance to Security, and I would meet them at the gate and escort them to our house. Of course, Japan is an exciting place to live even if you are not traveling about, but it can also be a dangerous place which can turn deadly without warning with natural catastrophes such as earthquakes, typhoons, and tsunamis which can ruin your day. We experienced two dramatic examples during our three-year stay. One evening at dusk, a fairly large earthquake rattled the house like it was a toy. It was the era when Godzilla was on TV and our young son—pressing three at the time— upon exiting the house like everyone else gazed upon a sparking transformer perched atop a telephone pole. Just like the movies! Sparks were flying everywhere, and he knew that Godzilla was just behind the roof line ahead. Almost with the speed of light, he reversed himself getting under his bed in a remarkable feat of athleticism. Only trouble was, the house was still shaking all over the place, and I had to retrieve him and race out the door. That was our biggest earthquake, but almost weekly there would be the gently swaying of the chandelier indicating the earthquake demons were at play deep beneath the surface.

Similarly, we had one really bad encounter with a typhoon. These giant winds—called *taifu* in Japanese, the origin of the word typhoon in English—can literally "blow your house down" like the severest tornados that rush through Georgia every spring. When this typhoon hit where we lived, it took out the window frames in our home, but luckily they landed on carpeting and other gentle landing areas and did not break. Several days later, the maintenance crews came by fixing each house one-by-one. We were lucky because at the height of the storm, we really could feel the house as it struggled to stay affixed to the foundation. Happily, we did not encounter a *tsunami,* another Japanese word that has entered the vocabularies of modern societies. But we did encounter political tsunamis, as soon it was to become an active time for security matters in Northeast Asia.

Mitchie and I became involved in breaking into living "on-base" for the second time in our career—remember we lived on Radford Terrace in Hawaii, not far from Pearl Harbor from 1960 to 1962 when we left for Omaha, Nebraska, and SAC Headquarters. Now we lived in Grant Heights, a family housing area where U.S. Forces lived and commuted every day to work at one of the military bases in the region. My commute to Fuchu Air Station (the difference between an air base and an air station is that air stations do not have active runways—basically, no airplanes) was possible by *densha,* or electric trains—sort of light rail trains—but you had to go in toward Tokyo and transfer to a train that would go out and westward. It took just too long. So, every day, I rode in a car driven by an officer colleague who took driving in Japan so seriously that he wore a crash helmet—just in case. I rode shotgun (the seat opposite the driver) and felt pretty insecure when my colleague was fully attired in safety belts and crash helmet. We never crashed so, like carrying an umbrella and preventing the rain, wearing that helmet worked. Thanks, Bob!

As I followed events in Vietnam and briefed the staff on a regular basis, I had one other requirement that I had to pursue. That was the completion of my Master's Degree for the University of Omaha that I had begun before leaving for Vietnam. Since the university did not offer Asian courses at that time, I did my Masters in history concentrating on European History, specifically the Interwar Period from 1919-1939 which unfortunately was only a two-decade period of peace before hostilities renewed. While trapped into European history—it really was good for me—I did ask my advisor, "Boss" Tricket, a jolly Falstaffian-like individual, who had a booming voice of authority and was an expert on many of the land battles of the First World War, to let me focus my papers on the impact of the European war on Asia. Ultimately, it led to my selecting as my thesis the negotiations between Viscount Ishii and Secretary of State Lansing to "normalize" relations between the U.S. and Japan as the United States was entering the war as an enemy of Germany and an ally of Japan. (Japan, which was an ally of Great Britain, had entered the war in 1914, and seized German-held areas in China and in the Pacific to "aid" its British ally.)

I had worked on the subject at the U.S. Library of Congress when in Washington studying Vietnamese. During the U.S. occupation in Japan, when we had access to all Japanese diplomatic traffic records from Japan's Foreign Office files, these files were copied and put on microfilm. These were and are still available at the Library of Congress. I did as much as I could, but I had not finished and being in Tokyo permitted me to pick up where I left off, but now using the Japanese files of the Diet Library located on the subway not all that far from Grant Heights. It was a tremendous experience because the one-time secret dispatches from Tokyo to its negotiator in Washington revealed, the Japanese objectives were clearly defined in welcoming the United States participation in the war. In essence, the Lansing-Ishii Agreement set out broad objectives for peace in the Asia-Pacific Region and included a Japanese pledge to stay out of America's way in the Philippines for a similar freehand on the Korean Peninsula and China. But, like many other things in U.S.-Japan affairs, it took on a much more complex function and is still debated to this day.

Here, I must acknowledge the yeoman ship efforts of my wife to translate the Taisho-era Japanese language that was much more difficult than the Japanese that I was studying and had emerged after World War II which controlled the number of standard characters (1800) that could be used on the front pages of newspapers. The Japanese she was translating was far more complex. Thanks again, Mitchie! I did finish the thesis and defended it in Omaha in 1968; it was one more thing that happened in a very busy year—this one of a positive nature, and it provided me with an earned Master's Degree a requirement to teach at the U.S. Air Force Academy—a story I will later tell.

Although we did not encounter a natural tsunami while in Japan— as I mentioned earlier—there was an abundance of political tidal waves that crashed down upon America and its allies in that fateful year of 1968. The first political *tsunami* was the North Korean attack on the South Korean Blue House—the presidential residence of Park Chung-hee—North Korea's arch enemy.

It was January 1968. My duties as Chief of Target Plans for 5th Air Force had generally been taken up with keeping the staff up-to-date with the situation in Vietnam. I was one of the few in the headquarters who had been to Vietnam, had received a Bronze Star for my activities there, and certainly was the only one who spoke Vietnamese on the staff. But as that fateful year of 1968 got underway, our focus became Northeast Asia, not Southeast Asia.

Luckily, I have the habit of making sure when one year ends, I am ready for the next. In this case, all the likely targets for the 5th Air Force in Northeast Asia were updated and ready. That really means that the target location matched exactly the planning data and DGZs (desired ground zeros) were aligned as required. Also, the most current intelligence information, including photos from sources we could not even give to pilots at this point, was reviewed and noted. We were ready, as far as intelligence was concerned, and I must say, I wish other sections and activities of the headquarters had followed my practice.

On Monday, January 22, we were alerted that at 2200 hours on the previous day, a North Korean assassination unit had made it to within 100 meters of the Blue House in downtown Seoul an attempt to kill the South Korean President Park Chung-hee. Of the 31 members of the attack unit, all were killed in their attempts to leave South Korea except two. (One was captured, and another one actually made it back to North Korea.) We at the 5th Air Force were fully involved in trying to make sense of this attack and were following closely the ROK Army's efforts to round up or kill the members of Unit 124[6] which had been responsible for the raid when the second shoe fell. Around noon, members of the 5th Air Force Headquarters Battle Staff were called to the Command Center and told the news that an intelligence-gathering ship, the USS *Pueblo* was under attack by North Korean ships off Wonsan.

I will not go into the details of the afternoon, but what happened was our Commander General Seth McKee attempted to rouse the air resources he had stretching from Misawa Air Base in northern Japan to Kadena Air Base in Okinawa (then still under U.S. administration), and American fighters also at Osan and Kunsan in South Korea. Considerable assets were available on paper, but transferring paper assets to fighting assets became a nightmare to the General who more than once sounded like Richard the III calling for "A horse, a horse! My Kingdom for a horse!"[7] In any event, air cover was not forthcoming, nor were punitive strikes on shipping or ground assets as the night set in and such activity was seen as endangering our own crews who now could be on North Korean ships as well as the *Pueblo*. By the next morning, the time for military response had expired; diplomacy was to rule the day for the next 11 months.

---

[6] See https://en.wikipedia.org/wiki/Blue House raid. Accessed 11 April 2017.
[7] Shakespeare, *Richard the Third* Act 5, scene 4, 7–10.

The event had repercussions in so many ways. The full attention of the 5th Air Force was now focused on Northeast Asia. Since many 5th Air Force resources had been temporarily deployed to Vietnam, a call for 150 fighters was sent out to the U.S. resulting eventually in the activation of Air Force Reserve and National Guard planes that flew to bases in Korea and Japan. Three aircraft carriers and fourteen thousand reservists were also mobilized.[8]Also, the Headquarters actually went on alert and kept all at the Command Center for several days to respond to the emergency. Some of the older officers and airmen could not take the intense pressure, and personnel changes were quick and career-ending in some instances. Obviously, it was a shock that was needed and resulted in a leaner and meaner organization that fit the time.

What this meant regarding the Korean peninsula was that the entire organization was preparing for the next North Korean provocation. If it meant an invasion was coming across the DMZ or via North Korean Special Forces and fast boats, no one knew. The message was clear; get ready for the next attack as it would be significant.

Indeed it was! The only problem was that the attack was not in Northeast Asia, it was in Southeast Asia—in fact, in Vietnam. During the late evening of January 30—only seven days after the turmoil of the *Pueblo*—more than 80,000 Vietnamese troops hit some 100 towns and cities throughout the entire length of South Vietnam announcing the largest military operation of the war. American and South Vietnamese forces eventually defeated the threat to the southern Republic, and the destruction of the Viet Cong—as opposed to North Vietnamese forces—was almost catastrophic, but the damage politically to America was immense. Support for the war in the States was beginning to erode. What had been seen as a military defeat for the Viet Cong, had, in fact, become a political victory with the announcement only two months later on March 31 when President Lyndon Johnson told the American people in a nationally televised broadcast that he would not run for another term. In addition, there had been another political casualty one month earlier that

---

[8] Sebastien Roblin, "North Korea almost Started a Nuclear War When it Captured a U.S. Spyship," The *National Interest,* captured from the Internet, Yahoo news on January 22, 2018 (however, the article first appeared in 2016).

foreshadowed Johnson's decision not to seek reelection. Secretary of Defense, Robert McNamara, whose countless "optimistic" reports about America "winning" the war in Vietnam could no longer be sustained. On February 28, 1968, he submitted his resignation.[9]

Excuse me for being distracted by this critical event in East Asian history, but I have always believed that the events of January 1968 were too perfectly executed to be just happenstance. The events in Korea became a classical military feint, and we fell for it as children before the masters. I have so strongly held the belief that there was coordination between the North Korean and North Vietnamese leadership in the January events of 1968 that on more than one occasion I have pushed that idea to high officials of both states. Before his death, I wrote a letter to the Vietnamese Commander Vo Nguyen Giap through the Vietnamese Embassy in Seoul but never heard anything in return. The attempts to assassinate the leaders of South Korea and South Vietnam within weeks and using almost the same number of sappers can support my theory, but I wish some historian with deep access to relations between these two states at this time can resolve the issue. I am not the only one who believes an absolute strategic masterstroke was devised and delivered by our enemies working in concert. (It was also reported that CIA Director Richard Helms believed the Soviets and North Koreans collaborated to "relieve pressure on Vietnam.")[10] Perhaps it only proves we should be reading Sun Tzu and not Clausewitz.

I was kept busy for the rest of the year making sure that the pilots of 5th Air Force units knew their targets and were ready to go at a moments' notice. So I made trips to locations in South Korea that had been added to our major operating bases, Kunsan and Osan. There were perhaps five or six locations with visiting Air Guard or Air Force Reserve aircraft including Iwakuni Naval Air Base in Japan; all had to be brought up and ready for action. In 1969, I was asked to temporarily take over as Assistant Chief-of-Staff for Intelligence at Misawa Air Base in northern Honshu. It was early April, and the cherry trees of

---

[9] See "Tet Offensive," Wikipedia for an excellent account of this important moment in East Asian history. Accessed on 11 April 2017: https://en.wikipedia.org/wiki/Tet_Offensive, pp. 1-30.
[10] Sebastien Roblin, 'North Korea almost Started a Nuclear War when it Captured a U.S. Spy Ship," *The National Interest,* captured from the Internet, Yahoo News on January 22, 2018.

that area were just beginning to get the idea that it was time to bloom. Spring does not come early to Aomori as it is part of Japan, often referred to as *yuki guni* or snow country.

And then, North Korea struck again—this time in the air.

As I recall, I had finished lunch on that April 15, afternoon—that by the way is not a good way to indicate time, as I am often quite a hungry fellow by 1100—when we received an alert of a possible attack on an EC-121 that was carrying out a reconnaissance mission over the Sea of Japan. The airplane, the kind President Eisenhower used as Air Force One when he was in office, was a Lockheed Super Constellation. It was sleek for a conventional, non-jet-powered aircraft, and flew at about 300 miles per hour. It was manned by 30 sailors and 1 Marine; all perished in the attack.

President Richard M. Nixon had become president in the election of November 1968, and the campaign rhetoric had been very critical of previous American responses to North Korean provocations; in essence, we (perhaps just me) thought that this was the beginning of a really big show. And we were ready. Believe me.

The 5th Air Force was ready; we waited, but it seems the new administration was finding out the difficulties of actually running a country, especially when an erratic enemy was behaving most unpredictably. No orders to respond came except to reduce the alert status later. I do not remember when our alert status was reduced, but shortly after, the regularly scheduled Assistant Chief-of-Staff for Intelligence reported in, and I returned to Tokyo to prepare for our next assignment and move to the U.S. Air Force Academy in Colorado Springs, Colorado. My new job was to teach Political Science to Air Force Cadets.

Over the years, I have often wondered if the attack on our EC-121 was a planned event to mark the birthday of the leader of the DPRK, Kim Il-sung, as that day certainly was his birthday. Just a coincidence? I think not.

Subsequently, we have seen special days in North Korea accompanied by special actions on the part of the North—especially as the 1988 Olympics approached, such "dirty deeds" were tried as deliberate state policy. As a professional military officer (retired), I have great difficulty in dealing with such a possibility. But, again, we are dealing with North Korea, but a birthday gift?[11] It is beyond contemplation.

[11] See Brook Benedict, "The EC-121 Shootdown: North Korea's Killing of 31 US sailors that has almost been forgotten," *News.com.au,* 13 April 2017. Accessed at: http://www.news.com.au/world/asia/the-ec121-shootdown-north-korea-killing-of-31-u...

EIGHT

Back to School

When we left Japan, we departed from Tachikawa Air Base and landed as a family at Travis Air Force Base in northern California. As we often did, we stayed with my uncle Lawrence, who had been wounded at Guadalcanal, married his nurse, and set off to build a new life in the San Francisco area as a court reporter. Being a court reporter was just Lawrence's cup of tea, and he was prospering with his principal office in Oakland, California—just down the hill from Piedmont where he had established his home.

Staying with Lawrence was always a wonderful experience thanks to the stories he regaled to us and his kindness. He was the youngest in my father's family and his children—my cousins—were not that much older than I was, so we had a lot of fun. While we were there, it came time during the week to pick up our Nash Rambler (which we had purchased in Japan through the Base Exchange) from the dock and have it cleaned up. For the trip across the Pacific, Cosmoline, a brown wax-like petroleum-based product had been vigorously applied to prevent rust. It was a mess. We could hardly see out the window as it was so covered with gook. We took it to a local car wash, explained to the owner that this was a really dirty car and got a special deal to run it through the wash several times, until clean.

Then it was time for good-byes and a trek across the country to visit our parents' home in Cincinnati. This was a special trip as Mom and Dad did not visit Japan while we were there so, it had been a full three years since everybody had seen each other. Another reason why it was special was my parents had sold the home on St. William Ave. and moved further west in Cincinnati to the Delhi area. Not only had they moved, but they had also downsized big time. Instead of the roomy two-story bungalow, they now lived in a one-floor ranch with only one guest room—and it was tiny. They had actually done that during my last year at Ohio State, but now I was four people, not one. (Thus, I will never sell the big house we have in Atlanta, as both Mitchie and I wish to have space for our kids, grandkids and possibly someday our great-grandchildren.)

After a few days of catching up and enjoying Cincinnati—it is such a great city—it was time to take the last leg of the journey and head west to Colorado Springs and the U.S. Air Force Academy. I was a "buck instructor." That basically meant I did everything someone else did not want to do, and I also taught five sessions of political science. It made for a busy life, but it was quite rewarding.

Because I had been in Vietnam (not many instructors at that time had been to Vietnam and served a full tour), as well as my self-taught specialization in Asian Politics, I soon found myself teaching courses on the Japanese and Korean scene, and American Government. The classes usually numbered around 20-25 cadets, and the expectations, not to mention pressures, were on all cadets to succeed. I must say, I was so happy to be on the giving side, not the receiving.

At one of the first big events of the new semester with the entire Cadet Wing in attendance, I was asked to provide some commentary on Vietnam and North Korea. Having just taken part in the response to the EC-121 shoot down, I ended up stressing the nature of a regime that would shoot down an aircraft in international airways and boast about it as a "gift" for the leader. Using some great intercepts from the unclassified Foreign Broadcast Daily, we were able to re-create the incident and held the cadets spellbound for the entire session. Since we were all hoping to increase the number signed up for political science, it was considered a successful first exposure to the student body. (Truthfully, it was so terrible that the Soviets offered and indeed helped in the search for any survivors. Their help was appreciated, but as an intelligence officer, I knew that their "help" could have self-serving implications. In any event, it did mark a new understanding between Soviet and American forces.)

The U.S. Air Force Academy itself is on a huge campus measuring some 18,000 acres. It is at the base of some mountains and makes a splendid site for an educational mission. In those days (1969-1971) it was very remote. The city of Colorado Springs had not yet reached the campus, so unlike the other academies, West Point and Annapolis, the cadets were stuck pretty much on campus until they became 1st Classmen or seniors when they could own a car. From a professor's standpoint, it provided a quiet and lovely place where distractions were really not a concern. My wife and I certainly enjoyed interacting with the other buck instructors and at times our seniors, but it was a small academic community out in the mountains where the deer, bears, and coyotes (no antelopes) roamed. In the severe winter, you could go outside to put your garbage in the containers and be greeted by eight or so coyotes that were just waiting—not to attack people, but the garbage. Also, small dogs or cats were not put out at night. If someone did, their pets rapidly became evening dinners for all variety of wild creatures. A big hawk or eagle would easily carry off a young dog or cat. Shall I say, life on the frontier was and still is, the survival of the fittest?

Football games quickly became a major item around which social functions were planned in the fall. And then right before Christmas, a performance of Handel's *Messiah* in the Academy Chapel marked the end of the semester. For football, we would often invite cadets to our house if there was an away game and 15 or so guests soon ate us "out of house and home." That is just an expression to indicate how young teenagers would go through your kitchen like vacuum cleaners. We enjoyed it immensely as our children at that time were about nine and five, and putting cadets with our kids just made for a great evening for all. And believe me, most cadets needed that kind of moment to relax as if at home. First-year cadets were pretty much held on campus for the entire year, so they particularly enjoyed such occasions. It really became a way for cadets to relax and have an unrestricted dialog between themselves and their instructor hosts. Attending the *Messiah* was always very meaningful as the service gave us an opportunity to celebrate the coming of Christmas with family, colleagues, and cadets.

Since at that time, the Academy tried to have serving officers do the teaching in front of cadets, it was imperative that the school keep an adequate number of instructors who possessed Ph.D.'s. Usually, for accreditation purposes, one-third of the faculty had to have an appropriately earned doctorate. One day my boss asked if I would be interested in returning to university to obtain a Ph.D. As I recall, Mitchie and I discussed this for all of thirty minutes; it was one of the best and most important decisions we ever made.

After considering our many options for graduate school, Mitchie and I decided that the Fletcher School of Law and Diplomacy would be the best for a more senior student who would be on an intensive two-and-a-half-year sprint to a doctorate. For the period during which I would be going to school full time, I was administratively transferred to the Air Force Institute of Technology (AFIT), and they would oversee my progress. As such, I was paid to go to school. I know no better way to obtain a graduate degree; you can understand my devotion to the Air Force and my willingness to stay some 28 years before retiring. Of course, there is a formal obligation for any such "special assignment." For each year one goes to school with the Air Force picking up all costs, one owes three, but the obligation runs consecutively, so you are reducing the number as you go to school— it really ended up being two for every year. In any event, both of us thought that that was a good idea, and in preparation during the summer of 1970, I took intensive Japanese at the University of Minnesota to make sure I had a certified base in that language which would become my principal language to offer at the Fletcher School. Receiving an A for that rough summer, memorizing as many as 50 characters per night, we were ready for the next adventure save one very important detail. We had two cars and did not want to drive two cars for such a long odyssey, so we had a special coupling put on the rear of the Nash Rambler that connected to the front of our 1966 Volkswagen "Bug." Almost as the wagon-trains that settled the West, we set off for Boston one car towing the other and the major challenge of Tufts University at the end of the Spring Semester 1971.

When we arrived in Boston, we had the benefit of a house hunting trip several months before. I had purchased a house in Bedford, Massachusetts, a small and delightful village along the Great Road that ran from Boston to Concord—the path the British took on Patriots'

Day April 19, 1775, marking the armed beginning of our Revolution. Bedford is not recognized for the role it played in those early days, but it was the Bedford Flag that was flown at Concord when the British realized they had perhaps underestimated the foe that they had angered. It became our home for the next two-and-a-half years and a delightful one at that.

The summer term began immediately, and I enrolled in Harvard University's 4th-year Japanese language class to get the Fletcher language requirement out of the way, if at all possible. It was quite an experience as when I went to class on the first day. I realized that I was the only 4th-year student. Now, I have had experiences with many universities, but I know of only one that will assign the head of the department to a course that has only one student. That is Harvard! My professor was Gen Itasaka, a renowned Japanese educator who made that summer one to never forget. Through his kindness, I met and had several interactions with Professor Edwin Reischauer, who had been President John F. Kennedy's Ambassador to Japan (1961-1966). He chose as our textbook the monthly journal *ChuoKoren*, which was basically like reading the *New York Times*. The only problem was every night there was another article. I had thought that 3rd year Japanese was tough, well, as the saying goes, one lives and learns. It was probably the most difficult summer I have ever had, but it ended successfully, and when I called back to the Air Force Academy the head of the Japanese Department actually thought he was speaking to some Japanese that he did not know. I finally convinced him that it was John Endicott at the end of the line. I am not sure if he was just trying to make me feel good, or it was a successful summer, but my Japanese improved.

The course routine was severe at Fletcher, especially as I took a full load and pushed to get as many requirements done as quickly possible. Soon it was time to celebrate Christmas, and we found out the joys of living in a small New England town. Volunteers from the local fire department visited our house in early December to find out how many young children we had. At that time (1971) Charlene was 11, and John II was 6. That was a difficult time as Charlene looked with a great deal of skepticism on the idea of Santa Claus and John was hyperventilating just at the thought of his arrival. It was decided the volunteers would deliver gifts for both children and Santa would personally give them their gifts.

On Christmas Eve around eight, there was a knock at the door. Since we did not have a fireplace, it was natural that even Santa would use the front door. Once the door opened, all bedlam broke loose, and even Charlene might have had second thoughts. But, Christmas was just one of the days that made life in New England more enjoyable. The sense of history among its people is truly magnificent, and things like Patriots Day and the 4th of July (Independence Day) were moments that signaled the rebirth of a true spirit of national awareness. The Town Square of each small town leaped to life with re-enactors dressed in Revolutionary attire—both British and American—and replayed moments only found in the history books. Boom! The cannon in the Square went off, plus muskets from the Minute Men and the Red Coats. Heavy smoke from the gunfire mingled with some from the hot dog and hamburger grills, and everyone celebrated as if the word of a great victory had just been received. For me, from Ohio, where that level of celebration is usually not found, it was an opportunity to relive history.

The passing of Harry S. Truman on December 26, 1972, saddened the nation, but there were probably many who felt that "Good old Harry waited until the day after Christmas to die, so not to ruin Christmas for his fellow Americans." Of course, other things were happening as a small incident that happened at Democratic National Headquarters in the Watergate Hotel in Washington, D.C. the previous summer was taking shape and would consume practically all who were involved—including President Richard M. Nixon. Happily, these events only became the subject of our evening dinners, and all seemed so far away.

The immediate issue was to complete the Ph.D. in the two-and-a-half years that the Air Force Institute of Technology had given me. Working with my advisors and mentors at the Fletcher School of Law and Diplomacy and Harvard, I made great progress and was nearing the completion of the required course work; only the doctoral dissertation loomed in the way. At this point, I had not chosen a dissertation topic as yet. Happily, the Air Force Academy invited me back to Colorado Springs to take part in a major international security affairs conference that had been an annual tradition—sponsored by

Columbia University. Since I was heavily into the security and political issues facing the nations of Northeast Asia, had been a nuclear weapons planner at several stops along my career, and was a specialist on Japan's security issues, I had been drawn to the subject of Japan's future policy towards nuclear weapons.

Thus, at the symposium, I delivered a paper relating to Japan's Nuclear Option. Already at that time, I was quite familiar with the Japanese government and public attitudes toward nuclear armament, and I believe that I gave a reasoned and cautious assessment that clearly set out Japan's particular circumstances. I did not know it at the time, but sitting in the audience was the Public Affairs Officer of the Embassy of Japan, Hisahiko Okasaki. After the presentation, he approached me and asked if I had picked a topic for my dissertation. I noted that I had not, but had considered the nuclear question and ruled it out as access to knowledgeable individuals would not be possible, and without that, there would be no reason to research that topic. At that point, Okasaki offered to arrange necessary interviews with specialists in Japan to help me gain the insights that would be necessary to adequately present all aspects of a very complex issue.

With that assistance to help, I submitted my proposal to my advisors at Fletcher, and we were off to the races. Basically, I had six months remaining of my 30 months, not all that long in that I would need to write about 400 pages. I set a routine of writing 18 pages of yellow legal pad per day as my goal. I would write, I determined whether good or bad, but 18 pages would be my goal. Once 18 pages were reached, usually in the late afternoon, I would put on my running attire and take off down Burlington Road running between one or two miles. That would burn off the frustration and get me ready to help Mitchie in the kitchen or pursue my hobby of baking. I also tried being a "Den Mother" for Cub Scouts and had quite a bit of fun. One Saturday afternoon, I took the entire "pack" to Fenway Park, home of the Boston Red Sox and had a great time—except one of my charges would burst into tears every time the crowd cheered. I really enjoyed being "Den Mother," but then Scout Headquarters found out about it, and I was "relieved" of duty.

In any event, these kinds of activities kept my primary focus on track, and I had written a major portion of the paper, which could be done by the research of available documentation and public papers. It was time to take up the kind offer by Counsellor Okazaki and see what I could learn from Japan.

With the wonderful cooperation of the Sanno Hotel in Tokyo, I was able to set up headquarters in this historic building that was once the headquarters for the leaders of the 2-26 Incident in 1936 when young Japanese officers tried to take over the government and seek a new "more righteous" Japan. After the war, it had become the Officers' Club and Hotel used by U.S. and Allied Officers in Japan. I had not taken much leave (vacation time) while at Fletcher so I had a good month available for my interview program. As an active-duty officer, I normally would have had to ask permission of the U.S. Embassy to visit Japan. But, since I was on vacation, not on official duty, getting permission was not necessary. It became the secret to my success. For approximately three weeks, I interviewed Japanese nuclear experts, strategic specialists, political commentators, and professors of many higher institutions on this issue of nuclear weapons for Japan. It was a most intense but rewarding time. My ability to use Japanese was put to the test, but most of the time my interlocutors spoke pretty good English, which eased my blood pressure quite a bit.

As I neared the end of my list of interviewees, I was asked by a professor of the Japan Defense Research Institute to come over and talk to a group of colleagues at this Defense Institute. At the end of my talk, my host handed me a wad of Japanese Yen and said it was for the talk. I was really surprised and said it was not possible for me to accept such a sum, but they insisted as the paperwork had been done and to undo it would be impossible, not to mention a slight to their "generosity."

"Okay, I said. "Give it to me, and I'll give it to the Embassy for the U.S. General Fund."

No harm, no foul. Right? Wrong. It was after that that my visit became really interesting and short.

It was in the afternoon, and I had gone to the U.S. Embassy to see the Air Force Attaché. When I walked in and put the money on this desk, all sorts of questions flowed. "Where? Who? When?" And so on and so on! So for the next hour or so, I explained that I was an AFIT-sponsored Ph.D. student and had spent the last three weeks interviewing Japanese on the nuclear weapons issue. To say the gentleman was incredulous is probably an understatement, as talking about nuclear weapons in those days was as taboo a subject as one can imagine. Filled with my information and my address, the Attaché bid me a fond farewell. I returned to the Sanno worried about the availability of a plane to get me back to the States as I was flying on a Space Available basis (Space Available or Space-A travel is when a military member "catches" a flight on a military transport) basis— actually, hitchhiking a ride back home to Boston.

It was slightly after I finished dinner that I received a call from the Embassy and my worries about transportation home were over, I had a seat reserved that very next morning—probably on the first aircraft out of town—and back to the States. The informed reader will understand from the Embassy's point of view, I "needed to get out of Dodge by sundown." Actually, it came at just the right time, as I had finished my formal interview program. I had what I needed to complete my dissertation, I knew that, and I am sure the Embassy was happy to see my back as I got on that aircraft.

I set to integrate the new data into my dissertation and submitted it in early November 1973, and defended in mid-December. As all doctoral students know, the final review and evaluation by the Ph.D. review panel can go either way. Just before my review was set, there had been another panel, for which the dissertation defender had prepared a party—Champagne, and goodies—for all his friends. Well, he failed. That sent a message throughout the school to not assume anything. With that clearly in my mind, I met the panel and passed with several comments on what a good book it would make.

With my mission accomplished, we reassembled the Rambler-Volkswagen convoy and on a rainy December afternoon headed west to the Air Force Academy in the middle of the gas crisis and a developing snow storm. Sometimes I think we should get medals for such things as a family transfer amidst and in the face of ice storms and fuel shortages, but that will have to wait until I am Secretary of the Air Force—or something like that. We made it, and I will say, just by the hair on my chinny chin chin.[12]

---

[12] "Little pig, little pig, let me come in/Not by the hair on my chinny chin chin./Then I'll huff, and I'll puff, and I'll blow your house in." Jacobs, Joseph (1890). *English Fairy Tales*. Oxford University. pp. 68–72.

Returning to the Academy, I had all of a sudden become the senior guy with a Ph.D. Thus, I was the ranking member of the Political Science Department. However, because collectively we had turned out more conscientious objectors than any other Department at the Academy, we were merged with the Philosophy Department, and I was made Deputy Head of the newly created Philosophy and Political Science Department. This shotgun marriage made for some interesting experiences and challenges in the management of anger and frustration on the part of the Poli-Sci faculty. It happened at the same time that the Air Force was introducing a new personnel evaluation system which allowed for very few "Outstanding" rankings to be issued to our staff. These were outstanding officers who had been recruited from around the world to serve as role models before our young cadets. Now having grouped them at the Academy, we were told that only ten percent could be at the top, and the rest would have to live a life of "almost been." In those days competition was so keen that a less than outstanding rating eliminated any chance of "below the zone" or early promotion, and in some cases would lead to an early departure from the Air Force. From a management standpoint, it was a difficult time.

However, from an academic point of view, it was a wonderful and productive moment for this new Ph.D. After returning to the Academy, I focused on getting the dissertation published in book form. Really that was the measure of a good dissertation "back in the day," and I was lucky to find an enthusiastic publisher who became a good friend—Fredrick Praeger of Praeger Publishers. It thus appeared soon after my return to the Academy on the international scene and was received very positively. I also had a life-long colleague and friend, Bill Heaton, who was also serving at the Academy, and we together wrote my next book, *Politics of East Asia*. I wrote the sections on Japan and Korea, and Bill did China. That was followed by my next major management feat, the preparation of the Academy's premiere book on security policy, *American Defense Policy*, 4th Edition. Practically every faculty member who wanted to contribute was asked to write a chapter, and the editor's job was to make sure that happened and to write chapters themselves. With the good support of the Johns Hopkins University Press, the book turned out to be a very successful edition and John Endicott and Roy Stafford the editors got quite a bit of good press as the collective input was well received. That is the time I learned to read sentences backward from the bottom of the page to proof the copy. (That is history; nowadays with the wonderful invention of spell check we leave it to the computer.)

The entire five years at the Academy passed rapidly. During that time, Mitchie helped established the Japanese Language Department and then started on her Master's Degree. Our children "enjoyed" school on campus at the Air Force Academy schools. I must say that both children ran into significant and surprising prejudice from playmates, or should I say, schoolmates. Our daughter, Charlene, dealt with it in a very sophisticated manner by going to the principal's office to complain about specifics (it was racist-based) that should not be permitted in a government school. Well done, Charlene! John II, being rather well-built took his own measures that brought a rapid halt to in-class bullying and name-calling. A punch here and a punch there, plus placing tormentors by their collars on hallway lockers, soon rectified the situation, but also led to visits to the principal who did not necessarily approve of the method used but was probably grateful for the lessons delivered. Well done John!

As the time for reassignment came into sight, I was approached by the ISA (International Security Affairs) Office of the Pentagon to assume the portfolio for Japan. It was a wonderful offer and was something that would have directed my career in another path, but I will never know because I stayed at the Academy for one more year so Charlene could graduate from Air Force Academy High as she only had one year to go. We made a family decision and turned down the ISA offer, and Charlene graduated in June 1978.

But there was another assignment on the horizon—one that would bring me to the Pentagon for the next chapter of my life.

NINE

The Pentagon

Now that I was in Washington, D.C., my life became more complicated, yet interesting. I was assigned to the Pentagon in the War Plans and Mobilization Office as an "Action Officer." That was the term used to make it clear that your job was to move and move fast. Action! It also meant that you did everything necessary, and you learned much about the logistical details that war entails. As many know, war is about logistics—the side that gets there "first with the most" (General Beford Forest)—is the side that at the end of the day is in charge of the battlefield. However, it is a matter of detail and timing/timing and detail. If it sounds like I was not terribly enthused with the introduction to the Pentagon, it's because I was not terribly enthused. In fact, upon arriving at the War Plans and Mobilization Office my boss greeted me with "John, welcome to War Plans. You are lucky; we only work half days." My mind immediately went back to my assignment in Hawaii, before Vietnam, when we took Wednesday afternoons off to play golf or tennis.

Wait a minute, the way he said that and the look on his face betrayed some sinister meaning, Yes—it was 0700 to 1900 hours—the "half-a-day" that we would work; not the "half days" of Hawaii when we only worked "half" of an eight-hour day. The times had changed! It was grind away, and details like the timing of supplies or conflicts in the delivery of supplies had to be resolved and all manner of items needed to be at the right place at the right time. The plans constantly needed reviewing; nothing could be taken for granted.

After the requisite introduction to the Pentagon and Action Officer duties, my boss asked me if I would take the job of Deputy Director of the East Asia-Pacific Office and eventually asked me to become the Director of the International Affairs Office. Would I like to do that? It was as if I was born again and was slated for heaven. You can imagine the multitude of issues that fell under this office's purview: Law of the Sea, Air Force relations with all our allies and enemies, overflight permissions, and duty as the Deputy Air Force Representative to the Military Staff Committee of the United Nations, among others. It was the time of the Soviet invasion of Afghanistan, and one of two places that U.S. and Soviet military could meet was the United Nations Security Council's Military Staff Committee. The other permanent members of the Security Council, Britain, France, the Soviet Union, and China also had Colonels representing them. It was a very busy time going back and forth between Washington, D.C. and New York, but for the old political scientists, it was my calling.

Back at the Pentagon, I had come to have a great relationship with the Secretary of the Air Force, Dr. Hans Mark. In my capacity as Director of International Relations, I soon found a person with a keen interest in international affairs and a great understanding of history. We formed a great working relationship, but as in many relationships, outside events can intervene and create all sorts of unexpected results. In this case, President Jimmy Carter was defeated in his reelection bid, and Ronald Reagan became our new president. Within weeks I found myself in my new job; outside the Pentagon and at the historic Fort McNair, home of the National War College, Industrial College of the Armed Forces, and the College of the Americas, as well as some of the most beautiful General Officer Quarters in the U.S. Army.

I became the Associate Dean for Academic Affairs of the National War College—a military college with a mission of educating and preparing senior military and diplomatic personnel for high policy and leadership roles in the Federal Government. My role was curriculum development and personnel recruitment. Many of the professors were from some of the top civilian institutions in the land. Some were from the military, like me, and several others from the various military academies. I also taught courses on East Asian matters and once a year led a group of about 25 "students" on a tour to some designated area of interest to our students. In the years I had at the National War College, I led trips to the Middle East and South Asia, the Philippines, and Japan. The Middle East-South Asian trip was most interesting as the school had not gone to either Pakistan or India in 15 years, and it was new to me, whereas Japan and South Korea had been my beat.

I do not want to minimize the trip in 1981 to Japan and South Korea; I did learn a lot, as well as my charges, but the Philippines excursion was unbelievable. We met and had great discussions with counterparts in the Philippine War College, but we also met President Ferdinand Marcos, his Foreign Minister, Carlos P. Romulo, and his outspoken and self-assured Defense Minister Juan Ponce Enrile. We were invited into the Malacanang Palace where we had more than an hour with the President in an engaging encounter where President Marcos, with elbows on his desk, leaned forward and got his message across to the amazed War College students—all Colonels or on the promotion list for Colonel. He spoke with emotion but was sitting on the top of a volcano that was about to erupt. He appeared fully in control, but events were soon to result in his removal and exile to Hawaii. Of course, that was not known when we exchanged opinions, but when our Institute conducted a major review of our (U.S.) policy toward the Philippines, it remained in the back of my mind as we recommended this leader be given a chance to reform his government. Accustomed to having his own way, our advice was not taken, and in time, he was replaced by "People Power" in the wake of the unbelievable daylight assassination of the popular leader of the opposition who had been in exile in the States, Benigno Aquino Jr. On August 21, 1983, immediately on deplaning, Aquino was shot. Having declared martial law to extend his rule past the two terms allowed by the Philippine Constitution, this man, who became president in 1965, finally took refuge in Hawaii on February 25, 1986, where he remained until his death in 1989. Having concluded a policy review in 1985/86 on the Philippines became instrumental in my appointment as Director of INSS in May 1986, but that is a story to be told shortly.

I had never been to South Asia before, so the chance to lead a National War College tour to India and Pakistan (Saudi Arabia and Bahrain, as well) I gasped with enthusiasm and great anticipation. To prepare for it, I studied intensely and arranged some special "briefings" for the National War College students. One of the special events was a private showing of the new movie *Gandhi*, which hit the theaters in 1982. We rented an entire movie house and had the entire NWC class, about 200 senior officers and selected diplomats and CIA professionals, attend a showing. For those who have seen it, you know that it is a very powerful movie that places Gandhi's entire life before the audience as well as scenes from Britain's attempts to keep the Indian Independence Movement under control. These two, as you might imagine, are very inter-related. To keep the independence movement under control, Gandhi had to be controlled. It was tough! This movie was immensely important in making our trip so successful. For example, during our visit, we spent a morning at the Indian Institute for Strategic Studies in New Delhi. Right across the street was the park in which Mahatma Gandhi was assassinated. As we visited, we were constantly reminded of relevant historical episodes open to us in the movie.

And while on the topic of movies, I would like to point out that the use of "historical movies" in the classroom can be a valuable teaching aid and resource. To be sure, films can assist a teacher who has to get much across in little time. A good movie can do that, and many fit the bill. I used the great Russian film *Alexander Nevsky* to counter the Nazi film *Triumph of the Will*; *Doctor Strangelove* to introduce the concept of deterrence; *All Quiet on the Western Front* to reveal the tragedy of WWI and *The Fog of War: Eleven Lessons from the Life of Robert S. McNamara* to reveal the role of civilian advisors in the security field. I also used *The Patriot* to demonstrate the intensity of our Revolutionary War and the war for the South. All these films and so many more can be masterful in the classroom, allowing the professor to draw out comments from the students and make for lasting impressions. Although some films take liberties with history, Oliver Stone's *JFK* comes to mind with some of the more controversial theories he blended into the storyline, students can learn much from a dramatization of history. And even if it is dubious and suspect, students can discuss why the filmmakers decided to do this.

India was fascinating, and we toured the cities of New Delhi, Agra, and Mumbai, and met with knowledgeable senior officials, but our trip to Pakistan included a discussion with General Muhammad

Zia-ul-Haq the leader of the nation and the Foreign Minister Mian Muhammad Nawaz Sharif who became the Prime Minister. In fact, we met the military and foreign policy elite of the nation as we traveled throughout the country, from Peshawar in the northwest, Karachi in the south, Islamabad in the north and Lahore in the east.

It was another one of those "important" assignments in my career that in many ways, led me to Woosong and SolBridge. Without question, there is nothing quite like an opportunity to attend the National War College, and I did so as a faculty member and associate dean.

After two years as Associate Dean of the War College, I was pulled up by the parent organization, the National Defense University, to become Director of Research and Publisher of the NDU Press. Our Chief Editor was Colonel Fred Keiley, one of the most enjoyable individuals I have ever met. His great facility with the English language and abiding interest in history made him the perfect "Mother Hen"— a term of endearment—for our NDU Press Team. As a publishing unit, the mission was to publish the works of men and women in uniform to demonstrate that the term "soldier-scholar" was not dead, but indeed thriving and alive within the modern military. The NDU Press not only published a significant number of books relevant to the military field, but it also had a conference agenda that would highlight security issues of the day and have seminars and conferences that would bring serving military together with scholars and specialists to issue policy-related studies of use to the security community generally.

One of the "fun" programs we ran was a series of dialogs with political and policy figures of the day. We held these intimate gatherings in the Ft. McNair home of the President of NDU, Lt. General Richard Lawrence. Several times we had Congressman Newt Gingrich from Georgia as our speaker. You need to know that these "get-togethers" were billed as "Dialogs with Leaders" and the stress should be on "dialog." Well, when we had Newt, it was never a dialog, it was a clear monolog. He has a significant background in history and is extremely well-read, so when our meeting with Newt began the Generals, and senior Colonels had met their match. These were never dull, and our guest speaker went on for the entire period almost without a pause for a breath. Actually, he was Professor Gingrich and held forth magnificently. These were some of the most interesting talks we were to have.

There was one event that I will never forget, however. We had invited General Al Haig to lecture on some aspect of our European or NATO policy, and he did quite well. His delivery method was very self-assured, and he was a master at detail, which was flowing all through his talk. At the end of the presentation, he asked for questions and was doing quite well until a Colonel, who had had his throat crushed by the boot of a North Korean soldier before the 1976 Panmunjom Ax Murder Incident raised his hand to ask a question. (Before the incident, U.S./UNC [United Nations Command], ROK, and North Korean soldiers could move freely within the JSA—Joint Security Area; incidents of spitting, shoving, and fighting were common occurrences.) As the Colonel asked the question he was barely audible—as a result of his encounter with a North Korean jackboot and a crushed throat. In the middle of the question, the General said something to the effect, "Out with it, Colonel! Cat got your tongue?"

Well, the silence in the hall was absolute and stunning. The once almost flippant speaker realized something was amiss. When he was told why the voice was so faint, he apologized and walked with our hero to his waiting car with apologies flowing. Now that General Haig has passed away, I remember both the beginning and the end of the incident, but his deep-felt apology saved the day and demonstrated to all in the hall that this great and accomplished figure had a sensitive side and he led by example. Certainly, if you make a mistake, he who is man enough to admit it is not diminished in status what-so-ever.

Soon, my days as Director of Research for the National Defense University were about to end. The University was undergoing a general reorganization that reflected the movement within the military for new and dynamic efficiencies that would reflect the times. The failure of Vietnam was now more than a decade behind us, our hostages long-held by Iranian terrorists were back safely at home, and a new more self-assertive defense community was in order. It was the Reagan Era and no longer would officers wear uniforms only once a week in Washington, D.C. "Wear them every day if you like," or words to that effect came out of the White House. The Pentagon found itself repairing the corridors and replacing light fixtures— even fixing deep holes in the walls that had been left as eyesores during the entire Carter Administration. Our morale was up; we walked with a new spring in our step and were recognized by the president as guardians of freedom, not as an embarrassment to be kept out of sight and very much under the watchful eye of the Assistant Secretary of State for Human Rights and Humanitarian Affairs 1977-1981 (Patricia Derian).

Out of this new era and recognition that we did not need to outsource policy issues to civilian think tanks came a new addition to the National Defense University; it eventually received the name: Institute for National Strategic Studies. To operate this new in-house think tank, I was asked to be the ranking military member, the Deputy to the Director—a civilian as required by its organizing statue—John Despres. Our mission was to "stand up" in military terms, to create a new organization that would have three component parts: a strategic studies center, a technology policy (following issues of our industrial base) center, and a wargaming center. All these elements would support both the Chairman of the Joint Chiefs of Staff and the Secretary of Defense.

It was a tall order as we were operating with Army support and in a very much joint environment. Military reforms were very much the theme of the day, with Senators Sam Nunn and Richard Lugar setting the standard by their military reform act that soon became law. All services were to reduce redundancy and move toward greater operational efficiencies. "Jointness" became a keyword, and the number of assignments in the other Services became a major promotion factor. Planning and policy reviews were to reflect this movement, and we began in earnest to build the organization and enter the policy arena. The NDU Press was incorporated into the Institute, and its output expanded, and gradually, we became engaged in policy review and even, in certain instances, policy initiation. It was 1985, and the situation in the Philippines was going from bad to worse. One of our first major actions was to convene a week-long conference focused on the situation in the Philippines. We assembled approximately 80 of the top experts in the defense community, basically locked ourselves in a secure area, and began deliberating the situation that included the assassination of opposition leader "Ninoy" Aquino and the increased instability arising from that 1983 event. At the conclusion of the conference, we invited Richard Armitage, the Assistant Secretary of

Defense for International Security Policy, to take the outbrief and submitted our recommendations for consideration to the highest level.

During these first years of the INSS, President Ronald Reagan announced his Strategic Defense Initiative, commonly called Star Wars after the 1977 movie of the same name. The entire initiative envisaged the use of space to create an interconnected series of space-based defensive systems that would make the U.S. completely safe from a surprise nuclear attack. It was a huge concept that involved out-spending the Soviet Union and providing a safety belt completely around America that would depend on space-based detection and killing systems as well as redundant interceptors launched from the ground.

Shortly after it was announced on March 23, 1983, I was sent to Japan from INSS to "feel out" the Japanese and their willingness to be associated with such a bold defensive program. Well, 1983 was still early for Japan to jump on this wagon that did not have a band yet. The trip was probably the least successful assignment in my entire career. Practically everyone I tried to see was "busy." Possibly being a Colonel at the time did not serve my mission well. One thing I came back with, however, was the great caution with which the entire concept was treated by the Japanese defense community. Later, others would at least make a sales pitch.

About this same time the first director of INSS, John Despres, had fulfilled a year on the job but was informed his SES appointment was expiring. Coming somewhat as a surprise for everyone, I assumed the post of Acting Director and began an active search for his replacement throughout the defense/academic community. Our search came up with five or six very suitable candidates for whom I would have happily agreed to continue to work. However, it was Washington, D.C., and believe me, nothing is simple in D.C. Since the Institute served both the Secretary of Defense and the Chairman of the Joint Chiefs of Staff (JCS), any nominees had to be vetted with both bureaucracies. One-by-one each of the six fell prey to someone or some organization that would withhold support or actively oppose it. Finally, the President of NDU said the process had gone on long enough, a duly appointed Director would have to be found and found quickly. He looked at me—this was only days after the completion of the highly successful policy review conference on the Philippines that took place in July 1985, and said, "What about you John? You have the academic qualifications, experience, and you know the job." (General Richard Lawrence who was the President of NDU at the time, retired to Texas and sculpted western scenes in his art studio up until he passed away in December 2016.)

Now, a similar experience regarding vetting was to be my lot. My name was distributed throughout the Pentagon, and all seemed to be going just fine. Then, all of the sudden somewhere within the halls of Congress came a voice of doom. "Endicott is a leftist, liberal, military academic who should not get this post!" I do know that it was a Congressional aide who went to Senator Barry Goldwater and tried his damnedest to prevent such an appointment being made. I'll not say who, as it only causes personal feuds to fester; however, the damage was done, and the process came to a screeching halt.

However, soon I received a call from Senator Goldwater's office: "Please come down for an interview; the Senator wants to get to the bottom of this"—something to that effect. One thing was certain, it didn't really matter "what," Goldwater said. The fact that he wanted to see me was all that mattered. On the agreed day, I went to his office and sat down with his office manager or person in charge of messy matters, anyway a young lady with whom I had a several-hour conversation. In essence, I laid out my entire professional career and was as direct as possible without revealing any classified information. At the end of the conversation we parted, but I did not know the direction her advice to the Senator would flow.

The next day I found out that Senator Goldwater told his staff and the young fellow leading the charge to "Get off Endicott's back!" (That one I remember very clearly.) Perhaps in his style, he might have added, "He's no pinko, Commie sympathizer, he is a professional Air Force Officer!" I can't say that for sure, but it is what I would imagine the fine Senator from Arizona to be capable of saying. That having been done, it was all arranged for me to become Director. May I say, it was a big deal, as the person who assumed the job would have to be a civilian, not a serving military officer. So, immediately I put in my retirement papers that gave me slightly more than 28 years of active service in the Air Force. It had been a wonderful 28 years, and I would have stayed for the additional two if a replacement had been found for John Despres, but that just did not happen.

I was given the rank of SES-4 or Senior Executive Service-4 that gave me a military rank roughly equivalent of a three-star or Lt. General. Going from a full Colonel rank to Lt. General equivalent on the same day of my retirement, May 31, 1986, caused some rather uncomfortable moments at the University which had several Major or two-star Generals, but over time it was the order of the day, and we all came together as a team.

Actually, I lost some good friends during this process; after the news broke that Endicott was the newly appointed Director of INSS, several of the academic candidates believed that I was a modern Machiavelli and maneuvered the entire search in a way as to produce the outcome I desired. Certainly, they give me a much greater power of conspiracy than I deserve. Now I understand why conspiracy theory can be so powerful, especially overseas where just about everything the U.S. does is seen as some huge conspiratorial process. Well, I would like to assure any of my former colleagues who believe that charge that it is far from the truth. I was almost a victim myself of the behind the scenes maneuvering that describes Washington, D.C., but a man of honor stepped in (helped by an aide who I will remember fondly forever) and got the conspirators off my back. Thanks, Senator Goldwater, I should have voted for you.

During these days 1985 and 1986, we participated in several significant trips to China as guests of the Chinese PLA National Defense University. On several occasions, we briefed the PLA NDU staff on the organization of our own NDU. We tried to convince them that the final realization of the U.S. NDU was a result of a series of compromises, and if given a chance, we would probably organize it differently. Whatever we said to indicate our organization was not perfect, was discarded. They went determinedly to replicate the organization we had crafted as a result of history and changes in administrations—both civilian and military. The sessions, however, resulted in many very good and productive exchanges. I recall most specifically when leading one meeting that my Chinese counterpart just before lunch asked me if there was any subject or question I had that he could answer. I responded, "Yes, during the Cultural Revolution did you isolate and protect the PLA nuclear forces from the Red Guard?"

My friend stopped short and said something to the effect, "let me get back to you on that subject. It is very sensitive."

After lunch, we reconvened, and he had a big smile on his face and noted he could let me know. It was, as we had expected, a case where the nuclear strike forces were indeed protected from the Red Guard assuring that nuclear weapons would not be used in any unauthorized fashion. It was not too much later that I found out that one of the top military figures to be involved in the return of Hong Kong to China was one of my friends from the PLA NDU. It was clear to me that involving such quality officers in the "handback" operation meant that China was serious about making the return work. Just as they were serious in protecting the command and control elements of their nuclear strike force in that period of uncertainty from 1965 to 1975 called the Cultural Revolution.

PHOTO GALLERY TWO

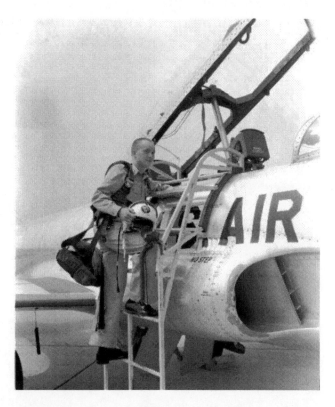

Getting ready for an Air Force ROTC orientation flight in a T-33 at Lockland AFB in Ohio, in summer of 1957. My first flight in a jet aircraft.

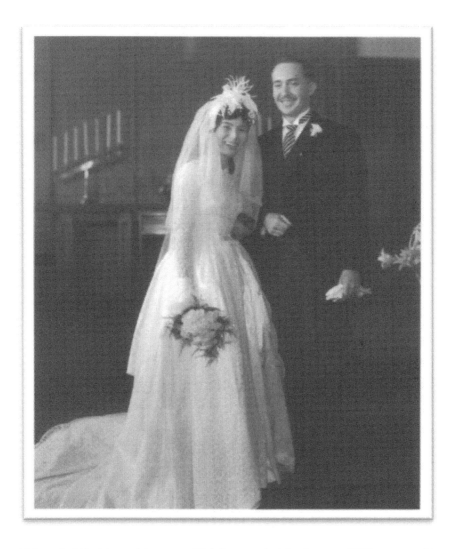

Although Mitchie and I were officially married in August 1959, we would have to wait until October to have our formal wedding ceremony. It was worth the wait!

At my desk as a Second Lieutenant and learning the ropes at Hickam Air Force Base, 1959.

Many of the pilots both U.S. and Vietnamese I worked with in the 522nd VNAF Fighter Squadron in Vietnam.

In front of an A-1H loaded for a strike mission with several of my U.S. and Vietnamese colleagues.

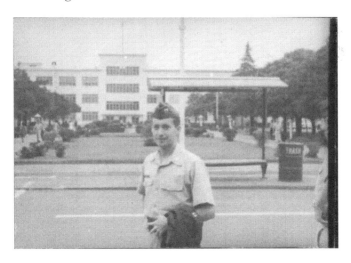

In front of Fifth Air Force Headquarters, Fuchu, Japan, 1967.

The Political Science Department of the U.S. Air Force Academy with Lt. Col. Ray Coble as the Acting Head. He is in the center of the front row, and I am in the second row, third from the left. I served there from 1969-1971 and from 1973-1978 receiving my Ph.D. at the Fletcher School of Law and Diplomacy, Tufts University with the Cooperation of Harvard from 1971-1973.

At Chartwell, Winston Churchills home in 1978.

John E. Endicott

On the Great Wall with General Hwang of the PLA NDU Institute and interpreter. The roads to the Wall were closed because of the snowstorm, but our vehicles were permitted access thus hardly anyone on the Great Wall. A scene seldom seen. Winter 1988/1989.

In Washington, D.C., with Mitchie and my PLA Institute Director counterpart. In those days distinct ranks were not being assigned for outsiders to know, just guess at.

A meeting in 1987/1988 with a Long March participant, PLA General Zhang Zhen. You can see I am no longer in the military, but the Director of the Institute for National Strategic Studies of the National Defense University. The NDU President, Lt. General Brad Hosmer is to his right.

Our Piper Warrior II that we purchased as part of Endicott Research Inc. activities.

John E. Endicott

The Retirement Ceremony held the day I retired in May of 1989 from 28 years in the Air Force and at the same ceremony sworn in as the SES-4 Director of the Institute for National Strategic Studies of the National Defense University.

Part III
The Georgia Tech Years:
1989-2007

TEN

A New Mission:
The Limited Nuclear Weapons' Free Zone

The time with the National Defense University went by exceedingly fast, and I had been there three years when one day I received a delegation from the Georgia Institute of Technology headed by its new President, Dr. John Patrick "Pat" Crecine. One of his best friends and associates, Dr. Mike Solomon, frequently visited NDU and introduced me to Pat who was on his way to change Georgia Tech from the "North Avenue Trade School" to a national university of international respect. I did not know it at the time, but he was looking for individuals to join him in changing the very nature of Tech. He had two major objectives, the creation of a College of Computing—that was his specialty—and the internationalization of the campus. Thus, he was also thinking about creating a School of International Affairs to add to the existing School of Social Sciences. He headed Tech from 1987 to 1994 and was instrumental in obtaining the 1996 Olympics for Atlanta. Using a comprehensive proposal with the most advanced computer effects available at the time, the Olympic Committee was adequately impressed to give the nod to Atlanta. Pat was a miracle worker but oversaw the greatest turmoil at Tech as he dragged the tenured faculty into the 21st Century.

I became part of the great experiment that did include the creation of the College of Computing and ultimately, the Sam Nunn School of International Affairs. Actually, we formed the School of International Affairs under Dr. Dan Papp and turned that into the Sam Nunn School when the Senator retired from the Senate in 1997. About a week after the visit, I received a letter from President Crecine asking if I would be interested in joining Tech as a full professor and center director. That sounded very good to the Endicotts as we were ready for a change in scenery, having been in the Washington "cooker" since 1978. My wife and I said "good-bye" to NDU on the 1st of June 1989 and Washington and Virginia on the 4th of July. We relocated to Marietta, Georgia, perhaps 20 miles north of Georgia Tech, and I began my transition from military and government-related activities to a full-time college academic.

Of course, the first several months were spent getting our house in order and moving the family things from Fairfax, Virginia, to Marietta, Georgia. I can recall giving several special lectures that summer and getting the office in shape and finding a secretary who could help me with the new center that we were working on. My office was really small and even smaller with my support staff installed. My assistant was a young flower who attracted many bees. It made for an interesting situation; so rather than two people jammed into a tiny space, we were two with an endless stream of visitors.

My first course at Tech was Japanese Politics, and I had all of 14 students. Of course, I was the new guy on campus, and the word was not out yet as to this retired military professor. Actually, it was a nice transition. The class, with only 14 students, turned out to be a seminar with a great exchange between myself and the kids. Tech still had the quarter system at that time, which I liked very much as Ohio State had the same when I went there, and soon I found myself in a rotation of Japanese Politics and Pacific Security Issues. Of course, the latter course allowed me to range throughout the Pacific and kept all of us up-to-date on the current situation in the Pacific. In these early days of work at Georgia Tech, I taught courses to introduce students to international affairs and to Japan thanks to the head of the School of Social Sciences, Professor Dan Papp, who put his most senior professors in front of the incoming freshmen. There was a reason for this. Most of the students had not declared a major yet, and it was a way to maximize our exposure to students taking electives and perhaps catch a few along the way. It was effective to grow the school, and it was great in getting us in front of students who were not too familiar with things outside of Georgia. In fact, as I look back when I asked my students in those early days of the late 1980s about their overseas travel it was amazing to see out of a class of one hundred, only a few had actually gone overseas, and not many had passports either. (By the time I left Tech in 2007, the figures were reversed; almost all had traveled, and the President was moving toward introducing international travel as a requirement for graduation.)

It was not until the fall quarter of 1992 that I moved to the big lectures dealing with international relations. The introductory courses for students in the School of International Studies were usually very big, and my first one had 151 students. It was INTA 1000, the very basic course. In a very interesting move, the really experienced professors in the school took the big classes to induce all the students to become majors. Ours was a new school, and we were hungry for students to sign up for the major. I must say I ran into somewhat of a culture shock. After having spent 31 years in government where the folks and I who did business, pretty much agreed with where I was coming from and where I was going. Lecturing to students who were only 19 or 20 years old was a different matter. Time and time again, I would say something that seemed perfectly right with my core beliefs and found myself being challenged by a student: "But why, professor?" I had to rethink all my basic beliefs that I had had unchallenged during the entire Cold War. No longer could I speak offhand about this or that threat without having a very modern and clear cut answer to their questions. It was wonderful. In truth, it was like going back to the Fletcher School and dealing with a wonderful professor who looked at life and international relations through his Quaker glasses (my mentor Professor Allan B. Cole). Who said you can't teach an old dog new tricks?

Also, soon after we set up camp in Marietta, our son, John II, let us know that a wedding was coming as he finished up his BS at the Embry Riddle Aeronautical University. That was great news, but little did we realize at the time that our house would become the venue for the ceremony itself. You can imagine when we finally realized the service would be held in our home how our life became focused. Moving into a house in August and then finding out we were to host a wedding in November really gave emphasis to all our house decorating ideas. Concepts had to be turned into drapes and appropriate settings with little time to waste. While it was a nerve-wracking experience, it turned out to be one of life's real pleasures. When Mitchie and I look back on that experience, few parents can say their son and new daughter actually married before the fireplace in the home we still call home. After a life of the "military gypsy" to still be living in a house purchased 29 years ago is a dream come true. We still treasure the memories of a service featuring a harpsichord centered trio, beautiful flowers, flowing gowns, sharp tuxedos, and a room full of new neighbors and colleagues from Georgia Tech to wish them well. In a sense, what a way to say hello to the neighborhood. The Yankees had come to "the further South." Welcome, Y'all!

(I have added that "further South" greeting as we received it when shopping at Garfinkel's in Atlanta for the first time. I handed our credit card to the assistant, and as it rang up, she realized it was from Virginia, not Georgia, and with a charming smile she said, "Welcome to the further South." While Garfinkel's has been long gone that lovely lady and her welcome will always be with us.)

At home, our daughter had already left the nest and had married a young lawyer she met while studying at Ohio University in Athens, Ohio. Remember I had taken part in the Ohio History Competition in 1953 to mark the 150th anniversary of Ohio's statehood? You can see it made an impression on me and Charlene could go there with in-state tuition as back in 1978 when she started college, I was still in the Air Force, and as such, a technical resident of Ohio. She enjoyed university life and taught figure skating and became a dorm manager. In that capacity, she earned money from two sources and helped dad out quite a bit, and learned the lessons of life. Upon graduation, she worked for several years in the Washington area as she prepared for the big day in August 1986 when she married her college sweetheart, Greg Noble. She tied the knot at a local church in Springfield, Virginia, and we hosted the reception at the Fort Myer's Officers' Club that is one of the military pearls in the D.C. area close to the one-time estate of General Robert E. Lee in Virginia. It came only weeks after my father's passing on July 2, 1986, and helped us all look forward after commemorating the past at the Cincinnati funeral. Soon she was calling Dayton, Ohio, home where she worked and supported her new husband as he started his career as a junior practicing lawyer.

Our son, John II, was also out of college having graduated from Embry Riddle Aeronautical University and had begun his married life working for E-Systems, Incorporated in the Dallas, Texas area. His educational background, as well as several certificates allowing him to work on large aircraft and powerful jet engines, assured a good job at the entry-level. We sold our Piper Cherokee airplane which we had purchased to cut the cost of flying hours as John received his pilot's license, instrument rating, and multi-engine certificates, but really not until we were sure he was on his way to a good career in aircraft maintenance.

The early years at Georgia Tech, from roughly July 1989 to March 1995 were marked by efforts to ease back into the classroom, create a new research center that finally settled on the name Center for International Strategy, Technology and Policy (CISTP), find new allies to "build the brand," and turn, once again, to work on policy issues involving Northeast Asia and nuclear weapons. (Remember, my Ph.D. dissertation was on Japan's nuclear option.)

Of course, in addition to my research agenda done within the Center and my teaching done within the School, two other activities increasingly demanded additional attention: Georgia Tech football and representing the School of International Affairs in the Faculty Senate. The football games were fantastic! Lunches in the President's Box to meet as many alumni as possible and interest them in the reforms President Crecine was actively pursuing and making sure some of our finest athletes paid attention to their studies. In a sense, it continued a tradition of tutoring athletes that I started at Ohio State. At State, however, it was baseball players, and at Tech football players. I must say, it seems that I got to know the football players much more than the baseball kids.

One of the first organizations that played a significant role in the start-up years of the Center was IDA, the Institute for Defense Analysis in Northern Virginia. I met an analyst William Crowley who wished to "beef up" the involvement of IDA in East Asian policy, and we became good friends and colleagues. We did several projects together that played a big role in facilitating the transition from government to the private world for me. You may recall that the early 1990s were punctuated by the U.S. reaction to Iraq's pressure on Kuwait for the forgiveness of loans used by Iraq in the war with Iran. By August 2, 1990, this pressure became an invasion of Kuwait by 100,000 Iraqi troops and its rapid fall to the forces of Saddam Hussein[13] and the announcement that Kuwait had become the 19th Province of Iraq. We became involved to encourage Japan to be a recognized "alliance partner" and help fund part of the cost of this war, and together with IDA hosted a critical meeting between Japanese parliamentarians and security experts of the Washington, D.C. area. The exchange that took place between the senior Japanese Parliamentarian and Lee Butler, the four-star former commander of SAC, which caused a halt in the meeting and a hasty call back to Tokyo. It was a moment when Japan realized the United States expected more than the normal response from our nominal ally.

America's visible reaction came some months later in the form of an air and ground war that began on January 16, 1991, and now known as the First Gulf War. By the end of February, the war was over with Iraq's retreat from Kuwait.

When this all happened, my wife and I were visiting Beijing to build relationships between Georgia Tech and various research institutions in China. While watching the CNN coverage from Baghdad, it soon became clear that the "mighty" Iraqi Army of over a million was not up to the standards now being demonstrated by the U.S. military—fully recovered from the Vietnam War and showing it daily on the rapidly collapsing defense situation of the Iraqi Republican Guard. Our visit quickly assumed a different character with visits to U.S. Ambassador James Lilly and various Chinese colleagues who could see visions of a Vietnam quagmire and America stuck in the deserts of Iraq. No one believed me when I said it will be over soon. The U.S. Army had reformed itself and integrated the new Abrams A-1 tank into its doctrine of movement and shock. Of course, much has been written about the American halt short of Baghdad and the resultant peace accords, but it was a new era, and no one was talking

---

[13] For interested readers, a quick summary of events can be found in a Milestones Report from the U.S. Government's Office of the Historian. See
https://history.state.gov/milestones/1989-1992/gulf-war

of Vietnam anymore. For those of us who had been spit on by peace activists during the Vietnam War, it was a good feeling to be on the right (correct) side of the American body politic.

Another major early development that helped the Georgia Tech community realize that there were some new players on the block happened mid-June 1990 when JETRO (Japan External Trade Organization) and MITI (Ministry of International Trade and Industry) of Japan asked us to put on a major environmental conference that came with a total budget that exceeded $340,000. For anyone remotely interested in social science funding, $340,000 is a mighty fine sum of money. We hosted environmental specialists from around the globe, but the highlight, for me at least, was working with one of our Georgia Tech resource specialists, Patrick O'Heffernan. He was deeply involved in this subject, and his advice and professional network proved to a deciding factor in the conference success. So, it was a time for building alliances, both personal and institutional.

On the other side of the globe, interesting things were also happening. The last President of the Soviet Union Mikhail Gorbachev had served notice on December 25, 1991, that the USSR was no longer a viable political entity and was replaced by the Commonwealth of Independent States (CIS). Both North and South Korea were admitted into the United Nations in September 1991, and by December 1991, both states had signed the Treaty of Reconciliation and Nonaggression; the U.S. had announced the withdrawal of nuclear weapons from South Korea,[14] in October 1991, and by April 1992 the two had signed the Joint Declaration of the Denuclearization of the Korean Peninsula. Things were happening fast and furious, and it really appeared that almost 40 years of chaos on the Korean Peninsula might be coming to an end.

I can remember sitting in my study one night in our new Atlanta home after the announcement that the U.S. would be removing its nuclear weapons from the Korean Peninsula. That was really big news, especially when it came to the consideration of some kind of peace accord to end the hostilities that had begun 41 years earlier on June 25, 1950. As I reflected, it dawned on me that concepts for a nuclear-free zone in Northeast Asia had always faltered on the fact that we had

---

[14] "U.S. to Pull Nuclear Arms from Korea," *Washington Post,* 19 October 1991.

some 700 nuclear weapons in South Korea.[15] If we were truly going to remove them, it would be possible to create some form of regional agreement in NEA that would reinforce the new treaties between the two Korean states. I believed from my time dealing in the area, that to be successful, the Joint Declaration had to be guaranteed by the regional big powers that included Russia, China, and the United States. It was time to begin. Once you got rid of the nuclear weapons, there was no need to object to a nuclear weapons-free zone.

I had had my "Eureka" moment!

After considering the unique situation in Northeast Asia, it was clear that what was to be recommended would come as only a first step. We had seen how the Cuban Missile Crisis had resulted in both sides becoming more rational and over time, reaching some significant limits on nuclear weapon inventories. I was hopeful that some form of agreement could be done that would become a process, but it would have to be "limited" or constrained as three of the big five nuclear powers would be involved. They might not mind some limitations on weapon types, but they could not be comprehensive, nor absolute. (The IAEA definition of a nuclear-free zone required that all weapons be removed from the zone. Since Northeast Asia was an area in which the territories of China, Russia, and the U.S. were found, this nuclear-free zone could not be all-encompassing, the major nuclear powers were not yet prepared to forego nuclear stockpiles completely.)

Thus, it was born, the concept for the Limited Nuclear Weapons' Free Zone for Northeast Asia. It was to consume many hours, days, and weeks in the coming 17 or so years while at Georgia Tech, and it still warrants time today. As the story of the LNWFZ-NEA unfolds over the coming years of this narrative, I will attempt to insert it with as much accuracy as possible. However, we have always kept the actual discussions between attendees as "privileged" information. Often, positions taken were at odds with the official policies of the nations represented. We always acknowledged that practice and I will continue it so that none of the participants in what became known as a Track II Initiative would be placed at risk in their home country.

My original idea was to use a nuclear arms control agreement as a first step toward the creation of a regional cooperative security zone

---

[15] Don Oberdorfer, *The Two Koreas,* Chapter 11, "Joining the Nuclear Issue," 2001.

where a secretariat established to oversee implementation of arms control agreements would increasingly assume the role of regional conflict resolution center and spearhead efforts of regional integration and ultimately produce a region free of conflict and confrontation.[16] Standing in the way, however, was the notion of what constituted a nuclear-weapon-free zone, and historical differences between the parties that ultimately assumed such significance that senior members of the initiative could no longer work together. My hope as I wrote in 2018, is that disagreements arising out of the era of colonialism and World War II will finally be placed in their correct relationship to the need to resolve the threat of a growing nuclear confrontation in the area. As the DPRK nears a demonstrated capacity to serial produce long-range missiles with nuclear warheads, perhaps it is again appropriate to examine this concept as a Track I initiative—official government to government negotiations. However, no sooner had I written this when new developments have occurred on the Korean peninsula capped by the first-ever summit between a U.S. President and North Korean leader.

By February 1992, I had developed the LNWFZ concept far enough to know, if I wanted to really see this through to the end, I had better introduce it to the folks in the Pentagon or perhaps face some difficulties later. Do remember that a full colonel is not a free element. As a regular officer, not a reserve officer, I need to let my former bosses know what kind of security-related things I am up to. Accordingly, with IDA assistance, we scheduled a seminar to vet the concept among policy-makers from most elements of the security community at that time. We had representatives from the DOD, DIA, CIA, all the Armed Services, some civilian academics known in the field, and several other research organizations like IDA. I presented the idea to 24 individuals who were not shy. For four hours, there was a good give and take about the merits and demerits of this idea. Finally, two admirals got into a heated exchange about "lines on water" and the fact that the U.S. Navy is against "lines on water" (weapons in specific areas; the Navy didn't want to have operational restrictions). The senior of the two finally took charge and said words to the effect,

---

[16] For a description of my thinking as I began work at Woosong University in 2007, please see: John E. Endicott, "Limited nuclear weapon free zones: the time has come," *The Korean Journal of Defense Analysis,* Vol. 20, No. 1, March 2008, pp. 13-26.

"if Endicott wants to make a fool of himself, let him do it. There just might be a window of opportunity out there; let him try." As I often say, it has been a few years, and perhaps it was not exactly that way, but it was what I took away. I considered it a go!

In March, the following month, we gave it a try at an international conference in Beijing. We had invited approximately 75 security specialists from all over Northeast Asia. States included, of course, China, the two Koreas, Canada, Hong Kong, Japan, Mongolia, Russia, and the United States. Taiwan was not there as the PRC would not issue a visa on this subject, but Mongolia was as it had been the host for Soviet nuclear weapons during the Cold War. The actual title for the conference "Economic and Security Issues in the Northwest Pacific" was held in a brand new hotel in Beijing that was adjacent to a modern department store. The economic topics on direct investment and future cooperative plans went very smoothly, but then I introduced the concept for a limited nuclear-free zone.

It became clear that our hosts were not happy with the proposal. As it was first envisaged, I proposed a 1200 nautical mile arc from the center of the DMZ as the zone for nuclear weapons limitation. China was incensed, or at least the head of the Chinese delegation, who was a member of the Chinese People's Congress, was blowing off steam in a manner seldom seen in an international conference. Literally, he was so angry that my translator paused and said, "Dr. Endicott, I will not translate this attack on your family lineage." That was just about as I remember it. The chief delegate was red in the face, and I really worried about a heart attack or stroke. I am not kidding!

Obviously, I could see that things had not gone well. Practically everyone at the meeting—except the Chinese—had responded favorably, but the fact that about 60% of China's nuclear arsenal could be found in that arc from the DMZ made it impossible for them to accept such interference in domestic affairs. And, very bluntly, I felt it was absolutely necessary to have China fully committed to such a plan for any degree of success. As you might expect, it is expensive to hold these international conferences and to come up with the required cash occupied much of my waking hours. So, the next meeting to follow-up on March 1992 was a quiet three-way meeting at Georgia Tech between China, Japan, and the United States.

We held the meeting during the first week of March, again among unofficial specialists, but we stayed with invitations to Chinese and Japanese who had been at Beijing, but the size of each delegation was reduced to save money. Regardless of cost, we started off our several day meeting with a Champagne reception in the evening just before dinner. As I was welcoming the individual representatives the chief delegate from the Chinese side—the same fellow who had castigated me in Beijing—came rapidly to my side, lifted his glass, and said something like, "Greetings! It is now time to view your concept in a positive manner."

I was dumbfounded! Here was the person who would have thrown me out a 20th-floor window only a year ago now sounding like we had a plan. Tremendous! Was it my silver-tongued eloquence that turned the Chinese side, or something else that I could attribute to the change? Of course, these words changed the atmospherics, and we concluded our meeting with a good feeling between all present—the Chinese, Japanese, and Americans had much to be happy about.

The true nature of what they were saying by changing their position on the limited nuclear weapons zone came strikingly clear during the second week of March when the DPRK announced they were giving official notice that they would be leaving the NPT. By their actions, the Chinese delegation had sent a strong message. China did not want to see a nuclear-armed North Korea. For me, with Chinese support to the idea, I could now approach the U.S. philanthropic foundations with some degree of optimism.

Exactly why should I be approaching U.S. foundations after such an announcement by the North? Many U.S. non-governmental organizations will support programs and research that support a peaceful resolution of critical international issues. A very high priority is placed on support for ideas and concepts that might reduce the danger of nuclear war. With the change in Chinese attitudes and obvious North Korean intentions to pursue a nuclear option, I had new data that could increase the chances for substantial foundation support.

Initially, I received support for individual conferences or projects very focused and limited in purpose. Often foundations will not provide funds for longer than three years, and they want to see results—very often—within the very near term. Using a mixture of foundation support and support from within Georgia Tech itself, I took the message of the LNWFZ-NEA to practically all the national capitals involved in the concept meeting with diplomatic, military, and academic institutions. There was one exception: I have never traveled to North Korea, but in place of actually going to Pyongyang, I used the next best thing: the New York United Nations offices of the DPRK United Nations Delegation. We kept the South Korea Delegation to the United Nations fully informed, as well as our own State Department. In essence, by 1995 we had indications of interest from all nations in the zone (China, France, both Koreas, Mongolia, Russia, and the United States) and from some countries outside the zone, namely France, Argentina, and Finland.

One thing was for certain—things were about to get *very* interesting.

ELEVEN

Making The LNWFZ-NEA a Reality

It was time to turn to something significant and unusual. I invited representatives from China, Japan, South Korea, and Russia to join me—an American—to focus on the idea of introducing a limited nuclear weapons' free zone into Northeast Asia. The reason I used the words "significant and unusual" was the timeline involved, five weeks. We invited a four-star Korean general, a three-star Japanese general, a two-star Russian general, and a two-star Chinese general to join me in my Atlanta offices of the Center for International Strategy, Technology, and Policy for five weeks from the end of January to the beginning of March 1995. Normally, a three-day meeting is tops; we were serious and wanted a draft treaty or agreement when it was over—unusual and significant in any person's language.

We agreed that the object was to inform the governments of all participants. We would examine the issues, determine areas where agreement was possible, and areas that provided only dead ends. We recognized our weakness from the outset. We were five individuals with no official status; thus, all we would be doing would be supplying what might be useful to further official negotiations on this very important subject. Before all the participants arrived, however, the general we had invited from China was unable to attend. He was replaced with a very capable academic from one of the top universities in Beijing. The team, as assembled, consisted of General (Ret.) Kim

Jae-chang (South Korea), Lieutenant General (Ret.) Toshiyuki Shikata (Japan), Major General (Ret.) Vyacheslav Bunin (Russia), and Dr. Xuetong Yan (China), and myself a retired Air Force Colonel with a civilian rank of SES-4, equivalent to a Lieutenant General when I was Director, Institute for National Strategic Studies of the National Defense University in Washington, D.C.

I will not go into the gritty details, but the first three weeks were spent in the longest sustained argument I have ever participated in. It was not doing my health any good, nor, I am sure, any of the other participants. Mitchie, my wife, clearly could see the impact these arguments were having on her husband and one night at dinner suggested that the group stop for a one day break and do something completely different. My deputy at the time, Bob Rudisill, a native of Tennessee, knew right away what was needed. "Why not a trip to the Grand Ole Opry (a country and western venue) in Nashville?" We all thought it to be a brilliant idea and made plans for all of us to spend the day in Nashville visiting the Hermitage, home of Andrew Jackson, Vanderbilt University, and the Nashville Museum that was having a special exhibit on the history of Mongolia. And finally, the trip was topped off with the evening show at the Opry.

Without a doubt, the day exceeded everyone's expectations, and when we boarded the 12 passenger van with yours truly at the helm for the three-hour drive back to Atlanta, all were in the best spirits seen in three weeks. It was a qualified success. However, there was one small detail all had overlooked. It was February. Now please do not believe the tourist ads that proclaim the South is the land of the sun and pleasant weather all year long. In fact, we can have some pretty nasty weather, and it usually comes in the February-March period. We had to traverse one mountain pass called Eagle Mountain, and as we approached, no one had turned on the radio to listen to road conditions, we were all having too much fun.

That is until we got to the top of Eagle Mountain and started to descend. The road all the way to the top had been dry and easy driving. As soon as I passed over the summit and started down the road, it turned into packed snow and ice. I was not traveling anticipating snow or ice, and we were easily traveling at 65 miles or more per hour as we hit the ice. After the fact, I know that the Lord was with us as we hit ice and started to spin completely out of control. There's not much you can do when you hit ice, but hope there is at least some snow or dry spot to regain control. Well, I cannot say how many 360s we did, but at last, at a somewhat slower speed, I did regain control. All the joy was gone from that van, and no one said a word. (Had they said anything, it probably would have been a few tried and true colorful expletives in English or their own language.)

The return to quarters in Atlanta was happily not further bothered by snow or ice, but we returned in silence as everyone clearly recognized that we had all just shared a near-death experience, and all I am sure were contacting their own divine being and quietly saying thanks.

That next Monday was like a miracle, issues that had divided us before became moot, and all focused on making a draft agreement that we could say represented a concept that all could agree to. We were now into verification issues and in need of some technical expertise that would satisfy all. I contacted the Sandia National Laboratory and explained our need and within several days we, as a group, were receiving expert advice about systems to guarantee accurate verification. It was again a contribution from a member of the security community we vitally needed; as we left, we were wholeheartedly in their debt.

Returning to Georgia, within several days, we had a working document and later published it as "The Agreed Principles." In retrospect, I now recommend a near-death experience to all who wish to get a group working together on a very difficult subject. Whatever the outcome, however, I know I lost five years off the end of my time on earth.

The draft agreement did not seek a total ban but accepted that tactical weapons would be a good starting place—smaller yield weapons that could be carried by fighter aircraft or fired from artillery. Each country that possesses such weapons would be offered the opportunity to decide how many would be subject to restrictions, and at the heart of the agreement was creating an oversight body charged with inspectorate duties. This would be a standing body, and it was hoped that over time if the initial obligations were adhered to, expansion of the contents of the agreement would follow.

Having gained consensus, it was time to introduce our work to the U.S. arms control community. We chose four destinations:

Washington, D.C., Boston, Mass., New York City, and San Francisco, Calif. It was some grueling itinerary, but all stood by and supported the work of the group. In Washington we had a session at the National Press Club and the Institute for National Strategic Studies at the National Defense University; in Boston at the Fletcher School of Law and Diplomacy of Tufts and Harvard University, and *The Boston Globe;* in New York City we briefed representatives from the North Korean UN Delegation and the Japan Society, and in San Francisco we went to the University of California at Berkeley and the Ploughshares Fund (one of our major donors at the time). The group had truly bonded and worked as a team to present the concept. Only at the National Press Club had we encountered any opposition and there it came from an Indian reporter who took our Japanese general to task for agreeing to a limited not total restriction on nuclear weapons. Do remember this was 1995, it was three years later that India joined the nuclear club, so to speak, and the reporter criticized our efforts from a high moral position that would have to be reconsidered three years later.

Generally, the overall reception was sympathetic but skeptical. Seasoned observers questioned whether the legacies of colonialism, World War II, the Korean War, and the Cold War could be overcome; some looked down their noses and questioned whether the international system in Northeast Asia was "mature" enough to support such an endeavor.[17]

One of the most difficult concepts to get across to our audiences seemed to be the fact that the entire affair was to be seen as a process in confidence-building. If our initial small steps could be realized, we hoped that it would provide the basis for further limitations that would provide the basis for even further progress. With a secretariat in place and manned by staff from all nations of the zone, we saw a significant center for the development of cooperative security.

We provided our work to our individual governments through our own channels, and we felt that progress had been made. On one level, at least, you could see four retired military officers and one academic had come together with a proposal that they felt comfortable with. I particularly chose to have military officers involved in the early stages of this effort as we had all seen combat or had been involved in

---

[17] *The Korean Journal of Defense Analysis, Ibid.* P.15.

preparations for defense at the highest levels. It was not a group that could be accused of being starry-eyed peace activists with no knowledge of the realities of war. We could, and did, stand eyeball to eyeball with members of our profession and argue for a peaceful course to ensure stability in Northeast Asia, the precursor to prosperity. It was a time when we appreciated our friends and respected our enemies and sought a better path forward.

With the focused group finished and a declared success—even if we were the ones who declared it so—it was time to broaden the consensus and seek wider acceptance of the notion. Our concept was to expand the participants. Rather than one expert representing each country, expand it to five, and mix the five with ambassadors, senior academics, practitioners, and peace activists. We also decided on a strategy to build consensus in areas outside of Asia, and once reasonable progress had been made, take the venues to Asian capitals. Thus, we made plans to have our first expanded meeting (plenary) in March 1996 in the city of Bordeaux, France. Our second was to be in Buenos Aires, Argentina, later in October of the same year.

As preparations progressed for the French meeting, I received word from our colleague in France, Michel Dusclaud, that one of our main sponsors, the French Foreign Ministry had asked that we postpone the meeting until October. While unexpected, we turned to our colleague in Atlanta, who was the Consul General representing Argentina, and asked if his government would accept a change in plans. Actually, it was an excellent opportunity that had we really understood what had just happened in Latin America, it would have been our first choice. What I am talking about is the Treaty of Tlatelolco that established a nuclear weapons' free zone for Latin America. It actually came into existence in 1967, but it was not ratified by Argentina until 1994. Thus, when Argentina invited us to meet in an expanded session in March 1996, it was only two years after their very intense experience with the ratification of this treaty. It turned out that our 25 delegates from all over Asia and the U.S. were matched with about the same number of Argentine experts who had struggled with the language of the Tlatelolco Treaty. We co-sponsored the meeting with the Argentine Council on International Relations with substantial support from the Foreign Ministry. Our 1st Plenary meeting turned out to be a tutorial from the experts of Argentina—a truly wonderful experience.

During this meeting, the language used in our draft framework was adjusted to meet the experiences of a group who had just gone through a similar drill.

Our American group now was headed by Ambassador (Retired) William Clark, former Assistant Secretary of State for East Asian and Pacific Affairs, and Ambassador to India, plus senior assignments to Japan and the Department of State. The group also included Dr. Harold M. Agnew, a former director of the Los Alamos Nuclear Lab; Richard Freytag, a successful CEO of a national bank who was also a Lt. General in the U.S. Air Force Reserve; William T. Pendley, an accomplished former Admiral active in the arms control area; Dr. Robert Kennedy, a former member of the U.S. Arms Control and Disarmament Agency; Selig S. Harrison, a nationally ranked journalist and scholar; and myself. The other teams were augmented by similar experienced individuals from China, Japan, South Korea, and Russia. When we all met in Buenos Aires, we were ready for their council and suggestions regarding the choice of words in the Agreement of Principles. At the closing session, we summarized our meeting, which became the 1st Plenary, and released it to the press.

In October 1996, we had our second meeting (Plenary) in Bordeaux, France, famous for its wine industry, but also the holder of historical ties with England and the Iron Lady of Aquitaine. (Actually Eleanor of Aquitaine who eventually became a Queen of England as the wife of Henry II. For lovers of history, it is in a class by itself. I'll say no more and hope you visit this jewel of France.) The meetings were getting bigger and as you might understand, more expensive. No matter the considerate support from our host countries, we still needed to get everyone to the venues, and that took money. We were lucky at this time to have the support of the W. Alton Jones Foundation of Charlottesville, Virginia, which stepped in and gave us a series of large grants that guaranteed we could continue meetings for several years. (In all, we received approximately $1,240,000 from this organization dedicated to a non-nuclear future for the world.) By the time we met in Bordeaux, our number had almost reached 45 participants with additional invited guests. As in all meetings, our purpose was to introduce what had been agreed upon and reach toward new agreements. At Bordeaux, we published the *Bordeaux Protocol,* which incorporated the suggestions from Argentina, and an Interim

Secretariat was formed to provide stable administrative support. The organization was actually the Center I headed at Georgia Tech, but it offered an organizational home that could provide students with an opportunity to gain some real-life experiences in international relations.

The meeting in Bordeaux, thanks to the support from the Foreign Ministry, the City of Bordeaux, and the Centre d' Analyse Politique Comparee' of the University of Bordeaux, was done at a level of splendor that encouraged success. Of course, the 2nd Plenary luncheon was held featuring five different wines. Need I say that we accomplished more than ever before and ever since in the afternoon session following. It was another lesson in group dynamics and negotiation. If you cannot have a near-death experience, five wines, and superb food also help.

Having published the *Bordeaux Protocol* which we thought to be of significant media import, an extensive press conference was scheduled to release it to the various media outlets in town. A session was prepared which assembled the head of each national delegation in a panel with myself slated to make some general introductory remarks. Near the appointed hour, perhaps twenty to twenty-five reporters began setting up TVs and communications equipment. Then all of a sudden, a major commotion swept through the media folks as tripods were dissembled, mics removed, and in fact, people began running for the exits. We, who were about to discuss our progress, were aghast until we heard that there had been a murder in town, the first in ten years, and our assembled reporters and TV crews became a mob as if a bomb was about to explode. We were unable to share our "Action Agenda" as the hall, except for the panel of experts, had emptied. Well, we learned another lesson. An old newspaper adage goes, "If it bleeds, it leads." That was indeed the case. Our stirring news finally hit the newspapers, but never the TV screens.

As I reviewed this very positive meeting with regard to the development of cooperative security using the free zone initiative as a base, I realized that the senior Russian official observer at this conference was the Honorable Sergei Ivanovitch Kislyak who at that time was the Chief of the Department for Security Affairs and Arms Control of the Ministry of Foreign Affairs for the Russian Federation. I remember distinctly the two of us sitting after dinner in the beautiful chateau owned by Professor Jean-Louis Martres of the University of Bordeaux IV. The rooms being used for dinner and after dinner conversations were without electricity—or it was not being used—as a beautiful shoulder-high candelabra gave us the light that flickered and glowed in an almost magical way. Anyway, the two of us, Director Kislyak and I discussed the course of the conference and the likelihood of eventual success. Later, he served as the top Russian diplomat in Washington, D.C., as Ambassador to the United States from the Russian Federation. This is an example of the impact of Track II diplomacy. The influence of such matters can never be directly fixed on certain events, but they play a role as presenting ideas and alternatives that might never see the light of day in the usual domestic setting.

Our next major meeting, the 3rd Plenary, was held in Moscow in October of 1997 and was a tribute to our very active Russian delegation that was headed by General (Retired) Anatoly V. Bolyatko with able participation and assistance from other Russian experts from research centers and policy think tanks. The official co-host was the Russian Academy of Sciences in Moscow. The highlight of the Moscow meeting was a trip to the Bolshoi Ballet. Here we had another example of group dynamics. To be able to invite all the delegates with their wives to such a grand cultural feature of Russia gave us some organization loyalty that paid off during times when we had to ask delegates to pay their own way to our meetings. We, in essence, were creating a group that now could talk without reservations and without recriminations. That is another extremely important aspect of negotiations on sensitive topics over the long term. Our principal achievement, as far as I was concerned in Moscow, was the very fact that we were in Moscow. Representatives from the Foreign Ministry and the General Staff became aware of our work, and it represented a significant advance in their collective awareness of a vital recommendation to improve the situation in the vast regions of Eastern Russia. We had no major press meeting, but we had achieved what we thought was possible.

Slightly less than a year later, the 4th Plenary meeting was held in Helsinki in October 1998 with the assistance of the Finnish Institute of International Affairs and the Finnish Ministry for Foreign Affairs. In addition, the Foreign Affairs Officer Markku Heiskanen of the

Japanese Office played a critical role. Coming only months after my triple bypass and related carotid artery surgery (see Chapter 13), I remember it particularly well. In fact, everything became much more meaningful as I appreciated each additional day given to me to work on this project. Plans for further expansion of the review group to include additional "official observers" from selected nations were put into effect at this meeting with invitations to all governments within the zone to send a serving official as well as Argentina and France.

The meeting in Helsinki was also a moment when all present came to appreciate what is known as the Helsinki Process, the process that began the integration of human rights issues into the Cold War dialog and the progress made generally in that field after the Conference on Security and Cooperation in Europe held in Helsinki from July to August 1975. The 1975 conference was seen as a great success, and our Finnish colleagues were as hopeful that this 4th Plenary meeting considering the nuclear issue in Northeast Asia could be just as successful.

Meetings with high officials of the Finnish Government were held, and presentations on the continuation of our own process were very constructive. The addition of three baskets of concern, as in the Helsinki Process, marked an addition that added a degree of sophistication to our program that provided a basis for many additional constituents to be in favor of such a pact. Items involving the actual composition and formation of the zone were placed in Basket I. Basket II became the area for Confidence Building Measures for the region: economic, political, military, cultural, issues including nuclear energy cooperation all became prospects for inclusion, and Basket III—became economic incentives to ensure that the DPRK would become actively engaged. These ideas were reported back to the governments involved as now actual serving members of various agencies were attending the meetings and taking notes. We were hopeful that their note-taking was good, but at the end of each meeting from then on, we issued a public declaration that summarized the outcome of that particular session.

The facilities for the conference provided by the Finnish Government were beyond all expectations. The final dinner was held in the Naval Officers' Club that in 1904 had been the Officers' Club for the Russian Baltic Fleet that was to leave from this port to meet its fate in the Tsushima Straits at the hands of the Imperial Japanese Navy. (In 1904 Finland was still part of Imperial Russia.) The great hall was decorated with large portraits of Russian Admirals who had taken part in that battle. It was an awesome feeling to be in such a setting of such historical significance. We had our dinner only days before the 94th anniversary of the departure of the fleet on its 18,000-mile voyage. The only bad note during the conference and a sign of things later to come was the surprise launching of a North Korean missile that traversed Japanese air space and impacted in the Pacific Ocean on the eastern side of Japan. It came as a severe blow to U.S.-Japanese relations as the Japanese were aghast that American intelligence did not alert Japanese defense forces to the impending test.

The leader of the Japanese delegation, Lt. General (Retired) Toshiyuki Shikata, was in a position to eat nails for breakfast at that time. Normally a person of great stability, you could see the internal rage that accompanied the news of the launch of a Daepodong-1 rocket that passed without permission throughout Japanese airspace and landed some 200 miles east in the sea.[18] Of course, the event had greater implications for U.S. and Japan relations. Japan, feeling it was not well served by its American ally, pursued a path to gain independent "weather" information by launching their own satellites after this. With U.S. radar installations in northern Japan, which were able to follow the launch, the Japanese were just seething that they had not been alerted. I can remember trying to calm down my friend, but it took more time than I ever expected. This was a serious issue, and we all hoped that U.S. intelligence would be made available sooner to this host country.

Having had four plenary meetings outside of Asia, of course, in this case not counting Moscow as in Asia, it was time for us to take the next plenary meeting to the heart of the dragon and reveal our work to the Japanese and do so in Tokyo. Actually, the first days of the meeting were in Hakone where the autumn air cleared our minds and increased our appetites. With very good friends in Japan, especially Tokyo, it was possible to have a meeting where our hosts actually paid most of the costs. The Japanese Team headed by retired Lt. General

[18] John Gittings, "North Korea fires missile over Japan," *The Guardian,* 1 September 1998.

Shikata developed their own funding sources and agreed to provide a research product, actually a report, at the end of the meeting. He had support from Teikyo University as our co-host. The meeting in Tokyo couldn't have come at a better time. The year before North Korea had launched a missile and reignited the arguments for Japan's own nuclear deterrent. Our presence was a "godsend" from my viewpoint, as it showed there was a viable alternative to going it alone and obtaining nuclear weapons to deal with the North Korean threat. Again, the greatest accomplishment for being in Japan was the fact that we were in Japan and presenting a counter-argument to those who demanded "nukes."

Along that line, many journalists and academics were invited to join our sessions when we moved to Tokyo, and a major news conference was held that was well attended and provided much ammunition for those who wished to retain Japan's peaceful orientation. We had our closing dinner in the Grand Ball Room of the Military Hotel used by Japanese Defense Forces personnel. It was indeed grand and happening on October 7, 1999, which was Mitchie's and my 40th wedding anniversary, made that day all the more special.

Now, with the 6th Plenary meeting scheduled for Beijing in the fall of 2000, we were aiming to present our work to the head of the dragon. But as 2000 arrived, a very special task was given to us by the U.S. State Department; would we be interested in becoming involved with the visit of an 11-person delegation from North Korea that would arrive in New York for normalization talks sometime in March. It is well known that the State Department budget is as lean as any budget in the world. Sums like 100,000 dollars are just not available that have not been placed in a budget the year prior. Funding unexpected opportunities for peace, unfortunately, are difficult to realize.

TWELVE

Getting North Korea Onboard
With the LNWFZ

While the narrative on the nuclear weapons' free zone has developed a life of its own, many other events were unfolding in my career that did not have anything to do with nuclear weapons' free zones. Sometimes there are unexpected outcomes. One such outcome or event in 2000 underscored the special role our research center played that ultimately supported our national foreign policy.

On one of my visits to Washington, I was asked by a State Department friend of mine if Georgia Tech would be able to help bring the DPRK delegation to New York for ten days to two weeks for substantive talks on the normalization of relations between the U.S. and North Korea. I responded that we could be very interested, if after their work was done in New York, we could get them to come to Atlanta for several days of talks with the experts in Georgia who were working with CISTP for the LNWFZ-NEA, or other matters of joint interest. A deal was struck, and we agreed to host their visit in New York, getting them to the U.S., providing suitable accommodations near the DPRK Mission to the UN, and then bring them down to Atlanta when business was over in New York.

Having made the deal, I started to gather the folks who could actually make it happen. I had talks with Delta Airlines, Coca-Cola, CNN, and my own funders at the W. Alton Jones Foundation and Ploughshares Fund, and of course, Georgia Tech. From my available funds, I believed we could come close to meeting the costs, but we had a big group and lots to do. Delta Airlines, seeing the importance of the meeting, responded with an offer of 2 business class tickets and 9 tourist class tickets to get them from Pyongyang and back. Coke agreed to bring the delegation down to Atlanta in a corporate plane and return them to New York, and CNN was very eager to provide any help they could provide, but they are in the news-gathering business, not in the fund giving business.

The meeting in New York lasted about ten days, and on the appointed day, I flew up and met the delegation at LaGuardia Airport and brought them down to Atlanta. While we could have selected any number of hotels in Atlanta, we chose the Marietta Hotel and Conference Center near where I was living. Its location was out of the way, somewhat more secure and gave the participants access to some of what I would say represented the Old South. It was a very pleasant venue.

A group of scholars, retired military figures, and policy-oriented individuals, along with CNN representatives, gathered. Former Senator Sam Nunn joined, and a contact was made for a one-on-one with former President Jimmy Carter. Former Ambassador John Kelly, Retired Admiral Pendley, Dr. Dan Papp, and others joined for these unique discussions. We had several round table sessions and dinner opportunities when the current situation was reviewed with possible options. Of course, the Limited Nuclear Weapons' Free Zone for NEA was presented so this DPRK delegation headed by Vice Minister Kim Gye-gwan could completely understand the objectives of the concept. It was March of 2000, and both sides were working to resolve the outstanding bilateral issues standing in the way of "normalization."

As far as endorsing the LNWFZ the DPRK delegation "took note of and understood the objectives" of the idea, but stayed away from outright support. The answer was always, "when differences are settled between the U.S. and the DPRK, we can address this 'very constructive' notion." (Offers to admit North Korean students at Georgia Tech, which would have sweetened the deal we were proposing, ended up in all conversations which addressed the bilateral relationship. Although these gestures were received favorably by the North Koreans, they could only occur after normalization between the two nations.)

After the two days of discussions, we flew back to New York, and they left from the Big Apple, having been introduced to the Big Apple and the Peach State. I can recall several conversations with delegates as they tried to understand how a retired Air Force Colonel who took part in the Cuban Missile Crisis would go to all the trouble to bring the delegation to the United States and also to Georgia. I thought it would be clear that I knew what nuclear war would do to Northeast Asia if allowed to go unchecked, but then again, maybe they did not do their homework on the old Colonel.

Evidently, the visit by the Delegation to New York was successful to the degree that another visit was called for in late September.[19] We (CISTP) were asked, once again to support a visit by three representatives from the DPRK for coverage of final details. We paid for the short meeting and received a briefing at a New York hotel near the United Nations. It seemed that all existing issues that needed resolution were going well, so well, in fact, that from October 9-12, Kim Jong-il's second in command, Vice Marshal Jo Myong Rok was invited to Washington, D.C. to meet with the Secretary of State and Defense. He carried a letter to President Clinton, as well.[20] Our Center was not involved in funding this visit; since it was a military figure, the Pentagon probably picked up the tab. It is a fair bet the North did not fund the visit as their embassies worldwide had been turned into "profit centers." (North Korean embassies and consulates around the world are tasked with funding their own operations through legitimate and not-so-legitimate means.)

It was quite an exception as he was invited to visit Washington, D.C. and meet with critical policy figures in a city normally out of reach to North Korean officials. This visit was evidently a success also, and led to the invitation for our Secretary of State at the time, Madeleine Albright, to visit Pyongyang and meet with Kim Jong-il. Her visit from October 24-26 was met with an invitation to the Arirang Extravaganza and special access to the leader of the DPRK. During that visit, the possibility of President Clinton being invited to Pyongyang was discussed besides commitments not to further test the Taepodong 1

---

[19] Arms Control Association, "Chronology of US-NK Nuclear and Missile Diplomacy," Recovered from: https://www.amscontrol.org/factsheets/dprkchron.
[20] *Ibid.*

Missile, as well as other matters dealing with the normalization of relations.[21]

The hope for a trip by President Clinton did not take place and time remaining for his administration was fast running out. The Republican candidate, George W. Bush had won the November 2000 election, and by December 28, Clinton announced that he would not be going to North Korea. It was a time of critical recounts from the November election, and according to his National Security Advisor, Sandy Berger, he decided to remain in the States in the event of a "constitutional crisis."[22] In any event, the movement toward rapprochement ended silently only to be cut off sharply when U.S. negotiators in Pyongyang revealed some very damaging evidence that indicated that all the time peace talks were ongoing, parallel nuclear developments were underway. Ambassador James Kelly, the brother of John Kelly, a member of our initiative, presented the U.S. case in Pyongyang and talks ended. By January 29, 2002, when Bush delivered his State of the Union Address, he included North Korea in the Axis of Evil.

From a personal standpoint, one could also see the rise of what came to be called, "The ABC Phenomenon"—Anything but Clinton. It generally was held to mean, anything that was started or left over from the Clinton Administration was going to receive very scant support or attention.

---

[21] *Ibid.*
[22] *Ibid.*

THIRTEEN

The Olympics
Come to Atlanta and Georgia Tech

The most important and constructive disruption that occurred at Georgia Tech in the decade from 1990 to 2000 was the coming and going of the 1996 Olympics. In a sense, when Tech began the process of competing for the games, we were still the "North Avenue Trade School" a not too kind term used to describe Tech—probably by folks calling the University of Georgia home—possibly not, but that rivalry was and is so intense that many a good story can be told. The first one deals with my arrival at Tech and a conversation I had with my great friend and mentor, Dan Papp, the head of the Social Science department that was to become the Sam Nunn School. We were on the phone; I was in Washington and Dan in Atlanta. I basically said, "Dan, I would be happy to accept the position and come to Georgia." There was a long pause, "John, you don't understand. You will be coming to Georgia Tech, not Georgia!"

Then there is the event some years later when I was having dinner with the newly assigned British Ambassador to the U.S. and the Lt. Governor of the State of Georgia when this rivalry came to the fore again. I will not go into names, but the Lt. Governor was a grad of UGA and was regaling the ambassador on the destructive nature of General Sherman's march to the sea. "And he destroyed everything of value that he came within sight of," the Lt. Governor proclaimed with great hand movements for effect. Of course, the dialog was getting pretty hot by this time, but he had left me an opening that was just too good for a Tech man to pass. "Right, and upon viewing the University of Georgia, he went right by." You might guess that I was never invited back for another dinner, but it was such a great moment, which proves that sometimes in life, the right people get their "just" desserts.

To set the matter straight, however, General Sherman, on seeing the University of Georgia supposedly said something to the effect, "Leave it be, they will need that university to rebuild the South."

(Once again, dear reader, I must apologize for getting distracted with my narrative as I pull things out of the deep parts of my memory. That's what happens when the old Colonel starts reminiscing about these moments.)

Continuing with my narrative and the Olympics, Atlanta gained the Olympics basically on the proposal created by an Atlanta lawyer and former University of Georgia football player Billy Payne. However, Georgia Tech President Pat Crecine brought Billy Payne's ideas to life with the most advanced presentation of the time using computer-generated virtual reality. It was a magnificent show that took the Olympic review team through all the aspects that Billy had imagined. The viewer could walk through the stadium, see the various venues, and dorms which were all done by computer.

On September 19, 1990, when the head of the Olympic Committee President Juan Antonio Samaranch of Spain opened the envelope and read: "The City of Atlanta," the entire city exploded. It had been a period of an economic downturn in the States and the economic activity associated with preparing for the Olympics acted as a buffer for the Atlanta area. Over one billion in public money was spent, and approximately 7500 rooms were added to hotel space between the time of the announcement and the opening of the games in August 1996.[23]

Atlanta put on one heck of a show. I still get chills when I think about Muhammad Ali carrying the Olympic Torch up to the cauldron to light the Olympic flame. It was one of those humbling moments in life, which make us appreciate the true spirit of the games. However,

---

[23] Olympic Games in 1996 – New Georgia Encyclopedia. Recovered from: http://georgiaencyclopedia.org/articles/sports-outdoor-recreation/olympic-games-1996.

tragedy struck during the games and almost tarnished the magnificent show Atlanta had put on for the world. On the morning of August 27, a pipe bomb exploded in the Centennial Olympic Park—a general meeting place and large open area created from urban redevelopment for the Olympics. Two persons were killed; sadly, these days, such events seem to be associated with a large gathering of people.

The Olympic Park was special to both Mitchie and myself as paving bricks were offered for sale to memorialize one's loved ones. We purchased four, and the names of both sets of our parents are still providing paving coverage for those enjoying the park. Every time we return and have a moment, we visit those red bricks that say Chie, Tadao, Alice, and Charles; no fewer words have said so much.

Perhaps the reason that the Olympics meant so much to us was the fact that the Georgia Tech Campus became the Olympic Village. As the beginning of the games approached, in the spring of 1996, all of us in the Sam Nunn School of International Affairs had to leave our offices and make way for Olympic personnel. In my case as Director of the Center for International Strategy, Technology, and Policy, I moved all of our computers to the basement of our home in Marietta, and on the table, we purchased from Georgia Tech that had been used for the five-week meeting of the Senior Panel, we conducted business. In fact, during those days, I was interviewed for a special on NHK in Japan, and more than an hour was recorded on video. I never saw the final product, but it was all about our efforts to bring stability to Northeast Asia.

The university built about eight dormitories on campus making it truly an Olympic Village and eventually purchased them from the Atlanta organizers at a 20% cost reduction. I cannot stress enough the impact the Olympics had on Georgia Tech. It truly became a first-rate international university since then and has never looked back.

My dear friend, Pat Crecine, who was President and worked so hard to bring the games to Atlanta and Georgia Tech, was relieved from his post two years before the games actually began. His reforms for the university were viewed as too extreme or too bold by many members of the alumni, and they began withholding contributions. In today's American university scene, that cannot be endured for long. Pat retired in 1994 and died of cancer in late April 2008. He had been a great friend with great vision and truly changed the world by changing Georgia Tech.

I need to mention a major part of the Olympics for myself: I was the official Olympic Attaché for the Mongolian Olympic Team from the time it was formed until very early August when my health told me to slow down. (I did not know it, but it was a symptom of things to come when one-and-a-half years later, I would have three major operations in three months to clear both carotid arteries and perform a triple bypass. I always maintained that my heart was fine, it was the lousy distribution system that was at fault; my love for fast food probably did not help either. At the same time, organizing and managing the meetings in Buenos Aires and Bordeaux in that same year also did not help.)

Before I stepped down from that attaché post, I hosted a preliminary visit by Mongolian officials and made attempts to prepare for their team and observers even when the Mongolians did not show up for hours after the appointed time. To my chagrin, fax after fax that I sent late at night from my second-floor office went unanswered. It seemed like no sense of urgency existed at the other end of the line, and literally, we found out the size of the team, the gender make-up, and items needed to prepare for their lodging when they arrived at Hartsfield International Airport in Atlanta. You can only imagine the chaos this created—but it was just the beginning.

By that time, however, I had stepped down and turned the job over to a great friend from the *Atlanta Journal-Constitution* our local newspaper. He was the son of a journalist who was on the scene in the 1930s in Japan and knew the most famous spy in the Second World War, Richard Sorge. His story about the Mongolian teams "break out" from the Olympic Village and a subsequent night on the town that resulted in the loss of their tickets home is a classic, but will not be repeated here.

FOURTEEN

Surviving a Health Scare

Without question, 1996 was a definitive year for so much that was going on in my life at the time, not to mention Georgia's with the hosting of the Olympics. Towards the end of 1996, we put the icing on the cake, so to speak, when we were able to convince Sen. Sam Nunn who was retiring from the Senate to join Georgia Tech and to lend his name to our Department of International Affairs turning it into the Sam Nunn School of International Affairs. While the international focus became clear in 1990 with the creation of our own department with Dr. Dan Papp as the leader, the addition of Senator Nunn put the school onto the front page not only in Georgia but much of the United States. The senator was not only a regional leader but clearly a national leader as well. His devotion to the reduction of nuclear weapons in the world ran exactly parallel to my own interests, and it marked the beginning of a very fruitful association.

1996 was also a good year for articles I contributed to books focusing on security issues in Northeast Asia. Three come to mind: "Denuclearization Initiatives: Will the Big Boys Play?" in William Clark and Ryukichi Imai's *Next Steps in Arms Control and Non-Proliferation*, published by the Carnegie Endowment for International Peace and Brookings Institution Press; "Japan's Emerging International Security policy" in Williamson Murray and Allan Millett's *Brassey's Mershon American Defense Annual 1997-1998; Current Issues and the Asian Challenge,*

Brassey's, 1996; and "Great Power Nuclear Forces Deployment and a Limited Nuclear Free Zone in Northeast Asia" in Whan Kilh and Peter Hayes, *Peace and Security in Northeast Asia: The Nuclear Issue and the Korean Peninsula,* M.E. Sharp, 1996. Not to bang my own drum, but these three books are essential reads for anyone who wants to brush up on their arms control knowledge and security issues for Northeast Asia.

I must apologize for not having the date for the next—and one of the most important meetings I had at Georgia Tech. The reason I don't remember is that the visit was done most secretly. So, I have no notes to jar my memory. Please let that be a lesson to anyone hoping to write memoirs sometime in the future. Anyway, the guest was spectacular—the long-time leader for democratic reforms in South Korea and ultimately Nobel Prize winner in 2000, and future President of the Republic of Korea, Kim Dae-jung. It was a hot spring or summer day with lots of Georgia sunshine to make matters hotter. Kim, who had run unsuccessfully for president in 1987 and 1992, hadn't announced his run for the president—he was elected in December 1997—so it could have been the spring of that year or the year prior when I met him.

Other aspects of his visit, while I cannot remember the date, were unforgettable. Already he was around 72 or 73. Now I have been around for a while, but I have seldom seen such a frail person walk into my office. I knew in advance of his visit and that he should not be required to walk too much, but when he came to our building on Marietta Street, in Atlanta, it was abundantly clear that he had suffered and suffered extensively at the hands of his captors—many times throughout his life. In reading about the life of Kim Koo another revered Korean leader, I learned how it was common practice in Korea at the time of Japanese occupation, for the police to break the legs of criminal suspects upon entry into custody. (No threat of running away.) While I cannot say that happened to this great man, it was apparent he had sustained severe injuries to his legs, and he walked with a shuffle of a person much older than his or her early seventies

While his body may have been frail, his mind was keen, and he was very inquisitive as I briefed him on the history of the limited nuclear free zone, and our hopes for the future. He was especially keen on the position of the DPRK which to that point was less clear than it would be in the 2000 timeframe. Anyway, he was clearly interested in the idea, and I was so grateful that he had set aside some time for our meeting and discussion. As our custom was always to keep things "close hold" so as not to embarrass any participant, I am relying on my memory for the brief encounter which probably took just about one hour as he had a very full schedule. I will say I have met many great persons in my life, but I hold the memory of the visit by the Honorable Kim Dae-jung one of my most precious. His commitment to democracy in South Korea places him apart from all others and deserves our collective gratitude.

In July 1997, with better notes and better memory, I had the honor of participating in a major conference sponsored by the City of Hiroshima and the *Asahi Shimbun* titled "Nuclear Disarmament and the Role of Nuclear Free Zones in Northeast Asia: The Role of Japan." It came just before the annual commemoration of the August 6, 1945 dropping of the atomic bomb on Hiroshima. It was a special meeting as the former president of the Union of South Africa Frederik Willem de Klerk was invited to discuss his role in turning back or reversing the policy on nuclear weapons development in South Africa. It was a remarkable setting in which we were briefed on a nation that had actually created a successful program and then disassembled it. In personal conversations, he wished us well in our regional endeavor but observed that it would be extremely difficult.

This was also an era when a neo-anti-Japanese feeling was evident within the U.S. security community. Many individuals had a fixed belief that having trounced the Soviet Union, the United States should be looking around to find its next foe. If we did not find one, budgets would be cut. Many of these specialists settled on Japan and wished those who wrote on Japan to support this idea of things like a coming war with Japan. I am not picking on the author who wrote a book of that very title (*The Coming War with Japan*, by George Friedman and his wife), but I came under pressure several times to add substance to this hypothesis. I never did, as my research—extensive as it was during the early 1990s—never supported that notion. My response was often if this is indeed on the horizon, all the more reason to support a multilateral security community in Northeast Asia. I will let this go for the moment, but having been on the receiving end of this kind of professional mass hysteria, I sympathize with those who have similar experiences as we strive to be the ideal democracy on this planet.

During this period, from the mid to late 1990s, I was busy teaching courses that included the Senior Seminar which picked a major topic of the day and worked to present policy recommendations in as real-life an atmosphere as possible. In fact, for the final "outbrief" for the course, we would invite senior government leaders to the class to review the findings and judge them as suitable for implementation. On several occasions, former Ambassador John Kelly participated and then was invited to our final dinner together where students accustomed to Big Macs and Whoppers were exposed to a full formal dining experience. It was the final touch that we gave to our students knowing that many prospective employers will invite applicants to a fine restaurant in the final stages of the interview process. Candidates who expect fast food and jumbo drinks stand a significant risk of having to continue their employment search. In the competitive market of the 21st Century, I believe this is a necessary touch. "Don't touch that wine until the boss does!" was heard a lot at these dinners.

Other courses I taught included "Pacific Security Issues" and "U.S. Foreign Policy." I was also teaching a "U.S. Foreign Policy" course in the spring of 1998, but then I underwent a series of operations that literally saved my life. It was February, March, and April of that year when I had the left carotid, right carotid, and triple bypass—in that order that permitted me to be at the computer today writing my memoirs. The story of the discovery of my condition is a story of true friendship that has spanned the decades. Dr. Robert Marmer of Atlanta and I were classmates from kindergarten through elementary, junior high, high school, and college. We both were friends from Ms. Buhrer's kindergarten class up through *the* Ohio State University.

One evening, in January 1998, we went with our wives, Natalie and Mitchie, to the movie *Wag the Dog*, and followed it with dinner at our local LaStrada restaurant. Bob looked at me and inquired how I felt. "Fine," I replied, "but I hear this high tone in my right ear every time my heart beats." Bam! Bob got up; came to my side of the table and started feeling under my jaw. You can imagine the scene; other dinners were looking at the two middle-aged men in some kind of embrace. Well, he told me to get to his office by Monday morning, and he would check me out.

I can never forget hearing a string of exclamations: "Wow!" "Never before!" and "Oh, My!" from my friend when I was in his office. After several moments, Bob calmed down and let me know he had never in his life heard worse noise coming out of the carotid arteries in a neck. The left was blocked 98% and the right, 90% it turned out. Bob also looked into my eyeballs and saw unprecedented cholesterol build up. He bundled up all his findings, sent me to a cardiologist friend, and the rest is history.

No, I can't leave it like that! I had the left carotid artery "cleaned out" in February. It was so bad that my doctor decided not to give me a general anesthetic, but a local. "John, I want you to talk to me during the entire operation. Do you think you can handle that?" Of course, putting it like that, as a man, I really had no option. "What do you mean, *handle* it? I was in Vietnam. Sure! Cut away." Well, the operation went quite nicely until he really had severed my artery and was preparing to do the "rotor-rooter" maneuver. All of a sudden, my naked body got nice and warm, and I realized what was happening. "Doc, are you warming me with my own blood?" "Shut up!"

Later as the operation proceeded, we ran out of inane subjects and turned to politics. That did it. As much as I like my doctor, we were not on the same wavelength when it came to politics. Our exchanges started to become more strident, and finally, I heard, "John, enough conversation. If we go on like this, I just might slip."

About a month later, we did the second carotid, and I must say, knowing what I went through with the first one, I was not at ease. He probably knew that by looking at my blood pressure, but staying away from politics, we finished the operation. As anyone knows who has gone through that operation, the recuperation calls for a mighty calm neck. I tried to be a good soldier and keep my neck as steady as possible, but the one-hour car ride going back home became a replay of some of the language I used to hear on the flight line when things were not going right. Sorry, Mitchie, I promise not to do that again.

Of course, I was not finished. February and March were over but the first week of April promised the double bypass that my doctor thought was needed. I was to find out that was not the case, and all of the sudden I was told I would have to change hospitals and have the "serious" one at the Eisenhower Medical Center in Augusta, Georgia. The fact was, I was covered by my military medical coverage, and I was told if you live within 200 miles of a facility that can do the major operation needed, then I would have to go to Ft. Gordon, the home of the U.S. Army Signal Command, as well as host to the Eisenhower Medical Center. My care was excellent, and the staff went out of their way to assure us that even though the doctor was young, he had performed over 2000 similar procedures.

I would like to acknowledge the excellent assistance of the Red Cross during this critical time in my life. The first week of April is the week in Augusta normally reserved for the Augusta National—one could say the most prestigious golf tournament in the world. Well, what does that have to do with your operation? All the rooms in the local hotels were taken up by golf enthusiasts. In steps the Red Cross that is operating a Fischer House on base which is in close proximity to the hospital. Its purpose is to provide lodging to patients, regardless of rank, who need to have family close by. The Red Cross Representative visited my wife, who was in the waiting room and offered a place for my wife and children to stay. It was wonderful and appreciated so much. Again, thank you, Red Cross.

The operation itself was eventful; very much so, and it ended up I needed a triple instead of a double. In baseball, that is always good, not so in heart surgery. As in all such events in life, it brought my family closer than ever. Again, it was a near-death experience, but I really do not recommend it as a means to have family bonding. Please try a camping trip, instead. After a week, I was out of the hospital and back home in Atlanta. I remember that three-hour drive with my wife driving as the most "far out" trip I ever took. So I would not feel any discomfort on the way home, the doctors had given me a "brew" that allows the world to go by with no cares at all. It was, however, a time to reset my clock. I believe the entire affair resulted in a "second chance," and I have tried not to waste it.

During this time, I was in and out of work and hospitals and medical breaks. In a sense, I felt like Mao in his later days when they would wheel him into a room to be present for some ceremony and then wheel him out. That was me. One such meeting was our February 1998 co-hosting and co-chairing of a roundtable session with the Institute for Defense Studies of New Delhi, India. To this day, I do not recall if I said anything coherent or not, but they kept applauding— probably just that I was able to sit up straight. The great support I received from all the crew at the Center and Sam Nunn School kept me going, but I still feel sorry for the 50 students who were in my U.S. Foreign Policy course that I told I would be out of class for a week or so, and never saw them again in that class. My wife had seen a significant change in my energy levels and my editor for a book I was writing at the time called me about the ups and downs in my writing style that were all signs of impending trouble. So, when we ended the year with the major limited nuclear-free zone conference in Helsinki both husband and wife, and of course the kids, were glad to see a dad that was actually recovered and almost "better than ever."

This is a very good time in the narration to say, "Thanks Bob, once again," and to Mitchie, who has been by my side since 1958.

FIFTEEN

A Nobel Calling

The nine years remaining at Georgia Tech before the transition to South Korea were full of work to consolidate and extend the role of the Center for International Strategy, Technology, and Policy and better integrate it into the regular activities of the faculty. Much time was spent finding funding sources for the activities of the Center itself, and sharing our experiences with INTA Majors (students who majored in International Affairs offered by the Sam Nunn School). Some of the funding came from research contracts such as IDA, Battelle Corporation, JETRO/MITI, the Strategic Studies Institute of the U.S. Army War College, and CNN, and grants from the W. Alton Jones Foundation, Ploughshares Fund, Department of Energy, Delta Airlines (tickets not cash but necessary for transportation), Carnegie Corporation, the Second Chance Foundation, and Coca-Cola (again no-cost round trip air to and from New York City). Finally, from 2003 on, we received 3.14 million dollars from the MacArthur Foundation to establish and run the Sam Nunn Security Program were we took selected doctoral candidates from across the technical spectrum at Tech to provide a one year tutorial in interacting with the U.S. security community.

In fact, from 2003 until my departure in 2007, the bulk of my teaching became associated with the Sam Nunn Security Seminar where 10 to 25 graduate students would meet with senior Sam Nunn faculty every week to discuss issues in government-research community interface. Toward the end of each semester the seminar was capped with a one-week to ten-day trip to various government and research facilities throughout the United States. It was a demanding schedule for students and professors alike, but the goal was to expose ethical scientific and/or technical experts in Defense Department programs that could use professional advice as to the adoption of new programs or upgrading of old. This was one of Senator Nunn's most frequent themes—the need to create independent specialists who could advise the government and not be beholden to corporate interests. We hope we added significantly to the pool from which to draw. That was our purpose, and thanks to support from the MacArthur Foundation, it was well funded. It was undertaken from 2003 and was going strong as I left in 2007.

My writing during this same time focused on articles about collective security, the defense policy of Japan, consideration of new denuclearization initiatives, the limited nuclear weapons' free zone for Northeast Asia, and a book co-written with Drs. Dan Papp and Loch Johnson, *American Foreign policy: History, Politics, and Policy.* In conjunction with an active publication schedule, presentations to nations, especially in Asia, dealing with advocacy of the limited nuclear weapons' free zone, took an increasing amount of time. Such trips included: a trip to Singapore to present the LNWFZ concept to the academic/security community by invitation of President S.R. Nathan of the Republic, lectures to fellows of the Center for War Studies of King's College, London, and members of the Royal College of Defense Studies (UK), a Guest Lecturer week at the University of Montesquieu IV in Bordeaux, presentation to a Wilton Park (UK) conference on nuclear non-proliferation, and in early 2005 bilateral meetings in the capitals of Finland, Sweden, Japan, Korea, and Mongolia. A trip to Canada, to Vancouver and the University of British Columbia, allowed us further understanding of the limited nuclear weapons' free zone, but also to understand the beauty of that particular corner of the world.

On practically all these trips, I was able to invite my wife, Mitchie. In a sense, this made for an acute difference from my travels during my Air Force years. We grew as a couple as all my activities could be shared with the person I loved. While in the Air Force, or the government for that matter, our daily conversations focused on anything but what I did at the office. Once in academia, I had an excellent sounding board and helpmate who could cool me down or spur me on—whatever the need.

As 2004 approached, I was very much involved in expanding the Korean related aspects of our curriculum at the Sam Nunn School. I had been very active in the Georgia Japan-America Society, but increasingly our efforts to expand Korean programs found me deeply involved. Involved meant not only academically, but also getting to know the leaders of the Korean community and eventually becoming the President of the Korea-Southeast United States Chamber of Commerce. This organization was rather broad in scope, involving all the seven states of the old Confederacy. Actually, that was a massive order for a group that was primarily concentrated in the Atlanta area.

We did, however, have meetings and tours of regional businesses as they came into the region and observed the major holidays celebrated in South Korea and the United States. Our annual New Year's party was a high point of the year and allowed for a great exchange between the more established mainline companies of Atlanta with, the newer, but promising Korean activities. While we played a very active role in making sure the American and Korean business leaders interacted with each other, I must be truthful and acknowledge that the State of Georgia had its economic development strategies in very good order. The Governor would take a trade advisory group to various countries where business was desired, and often we accompanied the group and became part of the greater government-driven initiatives. Soon the focus was on Hyundai and KIA Motors, and in both cases, successful significant investments were made in Alabama and Georgia. In both cases, the states played the driving role granting tax incentive and holidays, plus assisting in finding appropriate locations.

Later, I had the opportunity to tour both facilities in Montgomery, Alabama, and West Point, Georgia. As I had to stay overnight in Georgia, I chose a motel within an easy drive of the KIA Plant. I was stunned at how the supportive social infrastructure had been put in place. When I turned on the TV in my motel, the first five or six channels that I came to were in Korean! That blew me off my feet. Here I was in West Point, Georgia, once famous for textile manufacturing and old southern traditions and the TV was in Korean.

John E. Endicott

At breakfast, I noticed a few Koreans dressed in company jackets and matching trousers getting ready to go to the plant. Everyone was exchanging greetings and smiles abounded. I mean, people were happy. Of course, you would be happy too, if you ran into folks who were responsible for the "new life" of an old town. Rather than a defeatist attitude of many rust belt areas I have visited (remember my home was Ohio), you could feel a "can do" attitude on the part of everyone you met.

Then when I visited the plant itself—remember I was in the military for 28 years and I always check the food first—the lunchroom (very nice indeed) had three basic options: Southern, Korean, and Yankee (the sometimes pejorative term used to describe someone from the North). Grits, one of the mainstays of southern cooking and eating were prominently displayed, but if you wanted or needed kimchi, there it was down that accessible parallel food line. I was so impressed, not only was the food handled well, it seemed like everyone knew everybody else. Well, you know that can't be the case, but the willingness to exchange greetings and make everyone feel part of a team was in the air. I think that was a great blending of the down-home southern welcome and Korean recognition of efficiency and how to attain it.

I must say I did not find that same overwhelming welcome at the Hyundai Plant, perhaps because it was older and Montgomery did not depend on the Hyundai Plant as West Point depended on KIA. Please, I did not do a research project to ascertain that opinion. I went, I saw, and I compared. Things were better on the Georgia side than in Alabama, but perhaps those years as a Yellow Jacket (the nickname for Georgia Tech) had an impact.

So life, as 2007 approached, was increasingly becoming complicated, busy, and hectic. It was a blending of interests in Japan and the Japanese community, interests in the military activities of the region—especially the U.S. Marine Corps. One of the reasons for this was the relationship Tech had with one of its famous graduates General (retired) and Medal of Honor recipient, Raymond Davis. Believe me, we just came together and bonded, increasing involvement in the Korean community and making Korean studies a viable part of the Sam Nunn School's offerings, and promoting the Sam Nunn Security Program among the promising grad students of Georgia Tech generally. In between all this, I had become the Honorary Counsel for Mongolia to the State of Georgia. That position cost me money, but it was part of a service to a developing nation that I had so much respect for. I believe that I was able to increase the awareness of Mongolia's role in the 20th Century as well as its future in the 21st.

One of the projects was to make Americans aware that in 1939, Mongolia played a very key role in stopping an attempt by Imperial Japan to make significant inroads into the territory of the Soviet Union. (Actually, I should say the Kwantung Army rather than Imperial Japan, as it was the era of "dual diplomacy" when the Foreign Office tried to make right what the military did without approval.) What I am talking about is the May-September 1939 border war between Japan and Mongolia and its ally the Soviet Union. Certain factions within the Japanese military wished to invade and possibly slice off Russian territory east of Lake Baikal and place it in the Empire of Japan. Through good luck and unbelievable intelligence, the Soviets and the Mongols were made aware of Japan's intentions and took massive steps to thwart them. Stalin was lucky to have the master spy of the 20th Century in Japan (Richard Sorge) and a seasoned General at the time, Major General Georgy Zhukov, who believed in tanks, artillery, and airplanes, lots of them, in addition to prepared troops. Integrating Mongolian forces into his general defense plans, he prepared a reception that will never be forgotten by Japanese military historians. The Japanese planners remembering the glory days of 1904-1905 underestimated their foe, and when it was all over in September 1939, the Russians claimed some 60,000 Japanese casualties. While there is considerable debate about the correct casualty figures, the intensity of the Soviet response stood witness to a different Russia and a different Mongolia. In the end, the defeat was so devastating that the Japanese sued for an armistice in September 1939. Eventually, on April 13, 1941, both sides signed a non-aggression pact.[24]

The battle called Nomonhan by the Japanese (after a small village) and Khalklin Gol (after the river that flows in the area) by the

---

[24] For the definitive work on this subject (Japanese view) see: Coox, Alvin D. *Nomonhan: Japan Against Russia, 1939.* Twin volumes, 1985, Stanford University Press. Alvin was a good friend and we worked together in Tokyo during 1958 and 1959. For a Russian perspective the memoirs of Marshal Georgy Zhukov are fascinating, but unreliable when it comes to actual figures.

Mongol/Soviet Forces proved a godsend for Stalin as the Soviet response led by Zhukov was so severe that the Japanese were never willing to risk another such defeat in that theater. Eventually, he was able to transfer forces from the east to use in defense of the west as Nazi forces were pouring into Russia after the June 1941 invasion. One pauses to think about the "what might have been" aspect of this battle. Had the Japanese succeeded at Nomonhan indicating poor Russian defenses in the region, a later larger force might have been used in eastern Russia as the Nazis were driving into western Russia. Would the Soviet Union have been able to withstand a two-front war? Would Japan, involved in a massive war in Russia be interested in a Pearl Harbor attack, and if not, how and when would the United States have entered World War II? All such thought becomes academic as the Soviet General employed the massive use of tanks, artillery, and air in one of the largest air wars ever to that date. It was a tactic Russia would use over and over during the war, and it convinced the Japanese who had wanted to "go north" and seize Russian territory from Lake Baikal to the Pacific that another option would be better "going south." Of course, the southern strategy brought Japan to face America at Pearl Harbor.

You can see I enjoyed my time as the Honorary Consul in Atlanta for Mongolia. My wife and I met many interesting individuals and only occasionally had issues involving real diplomatic problems. I was trying to make at least Atlanta aware that Mongolia is more than Genghis Khan. It played a vital role in the 20th Century also. Finally, regarding Mongolia, may I mention one of the most important contributions I made to Mongolian foreign relations during my tenure? In one of the annual calls to return to Ulaanbaatar (UB) for Foreign Ministry instructions, the group of international honorary consuls was asked to comment on making Mongolia more tourist-friendly. Most everyone agreed Mongolia needed a place to feel that the visitor had met the greatness of Genghis Khan. A central monument needed to be erected to accomplish that and draw visitors to see and become aware of this greatness. A massive statue of Genghis on a horse was recommended to which all agreed. Today, outside UB about one hour is such a monument. It is huge, and it is Genghis Khan on horseback. Without question, it is magnificent and worth the time to see. I can say I voted for it—along with everyone else; it was just a good idea, and it's nice knowing that my vote and the votes of the other honorary consuls made it into a reality.

After significant activity devoted to peace on the Korean peninsula, regular meetings of the Expanded Senior Panel for the Limited Nuclear Weapons' Free Zone continued on an annual basis. In 2001 we had the 7th Plenary Meeting in Seoul, and in 2002, we had the 8th Plenary in Ulaanbaatar. We didn't have one in 2003 due to the Severe Acute Respiratory Syndrome (SARS) crisis that was visiting all of Asia, but led to an interesting meeting with the then Mayor of Taipei, Ma Ying-jeou who came to Atlanta to thank the Center for Disease Control (CDC) for help to deal with the crisis in Taiwan when the WHO demurred. While the annual meeting of the LNWFZ was skipped, 2003 was also marked by two visits by North Korean delegations headed by Ambassador Han Song-ryol. One visit was in February, and the other was in November. The November visit was accompanied by Director General Jo Sung-un who was head of the America Division of the DPRK Ministry of Foreign Affairs. On each visit, an extensive exchange of opinions was held, usually with a representative from the U.S. Department of State present. They were always good opportunities to introduce students at Georgia Tech with the intractable foe. And sometimes they even smiled (the North Koreans). We marketed the idea for a regional peace settlement and always had a rational discourse. In the end, however, it was always "the U.S. and DPRK must come to an accommodation; then all things may be possible," or words to that effect.

Another very significant meeting took place on August 27, 2003, in Beijing; we were not invited as it was at official levels and between the six nations that had a major stake in possible nuclear weapons in North Korean hands: China, Japan, both Koreas, the Russian Federation, and the United States It was the first meeting of what became known as the Six-Party Talks, and their focus was the dismantlement of a nuclear weapons capability in North Korea. Should we have proclaimed victory at this point? In essence, this was a continuation of the unofficial talks for a limited nuclear weapons' free zone that had started in 1995 at Georgia Tech within the Center for International Strategy, Technology, and Policy of the Sam Nunn School. Our work, by including official observers from all these states, was completely known to all. We paused but continued still inviting official observers to take what might be useful to their official efforts. In 2004, the 9th Plenary was held in Jeju Island, South Korea. It was supported by the Ministry of Defense, and the setting encouraged all to continue to press their respective governments on the qualities of a regional regime of cooperative security. In 2005, rather than have a major meeting, I decided on one-on-one meetings in the capitals of Finland, Sweden, Japan, Korea, Canada, and Mongolia. It was a very demanding schedule, where I tried to meet with the leading security organizations, both government and private within those nations to highlight the unofficial collective effort underway and to encourage their support and possible participation.

Happily, due principally to the earnest efforts of our colleague and former member of the Finnish Foreign Ministry, Markku Heiskanen, the work being done to achieve a Limited Nuclear Weapons' Free Zone in Northeast Asia was incorporated into a "national recommendation" by the Finnish Government to the Nobel Peace Prize Committee.[25] I was also told that several ambassadors and academics had also nominated me along with our entire organization for the Committee's consideration. This then became a matter for extensive comment in the media, at least in Atlanta and *The Atlanta Journal-Constitution* carried almost a full-page commentary on some of the candidates focusing especially on Senator Sam Nunn and myself. It was a very heady time, and one felt like the lottery ticket for $500,000,000 was in your hand, and it was almost time to distribute the prize. Well, it was not to be, and even the Australian bookies who do these things gave me odds of winning of 101 to 1. Not very good. They knew their business, and a favorite, the Director of the International Atomic Energy Agency (IAEA), Mohamed Elbaradei, came in the victor. It was an exhilarating experience, and on October 7, the day the results were announced, my wife and I opened the Champagne to celebrate, it was our 46th Wedding Anniversary after all.[26]

---

[25] I will have to admit I have never seen the recommendation, but am assured it happened by our colleague Markku Heiskanen. The recommendations are never publicly acknowledged by the Nobel Organization.

[26] I invite you to read: Mark Bixler, "Georgia Tech Prof could have Nobel calling," *The Atlanta Journal- Constitution,* October 5, 2005, pp. F1 and F3.

Photo Gallery Three

At my desk at Georgia Tech where I served from 1989 to 2007 as Full Professor and Founding Director of the Center for International Strategy, Technology, and Policy of what became the Sam Nunn School.

John E. Endicott

In a Mongolian Ger. The gentleman and his wife who gave me a horse. I owe him a saddle on my next trip to Mongolia.

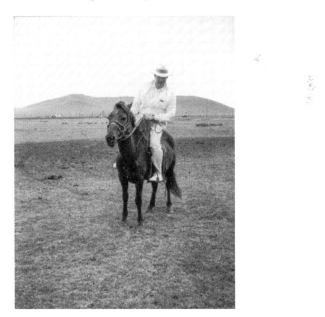

This fine Mongolian horse was given to me but has been far removed for decades. Here I am looking for the starter.

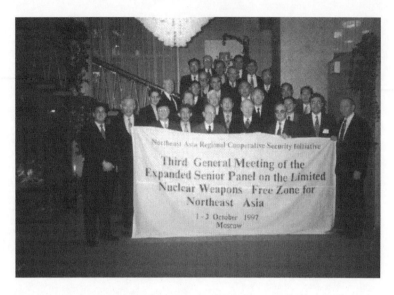

Members of the Limited Nuclear Weapons' Free Zone in Northeast Asia at
its 3rd Plenary meeting in October 1997.

Certainly excited about something as I deliver a speech at Nanjing University
in October 2008 marking the 30th anniversary of the Deng Xiao Ping
Reforms.

John E. Endicott

Members of the Tokyo 2007 LNWFZ Meeting having dinner on a flat-bottomed boat in Tokyo Bay.

Inaugural ceremony for the opening of SolBridge in the new SolBridge building in March 2008.

Presidential Inauguration Ceremony in January 2009. Chairman Kim, Mitchie and President Daniel Papp of Kennesaw State University, Georgia, our guest speaker are to the left of the podium.

Chairman Kim of the Woosong Foundation and Daniel Papp of Kennesaw State University, Georgia moments after my inauguration in January 2009.

50th Anniversary Reunion:

Botton line: "Jack" Endicott, Nick Noble, Greg Noble; 2nd line: Carol Mills, Alexandra Noble, Alice Mills (Sitty), Mitsuyo (Mitchie) Endicott, John Endicott, Kayleigh Noble (now Saxon), Charlene Endicott Noble; Standing: Gary Mills, Tina Mills, Gary Mills, Jr., Virginia Endicott, John Endicott II, Patty-Gene Watson.

Our 50th Wedding Anniversary Party in our home in Marietta, Georgia. Our children hosted us, neighbors, and friends. My sister, Alice, came with some of her children to take part—a wonderful moment in life.

Warming up to throw the first pitch at a Hanwha Eagles baseball game. Mitchie, Dr. Lee Ji-en, interpreter,and Dr. Lee Dal-young are off to the side watching; I wore Number 14 in honor of Pete Rose of the Cincinnati Reds.

John E. Endicott

Receiving an Honorary Doctorate from President Bruno Sire of the University of Toulouse 1 Capitole in recognition of efforts to promote international peace as seen in the nomination for the Nobel Peace Prize, October 8, 2010, during the 13th Meeting of the LNWFZ-NEA Plenary in Toulouse.

SolBridge International School of Business

Part IV
The Woosong-SolBridge-Endicott College Years

SIXTEEN

Land of the Morning Calm

In the fall of 2006, we had the 10th Plenary in Shanghai with the wonderful cooperation of the American Consulate General; it also marked our last plenary while associated with Georgia Tech. This meeting did have representatives from the DPRK in attendance who became constructive dialog members once they made their introductory remarks. Inevitably first comments were strident and directed to the "keeper" who had accompanied the delegation from Pyongyang. Once the commercial was delivered, their contributions became constructive. I should point out that the only times the North Koreans joined us for the multinational meetings were for meetings held in China—but not always. For our first Chinese plenary in 2000 in Beijing, we received a call at 0300 on the morning of the meeting letting me know that the expected delegation would be unable to attend. Something had happened at the other end of the line between the U.S. and North Korea, and that group had to remain at home. However, as you can see, we had many opportunities to make sure the North Koreans were players in one-on-one sessions.

About this time, my life became slightly more complicated. In the many trips to South Korea, I had met a former South Korean Air Force pilot who had contacts with friends in Atlanta—Young Kim; he and his wife-to-be treated me far too well when I visited Seoul, sometimes giving me a typical gift of welcome, for example, a case of Korean pears. These pears are huge and delicious, but when one received a case of eight or so for a three-day stay, it is over the top. And there is no way to bring these back into the country. I hope you have tried these pears—one fourth is enough at one sitting so you can see six to eight almost warrant an export license when received as a gift.

Young Kim introduced me to Paul Kim, his friend of many years. Paul is an Australian-born Korean who heads Benchmark Associates Incorporated. One thing Benchmark does, among many others, is to find candidates for executive opportunities. So, one day in early February 2007 (I remember it was February as the Lunar New Year was on February 18 that year; we had timed our arrival, so it overlapped with the latter part of the holiday which caused some considerable trouble in making meeting arrangements), I was meeting with colleagues at Sogang University in Seoul, the Jesuit University of Seoul, in fact, the university that former President Park Guen-hye graduated from in 1974. In the middle of a meeting to arrange an exchange agreement between Georgia Tech and Sogang, I received a call from Paul, who at this time, I did not know.

"Hello. Is this Dr. John Endicott?"

"Yes."

"This is Paul Kim, and I have an offer you cannot reject!" It reminded me of that famous line from *The Godfather* (1972)—"I'm going to make him an offer he can't refuse"—and that's pretty much what Paul did. In the course of the conversation, I found out that Woosong University in Daejeon, South Korea was looking for a new president and a vice chancellor for a new international school of business. Paul wanted to meet with me to discuss the particulars, and since I was staying at the Lotte Hotel in downtown Seoul, a meeting was set up for an afternoon that was free.

The afternoon meeting literally changed my life, and of course, my wife's as well. Paul is an energetic and engaging person. I think he could sell anything he was required to sell. During the meeting, he explained the basic drive behind the personnel search; the university's foundation, the Woosong Education Foundation, wished to internationalize its campus and first on the agenda was the creation of a new business school that would revolutionize the way Korean colleges teach: it would use English as the language of instruction, follow an American business school curriculum, seek professors and students from all over the world, and specialize in its Asian characteristics. They were looking for someone who had created organizations or been in on the creation of new institutions, someone who understood Asia and its people, and someone who had demonstrated an ability to fundraise and improvise, not to mention, someone who was flexible.

You must believe me when I say this took me completely by surprise. I had been approached by organizers seeking to start the foreign university enclave in Incheon, later to be called Songdo, but their message was still not quite focused. Woosong, on the other hand, seemed to have a desire to do something and do it fast. Paul was quite clear in the financial incentives that were involved, as well as the expectations that went with them. Without question, it was an offer that could not be refused. But, after a long conversation, it was clear to me that this kind of decision was not to be made by myself. I explained to Paul that as a life-long student of Asia, the offer was magnificent and very tempting, but my wife, although a U.S. citizen, was born and raised in Japan. Her degrees from Jissen Woman's College in Tokyo and the George Mason University in Virginia prepared her for much, but life in Korea? That was an entirely different challenge.

"Paul," I said. "You know South Korea and Japan have not always been the very best friends. I have to talk to Mitchie and get her opinion."

In essence, I really did not mean "opinion," I meant "permission." After a life of an Air Force wife and years having to create short term relationships and follow her husband around, it was time to let her make the decision. I did not want her to feel uncomfortable in a high visibility post—and possibly in danger. Remember, I was not necessarily very kind to our friends up North and they knew it. Also, there can be latent tensions between Japan and South Korea, which can turn unpleasant at times—and unpredictable (case in point, the ongoing diplomatic tussel between both nations in 2019). I thanked

Paul, and we agreed to stay in close touch. My next stop was a long conversation with the woman I love.

Upon my return to Marietta, a short 20 miles north of Georgia Tech, my wife and I gradually turned over the idea of leaving our comfort zone and our tenured full professorship relation with Georgia Tech. At 71, I was not necessarily a spring chicken, and we both knew that taking the helm of a start-up organization meant a life of endless stress and a bag of unknowns. It was only nine years before that I had gone through the carotid artery mess and a triple by-pass. Would the machinery hold up; how about the brain? What about our house? Our children now all living within three miles of our home—that is a situation most all retired military would give their "eye teeth" to have—what would they have to say?

Well, these are the kinds of thoughts that ran through our minds, and I was not all that sure that a Ph.D. in International Relations would hold up in the quest to build a new international school of business. At the Fletcher School of Law and Diplomacy, I had taken courses in international economic development, but I was not an economist, a businessman, or an accountant. Perhaps I knew a bit about marketing as I had actively "sold" and marketed the limited nuclear weapons' free zone, but that was all experiential learning, which had nothing to do with the academic field of marketing. I did have a good deal of leadership experience at the Air Force Academy, the National War College, and the Institute for National Strategic Studies and at Georgia Tech—all with educationally related individuals. Much of that was in a "start-up" mode, and at that, I had done a pretty good job.

Now it was time to consider an old Japanese saying: "You have not lived unless you have jumped from Kiyomizu Dera at least once in your life." Kiyomizu Dera is the beautiful Buddhist temple on the outskirts of Kyoto, Japan. There is a magnificent vista from the veranda of the temple, but straight down it is probably about 100 feet. That is the spot from which the great 11th Century Japanese samurai, Yoshitsune jumped with his trusted lieutenant Benkei (Saitō Musashibō Benkei) when cornered by the men of his half-brother Yoritomo. (Yoritomo happened to be the Shogun and at that time not too happy with the fame of his half-brother.) Of course, they jumped, but the fall was moderated by the branches of the tall pine trees onto which they jumped. Crashing down limb by limb, they landed, got up, and ran to fight another day. Was it time for Mitchie and I to face our Kiyomizu Dera moment?

Yes, it was. Mitchie, bless her heart, looked at the situation, and responded, "Let's do it!"

After several days of deliberation, I called Paul, and we threw our hats into the ring. Of course, it was not automatic. Paul flew out to Atlanta and met me at Tech for a beer with one of my best friends at Tech, Lou Cercio, a retired Army Colonel and an expert in plasma fusion. We talked about the proposition and indicated we were interested. For sure, it was not over. The folks at Woosong had put out a worldwide search, and there were others who were interested in the challenge. Whatever was happening with the process back at Woosong was unknown to us until one day, Paul called to ask if we could travel to Daejeon and meet with those charged with reviewing the finalists. We were delighted and made plans to visit South Korea together in May 2007.

Arriving in the evening, we were put up in an airport hotel for the night as we faced a three-hour car ride the next day to reach Daejeon. Nowadays, one can take a train directly to Daejeon in less than two hours, but in 2007, direct rail service between Incheon International Airport and Daejeon hadn't begun operation (in order to reach Daejeon by rail, one had to take the airport express train to Seoul Station, and there, transfer to the KTX—South Korea's high-speed train). Our host was a man who was to become our dear friend and colleague, Dr. Jung Sang-jik. He was basically the action officer for the new business school concept, and you could see he was happy to see us. On the way down to Daejeon, I saw the dramatic changes that had been realized in the highway system since being in Korea. Being in the Air Force at that time meant one did not drive about the country, but visited small air bases hither and yon, using an 0-1 observation plane or some other small administrative plane. I had just not used the highway outside of Seoul. Once on it, it was like any U.S. interstate highway, and we made good time.

We had the normal meetings with the Foundation leadership, did a lot of talking about education philosophy, visited the 40 million dollar complex that was then under construction with the outer shell fairly well complete, but much to be done on the interior, and finally I entered into a meeting with the Chairman of the Foundation asking my opinion of the proposed name of the college.

"What do you think of SolBridge?" he asked.

I can still remember my answer. "Well, it certainly worked for Cambridge. What does 'Sol' mean?" I said with a smile. I certainly wasn't being facetious or anything with my comparison.

Chairman Kim Sung-kyung then explained that "Sol" was Korean for pine tree and of course "Bridge" was a bridge—a pine bridge to "success, joining East with West."

That was the end of the meeting except for a question regarding the viability of the institution. I opined I thought the idea of turning outward and overseas for students was a great idea in light of South Korea's population decline. It was then, as it is now, over ten years later, a very illuminating remark to say as it was also the vision, by a strategic planner and educator, Chairman Kim.

During the visit, I was asked what historical site I really wanted to see. For me, it was the tomb of the great hero of the Paekche Kingdom, General Gyebaek, who is renowned as one of the most loyal military figures in history. His fame came at the end of the Paekche Kingdom when he was presented with a near to impossible task: defend the kingdom facing incredible odds. His force was approximately 5,000 and Silla, the kingdom to the east had 50,000, and thanks to the presence of Tang Chinese allies, a considerable backup of more than 100,000. (The Japanese eventually sent approximately 30,000 to fight in support of a new King of Paekche, in an attempted revival of Paekche power, but the attempt was defeated in 663 at the Battle of Baekgang[27].)

Facing a very bleak picture, General Gyebaek went to his wife to explain the situation. His defeat would mean slavery at best for his wife, and probably death. Mutually they decided to end the uncertainty and kill their children and then his wife so the general could fight without reservation. That is a pretty high measure of loyalty to the king, and it serves as an example of the ultimate sacrifice for duty. The general, indeed, was killed in battle, having successfully fought back four individual thrusts by the enemy. On the fifth, however, he and his loyal retainers were eliminated. Members of the royal family ruling

---

[27] The accounts of the Paekche Kingdom are extremely interesting and will serve as a basis for a thirst for more. See *A History of the Kingdom of Paekche* by Jonathan West.

Paekche took refuge in Japan, and that event serves as one of the more visible Korean ties with Japan and the Japanese Imperial Family today. However, in this short visit to Daejeon, I was unable to make such a side trip, and Mitchie and I returned to Atlanta to consider what had transpired on our first visit to Woosong University, and to make a decision.

SEVENTEEN

Hello Woosong!

As is clear from events of the past ten years, Mitchie and I made that decision to leave the security of tenured life at Georgia Tech and strike out for "points unknown." It really was not as dramatic as that, as South Korea had frequently been on my agenda from my very first visit in the early 1960s.

What I do remember is Kimpo Air Base and the steaming hot table as I ate breakfast in the mess hall at 0500 or 0600 hours in the dead of winter. It was minus 20 degrees Fahrenheit, and SOS (chipped beef on toast, but in military parlance, "sh*t on a shingle;" I'll let you, dear leaders, figure out the missing letter on your own) never tasted so good in my life. Just the thought of thick white sausage gravy on biscuits makes my mouth water, kind of like Pavlov and his dog. It's probably not the most nutritious dish on the planet, but it sure tastes as if it is. What I also remembered about that trip was when I noticed no trees on the mountains. There are several reasons for this, including Japan's occupation of the peninsula and the Korean War. Later, Park Chung-hee's Saemeul Movement would put a lot of men to work planting trees and reforesting the hills and mountains—very similar to the Civilian Conservation Corps as part of FDR's New Deal programs.

That first trip to South Korea was one of the times that I was augmenting a PACAF Inspector General's inspection trip to the various air elements throughout the Pacific. Since then, I had been drawn to Korea many times in my Air Force and DoD career, so clearly the points were not unknown. What was unknown was how a fairly seasoned specialist on Northeast Asia would handle the requirements to succeed in heading a new international business school that was basically a "start-up" operation.

Closing down the operation at Georgia Tech was not an easy matter, and my very able assistant Ms. Angie Levin shouldered the many responsibilities of following through with the preparations for our Limited Nuclear Weapons' Free Zone plenary meeting that we had been readying for Tokyo for October 2007.

Indeed, the meeting went off without any major problems, and for that, we could thank our Japanese host, Professor Toshiyuki Shikata, a retired Lt. General of the Japan Ground Self Defense Force who worked tirelessly to make the meeting both substantive and enjoyable, even including an evening dinner trip on Tokyo Bay. Rather than describe the events, permit me to share the report of the meeting and notations about our planned subsequent meeting for Daejeon in 2008:

Initial Report of the 11th Plenary of the LNWFZ-NEA
October 3-6, 2007
Tokyo, Japan

The 11th Plenary of the Limited Nuclear Weapons' Free Zone for Northeast Asia (LNWFZ-NEA) took place in Tokyo, Japan in early October. It was marked by an extremely positive Keynote address from the Director of the Arms Control and Disarmament Division of the Disarmament, Non-Proliferation and Science Department of the Ministry of Foreign Affairs of Japan. Followed by "Country Reports" from all the Team represented—Argentina, China, Finland, France, Japan, Mongolia, the Republic of Korea, the Russian Federation, and the United States—the meeting got off to one of its most positive starts since the Expanded Senior Panel began meeting in 1996. All teams reported about the changed environment that included the Korean South-North Bi-laterals and the resumption of the Six-Party Talks in Beijing.

In addition to the keynote address and introductory remarks by the co-hosts, formal presentations were made by Dr. Toshiyuki

Shikata of Japan, Dr. Lee Kwan of South Korea, Professor N. Akiyama and Ms. W. Mukai of Japan, General A. Bolyatko of Russia, Dr. Lim-chae Hong of Korea, and Professor H. Takesada of Japan. Dr. J. Endicott made a detailed report of the activities of the Secretariat since the 10th Plenary meeting in Shanghai in March of 2006.

Presentations and commentators discussions primarily focused on the developments related to the Six-Party Talks, confidence-building measures in the context of current conditions, and economic incentives for DPRK participation in the LNWFZ-NEA concept. Conclusions of the 11th plenary meeting included the following points:

—Continued support for positive exchange and dialog between South and North Korea.

—General endorsement of progress made thus far in the Six-Party Talks.

—The need for rapid resolution of the abduction issue and greater bilateral dialog between Japan and the DPRK.

—The need for positive reinforcement of the global arms control regime and awareness that traditional concepts of deterrence must be expanded to take into consideration the role of non-state actors.

—The revalidation of the principles of step-by-step nuclear arms reduction in the region.

—A balance between economic incentives and progress on denuclearization by the DPRK is seen as crucial.

—The further development of special economic ventures with the DPRK, both public and private.

—The single-state NWFZ concept implemented by Mongolia could be considered by other nations and in other cases where appropriate.

—The complete dismantlement of the DPRK nuclear program and facilities is essential for maintaining peace and prosperity in the region."

(From the Press Release of the 11th Full Plenary Session of the Expanded Senior Panel, Tokyo, Japan, October 6, 2007.)

The meeting stressed the point that the current period is one of transition in many of the states of the region. Government leadership has or will change in Korea, Japan, Russia, and the United States. In this circumstance, an opportunity presents itself for new ideas and creative concepts. It was emphasized that the concept for limited arms control in Northeast Asia is one of those ideas whose time may well have come

As the Chairman of the Interim Secretariat of the LNWFZ-NEA, Dr. John Endicott moved to assume the Co-Presidency and Vice Chancellorship of Woosong University and SolBridge International School of Business in Daejeon, South Korea, the Plenary session decided to move the Interim Secretariat to Woosong University and to accept the invitation of the Chairman of the Woosong Foundation, and the City of Daejeon to conduct the 12th Plenary in Daejeon, Republic of Korea in 2008.

Tasks for the 12th Plenary Session of the LNWFZ-NEA:

—Meet with Chairman Kim Sung-kyung and appropriate Woosong University officials to review this commitment.

—Decide on the Woosong LNWFZ Team and the role of student volunteers.

—Meet with the Daejeon Visitors' and Convention Bureau officials to apportion support responsibilities.

—Brief Ministry of Foreign Affairs and Trade, Unification Ministry, Defense Ministry, and Education Ministry about the concept and the decisions regarding the 12th Plenary to receive their cooperation and support for Fall of 2008.

—Inform North Korean officials in New York or Pyongyang of the results of the 11th Plenary and invite their participation in the 12th Plenary.

—Inform the Secretary-General of the United Nations, His Excellency Ban Ki-moon on the results of the 11th and intentions for the 12th.

—Seek needed partnerships and supporters for additional funding, if necessary. For example, Delta Airlines, Korean Airlines, Korea Foundation, Carnegie Foundation, MacArthur Foundation, etc.

—Prepare scope of Daejeon Conference and take advantage of the unique institutional resources in this area. Participants could include:

—Faculty related to Woosong University—worldwide
—Local research institutes (KAIST, KAERI, etc.)
—Local universities and education officials
—Local defense organizations
—Local media
—Seoul-based officials from MOFAT, Unification, Defense, Education, etc.
—Regular participants from China, Japan, both Koreas, Mongolia, Russia, and the United States, and observers from Argentina, Finland, and France. Note: Canada and Great Britain should be approached about participants—possibly from their diplomatic representatives in Seoul.
—Special effort made to have DPRK participation.

Of special importance will be determining the budget for this meeting as soon as possible. The Tokyo conference cost in the neighborhood of $100,000.

John E. Endicott, PhD
Co-President, Woosong University
Vice-Chancellor, SolBridge International School of Business
Daejeon, ROK[28]

* * *

Again this meeting in Tokyo put before the general public the activities of a volunteer group that was actively seeking a peaceful

---

[28] Original document recovered from my 2007 e-mail file dated: October 15, 2007.

alternative for the resolution of the tensions in Northeast Asia. As you could see from the text, the setting was somewhat positive, and the final report useful (hopefully) to the representatives of the governments who attended.

Not only was the beginning of October 2007 starting off nicely with the completion of the 11th LNWFZ-NEA Plenary, but we finally received our household goods from Atlanta. The shipment had been sent in July with all estimates indicating a six-week trip at the most. Well, languages being different as they are, our goods ended up in Incheon being charged for storage when they should have been on the road to Daejeon. Of course, when such things from home arrive, it is time to pay the bill and offer thanks for their final safe arrival. Things like our bedroom dresser that had traveled with us since Omaha in 1962, precious books that I really needed by my side, and the silver tea and coffee service that had been the centerpiece for all the military entertaining of our first three decades together. Well, I probably don't need to tell you how much Mitchie was delighted—you know, the old saying: Happy wife, happy life!

With that, our five-bedroom apartment in the Taepyongdong area of Daejeon was ready for comfortable living. Actually, we ended up using one bedroom for the computer and books that we brought, and another bedroom became the "changing room," a somewhat fanciful name for "large closet." That left two guest rooms and our master bedroom, plus the kitchen, eating area, and living room. It was quite sufficient for two folks. And, unlike most folks in South Korea, initially, we entertained many of our staff and faculty in our apartment. The first such affair had all the makings of a Laurel and Hardy movie. Let me explain.

One Friday evening, we invited our SolBridge senior staff, so the Acting Dean, the Vice Deans, and several faculty members showed up one by one to be admitted to our tenth-floor apartment using the security system that was, of course, all written in Korean. Being a Japanese specialist with only introductory verbal Korean under my belt at the time, we, of course, pressed the wrong button, several times, very slow learners, eventually hitting the all "hands on deck button" which must be reserved for the next war. We ended up being visited by all sorts of folks, and it ended up as a wonderful way to meet the security staff and have another of those unique cultural experiences that played such a significant role in bonding our friends and colleagues in the past. We eventually learned that the best way to entertain was using a university facility or resorting to the omnipresent family restaurants that make life enjoyable here in Korea.

We enjoyed our first apartment and were fortunate to have it for four years, but we did find out its Achilles Heel—the centralized hot water system had to be shut down for two weeks every summer for maintenance. You can imagine the first time it occurred, we had no idea why the hot water did not flow from the hot water spigots. We heated water in big pans and carefully carried them to the bathtub as they were just below the boiling point. As some comedians have said, "don't try this at home"—well, they're right, you don't want to carry pots, buckets, or whatever vessel filled with boiling water around the house! Most of our Korean neighbors went to their relatives' home, visited old fashioned bathhouses, or took their vacations because they could read the public notice when the hot water stopped. When we finally left that apartment as the owner wished to sell, individual hot water heaters became an item of highest priority in any new quarters.

I think our settling-in process had only one other "babes in the wilderness story," and that dealt with supermarkets. I must share it for any of you who may come to South Korea for more than a week. In that case, this tale has grand significance.

As we set up housekeeping one of the first items of business was to increase the supply of food to augment significantly the "Welcome Lady" supply of milk, bread, and coffee that got us through the first several days. However, come Saturday morning, we launched out around 10:00 to find food for our lager. Actually, we found several small mom and pop convenience stores and regularly used them as we could not find any supermarkets—the kind we had become accustomed to in Atlanta, like Kroger's.

Several weeks went by, and our searches still yielded no really big stores: they were all about the size of 7-11 Stores, and the pricing was about the same—you were paying for convenience. In a sense, I am not complaining. We met some wonderful people in the time we were searching, some of whom we still visit, just to let them know we appreciated what they do, but we were looking for substantial food, not just snacks.

One day, my dear Mitchie decided to follow a lady from the apartment who was pulling behind her a large empty shopping cart—the kind that leans toward you with two wheels, but enough space to carry a bit of food. As she followed the lady, all of a sudden, she went downstairs into the basement (B1 in South Korea) level of a major shopping complex. Mitchie follower her down and there it was, a big modern well-lit grocery store just waiting for customers. Now, whoever heard of grocery stores underground? Well, the Koreans, that's who. In South Korea, many of the larger stores have their parking garages on the top floors with the stores below. With this revelation, we made sure to brief all incoming faculty and staff so they would not lose weight on our account!

Back at SolBridge, we were also making progress. We received word from former President Jimmy Carter that he would be unable to speak at our opening ceremony. Well, I was not holding my breath, but he had come to several things I sponsored at Tech over the years. I was hoping he might be visiting South Korea and drop by. No such luck, but we were about to begin a program that has been a constant companion since our first speaker, Dr. Nayan Chanda, kicked off our Distinguished Speaker Series which some years later, we changed to our Platinum Lecture Series. Dr. Chanda spoke to us on the evening of October 26, 2007, as he was in Korea to launch the Korean version of his latest book: *Bound Together: How Traders, Preachers, Adventurers, and Warriors Shaped Globalization.*

He was an old friend of mine, and his presentation set the tone for the mission of SolBridge in the years to come. In fact, years later in 2015, SolBridge won a Creative Korea award of $7 million from the Ministry of Education for having the best globalization programs in all of Korea. We listened to Nayan.

As the SolBridge staff and faculty met on a weekly basis, perhaps I really should use "daily" basis at this time, we met as a committee of the whole and worked to stamp out fires that would arise for not meeting some Ministry deadline or some other immediate requirement. In a sense, the eight faculty we had and our very trim staff at that time were working as a team and on a daily basis creating the regulations, academic curriculums, and the procedures we would need when we finally moved from our temporary quarters on the seventh floor of the

Woosong Library building to the new and grand facility to be known as the SolBridge building.

We had a unifying document that spelled out the grand design for the early operation of SolBridge; it was indeed, our master plan, and was since the beginning of September. You can see, it was our intention, but in the early days of welcoming students, teaching classes, and settling in, it served as our guide—if we ever had time:

Vice Chancellor
SolBridge International School of Business
Co-President
Woosong University
August 29, 2007

Management and Oversight:

Dr. Endicott will chair the following SolBridge Leadership committees:

> Finance and Budget
> Evaluation
> Employment and Compensation
> Development (Curriculum)

In addition, Dr. Endicott will oversee the Quality Assurance and Student Affairs Committees.

Comment: Chairing the above four committees will involve Dr. Endicott in the major leadership committees for administration and academic affairs. In the case of the Finance and Budget Committee and the Employment and Compensation Committee, Dr. Endicott's direct involvement will assure that his personal judgment is reflected in the financial and personnel direction of the institution. With regard to the Evaluation Committee, Dr. Endicott will chair, but substantial input should come from faculty members acting in the capacity of a peer assessment body. In this case, Dr. Endicott will encourage a peer assessment process by the faculty, the results of which would be provided to Dr. Endicott for subsequent counseling and professional enhancement of the faculty members being evaluated.

With regard to the Development/Curriculum Committee, Dr. Endicott will act in the interim as the Chair until the Vice President for Education Programs arrives.

Quality Assurance and Student Affairs Committees should provide input to Dr. Endicott for his awareness and action as appropriate. In both these committees, it would be good to have some kind of student involvement. On specific occasions, the students might be asked to absent themselves from deliberations, but on the whole, a student representative, possibly elected, would ensure feedback from students that would help in the overall management of the institution.

All committees mentioned above will, in the process of organization, draw up articles dealing with membership, terms of membership, meeting schedule, and general areas of competence.

As an immediate management measure, Dr. Endicott implemented a weekly faculty meeting, which was first held on Tuesday, August 28, 2007. Initially, meetings will be held at 1500 hours on Tuesday with all faculty present on campus attending. This general meeting will be used to disseminate information by the Vice-Chancellor on programs and events of the School and to respond to issues of interest to the faculty generally. It will also be used as the prime vehicle to build a collegial environment for all taking part in the SolBridge new age.

Information Technology Support:

All faculty members will be provided with adequate computer support that would include, at a minimum, Internet Explorer, Microsoft Excel, PowerPoint, and Microsoft Word. Capabilities to write in languages other than English will be encouraged. The Woosong University web and network e-mail system will be one of the prime methods to send and receive information and communications necessary for the operation of the school. All personnel will be expected to become competent in these IT tools, and faculty members will establish list-serve networks to interact with students on a timely basis, allowing for the broad distribution of reading assignments and other academic and research-related requirements. Dr. Endicott will work to assure these minimum IT networks/capabilities are available to all faculty. He has directed that a faculty "list-serve" be set up for faculty communication. This will assure ready contact with all in the SolBridge family.

Business Library Support:

Of vital importance to a school of international business is ready-access to online journals, newspapers, and government, corporate and NGO reports covering the business and finance worlds. The faculty will be expected to use these facilities to support their own efforts at research and publication—a key aspect of any international business faculty. Dr. Endicott will coordinate with other organizational units within Woosong University to assure the faculty and student body of SolBridge has immediate access to these critical IT assets.

Maintenance of Student Enrollment:

The first semester of SolBridge may witness student enrollment figures of only 6 MBA, and 24 BBA students enrolled. SolBridge can claim to have one of, if not the best, student-teacher ratios in the world. While it is uncomfortable for some to see such enrollment numbers, it is not unusual for new institutions to have similar low enrollments. The results of intense efforts to begin with greater numbers ran directly into the problem of our principal building not being finished by the start of school. Students worldwide can be instantly aware of the status of our efforts through the "beauty" of the internet. Temporary facilities, however, are being used which are very handsome in their own right. When we do move to the new building, it will be one of the finest in the world. The word will get out. We will make certain of that. Dr. Endicott has been asked by CNN if Woosong/SolBridge might be interested in having some of its students interviewed for a program being done from South Korea by CNN. Whether they will choose to come to Daejeon is not clear at the moment, but Dr. Endicott responded positively. Such opportunities will begin to showcase our campus to the world—facilities, faculty, and students alike. (What we need is their visit in January or February next year; we will really have something to showcase.)

Enrollment for next semester is very promising and could reach a total of 250 for the 2008 academic year. That will begin to put pressure on faculty numbers as a faculty to support 250 students in core and regular courses, which could require a steady increase in faculty size, possibly twice as high as for the first semester. (This issue will be addressed by at least the deliberations of the Finance, Employment and Curriculum Committees.)

Dr. Endicott will, in close coordination with the Vice President of International Affairs and his Deputy, Associate Professor Isabella Kam, offer to travel to particularly promising student recruitment zones. In this case, Dr. Endicott has agreed to travel to China during winter break and before returning to Atlanta for Christmas. He has particularly good contacts with Tsinghua University in Beijing and FuDan University in Shanghai. There might be other locations where Dr. Endicott's visit would yield some increased student interest. He will be most pleased to lead and participate in such recruitment visits. These can be integrated into his schedule with coordination with the President and Chairman. With respect to trips abroad, the recruitment office should play a lead role in appropriate recommendations

Enrollment for 2009 and 2010 should be set at an agreed target in line with supportive increases in faculty and staff. In conjunction with the Budget Committee, out-year planning figures should be provided that will set the parameters for reaching a goal of 1500 total Daejeon based students of SolBridge International School of Business. An expansion of this magnitude would require faculty figures in the vicinity of 75 (for a ratio of 20/1) or 95 for the more desirable 16/1 ratio. This represents a significant personnel augmentation effort.

Our personnel database currently houses the names and specifics on some 900 candidates who would be appropriate for SolBridge to take a serious look, according to Mr. Shaskey. These qualified candidates have indicated a desire to come to Daejeon and SolBridge. (In the meantime, Dr. Endicott will review available office space in the new building to ensure our facility support structure is adequate; briefing on the specifics of the new building is needed for Dr. Endicott.)

Key to this increase in student enrollment is a greater PR footprint for SolBridge in the coming months and years. A separate PR plan should be created for SolBridge that incorporates the activities of the faculty, students, and leadership of the College. I believe the 2007 plenary of the LNWFZ will receive some good publicity, but if we bring the 2008 plenary to SolBridge, we can involve students, faculty, and the media in the enterprise. Depending on world-wide events of the time, it could be very successful in increasing our PR footprint. Another aspect of our PR effort should include the Railroad Technology College and will involve Dr. Endicott discussing several concepts with that College.

As part of the PR Plan, Dr. Endicott intends to write a weekly "Letter from Daejeon" that will be available on the internet, possibly through the CISTP web site, or the SolBridge web site.

* * *

I think the reader gets the picture from the above that there was plenty to do. Our desires to reach 1500 regular students have still not materialized, but we are at 1642 much closer than the 30 when the plan was written. The 2008 LNWFZ conference, more on that later, turned out as one of the most successful ever, and my "Letter from Daejeon" actually became a monthly substantive article written for various newspapers of South Korea, and not as a blog aimed at folks back home. They chronicle my adventures in and around Korea over the past thirteen years. (The most recent version described a trip to NingXia and Inner Mongolia in Northwest China in search of the Genghis Khan legend.)

Our first semester ended in early December, and we concluded the year with our first Christmas Party. Here is our first invitation:

Season's Greetings!

SolBridge International will host the first Christmas Party on Dec. 6th, Thursday, at 6 PM. It will take place on the 7th floor of the library. You are welcomed to bring your family and significant others. Please be sure that each person brings a small gift for the gift exchange (anything below 5,000 Won.)

We hope to see everyone at this festive gathering.

In a sense, it seems so quaint. It was sent to only 15 addressees and, of course, their families. What I do recall, besides some really good times, was the pizza that stole the entire affair. It was great. All felt lucky.

EIGHTEEN

SolBridge Takes Off

As 2008 came rushing into being, I began to experience some of the customs and traditions found in Korean culture that I began to respect and quite frankly, admire. The first would be the Opening Ceremony that is associated with the first day of work in the New Year. Of course, I am now talking about the Western New Year that is celebrated on January 1. Korea, in a sense, is caught in the middle of many things, in this case, it does begin the solar-based New Year, but then again, in January or February is the Lunar New Year, and that warrants a discussion of its own. For this event, I am referring to the first working days after January 1—which is a holiday in its own right.

On January 3, 2008, Woosong celebrated its Opening Ceremony to begin the work year. We held it in the 4th-floor auditorium of Woosong Tower, a room that holds approximately 250 people. It is a very formal celebration with the leadership of the university meeting the assembled faculty, and after reciting the Korean Pledge of Allegiance and singing the national anthem, the two groups exchange bows in mass, and then, the Chairman of the Foundation and the President of the University give welcoming speeches. Afterward, all go off to have lunch with as many of the faculty who can show up on this important day. As the faculty steps out of the elevators they are met by a reception line of university leadership; everyone exchanged New Year greetings individually and then entered the SolPine Restaurant—the school's premier restaurant, staffed by students from Woosong's

Culinary Arts Department, where students get to showcase their culinary talents. It is quite festive and signals the end of the holiday season and the beginning of the work year.

In the States, I have never had this kind of experience in a university setting, but it did remind me of the early days in the Air Force when all officers visited the commander's home on New Year's Day, greeting the General and his wife, and leaving their cards on a silver tray by the door. All wives wore white elbow-length gloves and the officers in their formal dress attire. From my recollection, all that ended with the Vietnam War Era. My wife and I had that pleasure at Hickam Air Force Base in Honolulu in the early 1960s, but by the time we arrived at SAC Headquarters in 1962, those aspects of a refined era became casualties of the Cuban Missile Crisis and the increased operational tempo associated with MAD—Mutually Assured Destruction. In any case, they just disappeared as did Wednesday afternoon physical training options that included 18 holes of golf. In a sense, these things were considered relics of the old "brown shoe days" (a term used to describe the old military rank and file), and did not survive a continuing status of alert. Why was it that everything changed just as I was approaching the window? But I digress.

Part of the excitement of opening a new college that would draw the majority of its students from non-Korean sources was the frequent calls to appear on television to explain the concept or meetings with members of the print media sector of public relations. The first television call was from the Arirang Television Organization that was a national government-supported channel. I appeared on the program "Heart-to-Heart" that aired in the evening on January 22, 2008. Besides plugging the new school, it gave a great opportunity to introduce our Korean/English-speaking audience around the world to the limited nuclear weapons' free zone concept that we were still hoping would have a happy ending. I cannot say how productive this half-hour show was to either the school or the nuclear-free zone, but in conjunction with a major ad campaign announcing SolBridge, I found myself being pointed at by increasing numbers of people. It used to happen just because you were a foreigner, but by 2008, it represented the results of a major advertising campaign. Would it pay off for the school? That was the question.

* * *

As we approached the Grand Opening of the SolBridge International School of Business that was now set for March of 2008, we sent requests for some short videos from folks around the world to get their blessings as we opened the new school. Some came back with supportive tracks, others came as nice turndowns:

> Dear Professor Endicott,
>
> I am Secretary-General Ban Ki-moon's special assistant in charge of his schedule and correspondences. SG Ban was glad to receive your email and instructed me to send this email on his behalf.
>
> First of all, SG Ban sends his greetings and congratulations on your assumption of new capacity as Co-President and Vice-Chancellor of Woosong University and SolBridge International School of Business of Daejeon. He says that a world-renowned scholar and Korea expert like you bring so much to Woosong University.
>
> However, he regrets to inform you that in line with the UN internal rules and practices, it would be difficult for him to send his video message to celebrate your opening of the new school. His messages in his capacity of SG of the UN are issued only to those occasions which have direct bearings on the work of the UN and go through a review process by various offices in the UN.
>
> Nevertheless, SG Ban sends his personal best wishes for your new endeavor and the success of your new school as well as his thanks for the important contributions you have made toward peace and security of the Korean peninsula over the years.
>
> Sincerely,
>
> Yeocheol Yoon

Special Assistant to the Secretary-General
& Chief of the Scheduling Office
Executive Office of the Secretary-General[29]

* * *

Not all replies were negative, in fact, most were wonderful and included notes from the President of Georgia Tech, Wayne Clough, the former President of Emory University, Ambassador James Laney, and several other close friends and associates over the course of my career. The schedule of events became so full that we put them in our memory bank and rushed to take care of immediate issues. It was a startup after all, and things moved so fast that I even missed the ribbon cutting of the new building, but that is a later story.

By February 13, 2008, we started the move from the Woosong Library to the new SolBridge building some ten minutes away by car. Two days later, all the staff and faculty were in place, and we were starting to look like a real operation. The building is an imposing structure of fourteen above-ground floors and three below. So, when we moved in, only the ground floor to the 12th floor were complete. That meant the basic requirements were ready—main entrance, school cafeteria, library, auditorium, administrative area on the 5th floor, classrooms on floors 6 through 9, and faculty offices on floors 10, 11, and 12 were ready and looked really good. Finally, on March 5, we had the formal opening of SolBridge.

Amid the required massive floral arrangements from various well-wishers and supporters, the opening ceremony took place in the 4th-floor auditorium easily holding the students and guests. Amid the confusion of groups being taken on tours of the building, I missed the ribbon-cutting ceremony as the time came and passed as I described the building's great features to my guests not quite realizing that the trains run on time in South Korea and there were already enough scissors cutting the ribbon. "One, two, three" went the count and down came 15 or so scissors slicing the ribbon to pieces and formally opening the SolBridge International School of Business. I did survive.

---

[29] This letter was sent by e-mail on February 5, 2008 and was obtained from my WSU e-mail file, July 27, 2017.

Sadly, although the excitement of the grand opening had kept everyone in a high state of euphoria, only days later, I received word that my mentor and friend, President Pat Crecine of Georgia Tech was losing his battle with cancer. Indeed, not long after that, he passed. His service to the City of Atlanta and Georgia Tech was significant indeed as he saw that a new school of International Relations was formed as well as a College of Computing. But his contribution to bringing the Olympics to Atlanta in 1996 stood almost at the level of Billy Paine's contribution; alas, only a few knew of this effort. Of course, his counsel and advice to me as I took on the responsibility of university president I will always treasure.

Besides the opening of SolBridge, 2008 was to see several very exciting moments. For example in January, I received word from General Shikata in Tokyo, that he was holding a meeting to discuss East Asian security issues in March and it would be held in Ho Chi Minh City—the old Saigon. I had not been back to Vietnam since departing in May of 1966, so, enlisting Mitchie as my traveling companion, we attended the meeting and visited Saigon from March 28-31. It was breathtaking for me as we stayed in the Majestic Hotel, the grand old French building that had recently been completely renovated. Although we did not have much time in Vietnam, I tried to show Mitchie those areas that loomed large in my experience—like Cholon the Chinese district where I lived, and the various hotels and government buildings that played a role while I was there—not to mention the memories I have of the time I spent here during the war. One of those memories was having breakfast on the top of the Majestic with my colleagues where we enjoyed *pho bo*—a beef and noodle dish that is served for breakfast or lunch. *Pho bo* and coffee *sua*—a rich dark coffee laden with condensed milk—is a wonderful way to start the day. I introduced Mitchie to its delightful taste and aroma as we watched a flooded Mekong just floors below.

It was also during this trip that I experienced a memorable moment that I shared earlier with you. We were in the Majestic and getting ready to turn in for the night when I noticed a pretty hefty book on the nightstand—much like the Gideon Bibles one sees in the States. I picked it up, and it was a history of Vietnam, and about 700 pages long—quite impressive. Curious as to what the book had to say about the U.S.-Vietnamese relations, especially during the Vietnam War, I mentioned to Mitchie that this is a good chance to see how that period of 1965-1975 is treated in the book. Looking at the index, there it was, something like U.S.-Vietnam relations. The entire account of that period was summarized in about one-and-a-half lines, basically noting that during that period the United States and Vietnam had major differences, which were now on the mend—or words to that effect. I could not imagine such a neutral treatment and must say it reflects my every contact with Vietnamese students, faculty, administrators, and just plain folks that I have come in contact with. They are all focused on the future—most know the role I played and of course my government over those ten years—but they are all ears as to what the future might bring and a positive relationship with America. In Northeast Asia, the memories of colonialism, World War II, and abuse of power burn deep into daily worldviews, but here in a line-and-a-half was a decade dismissed, but a future possessed. I was impressed, and I remain impressed.

I do not want you to think that there is not any memory or lack of opportunity to remember those years. Mitchie and I visited a museum dedicated to that era and took a photograph in front of one of the existing A1-G aircraft that was used by the South Vietnamese Air Force. It was one of many armaments used by the U.S. and allies as we attempted to defeat, first the Viet Cong and later the more professional and regular forces of the North, that are on display in a museum maintained in Ho Chi Minh City. Not only armaments, but pictures are on display that can remind the visitor of the intensity of the time.

(Today, our university has formed many relationships with partner universities throughout Vietnam. In October 2017, with the Chairman of the Foundation, Dr. Kim Sung-kyung and a total delegation of eight staff members, we signed an MOU with the Foreign Trade University of Hanoi and met with its President, Dr. Bui Anh Tuan. I don't mind saying we had hit it off when he visited SolBridge in the spring, but in Hanoi, we worked through any problems that arose, and an obvious bond resulted. When I was on the plane heading back to Incheon Airport, I was told he was a retired General in the Vietnam Army. Well, I know there is a link between those who serve their countries in the military, and here was a clear example. He has already announced that the first cohort of 14 students will spend the next two years to prepare for two years at SolBridge and completion of their BBA's. I can't say "mission accomplished" just yet, but certainly, a good start was had.)

March 2008 really stands out in the life of SolBridge for another reason, not just that we started to use the new building, but the Corporate Advisory Council was also becoming more than just an idea. Our Vice President for International Affairs, George Peterson, put thoughts on paper and started the process of building its objectives and mission. While the first meeting did not take place until September 8, 2008, the work of identifying candidates, meeting with them, and establishing the meeting date took about six months. We finally held the first meeting with five wonderful business professionals:

- Dr. Lilly D'Angelo, R&D Director, Greater China Campbell's Soup Company.
- Mr. Trey Freeman, Managing Director, AIG Global Real Estate.
- Dr. Yoon-soo Kim, Managing Director, and Seoul Branch Manager, Bank of New York.
- Dr. Jae-ha Park, Chairman, Intellectual Ventures Operations, Korea
- Mr. Christopher Wood, Resident Director, and General Manager, Estee Lauder, Korea.

Each person had a keen interest in education and were all deep into international business. As the council expanded, we invited senior academics to help review our programs and offerings to our students. The Corporate Advisory Council was one of the best assists for the development of SolBridge and here and now I would like to note that in our first meeting as we discussed our curriculum, the response was to ask about the role of soft skills in our programs. They made us acutely aware that what made a successful business person was the ability to successfully interact with co-workers and clients. They cited so many examples of smart graduates not being able to communicate with colleagues or did not even want to acknowledge the existence of colleagues, and an inability to work as a team and contribute to overall success. They pleaded for us to stress soft skills, and stress soft skills we did—and we still do.

The spring of 2008 was a time of back-to-back lessons: the first demonstrated the non-interest in the details of arms control by busy businessmen; the second came in the form of a great opportunity to hold and sponsor a nation-wide reunion of alumni from the Georgia Institute of Technology. The Georgia Institute of Technology is very famous in South Korea. In fact, I immediately noticed that when I first came to Korea as an emissary from Georgia Tech in 1989, and not the U.S. government. As soon as I said I was from Tech, doors opened, and the opportunity was made manifest; I was really surprised. So, when the Alumni Office at Tech brought up the subject for an alumni meeting in Korea, I immediately offered our new SolBridge building that was an architectural gem. Located only 55 minutes from Seoul by express train and only five minutes from Daejeon's main station, I thought that here was a great opportunity to salute Georgia Tech, and spread the word about the new SolBridge.

We made all the arrangements and sent out invitations to about 400 names on the Tech list of graduates. The night of April 17, was to be an exciting gala where we would introduce Tech grads to another exciting educational institution, however, most e-mail addresses were wrong. People just move too fast, especially young graduates and this is a very dynamic country. When the night of the reunion came, only one person came, a fellow who was working in Daejeon nearby at KAIST, the Korea Advanced Institute of Science and Technology, a school very similar to Tech except it is nationally supported. It was a colossal disaster. Well, the only thing to do was learn from the experience. What we learned was: first, graduates in Korea honor their high school more than their college when looking backward; second, even though Daejeon is only 55 minutes from the Seoul Station it's getting to the station in Seoul that takes time—lots of time, so getting to Daejeon is just not easy; third, since SolBridge had just opened, no one knew about it, and it was not a draw in itself; and finally, the speaker was not the President of the university, but the Dean of the College of Computing, Dr. Richard DeMillo, certainly a friend who deserved better. We were learning fast, but how many cultural "lessons" remained ahead? Thank goodness I don't recall this event very often, as I am told that the mind is very considerate in forgetting such bad memories.[30]

March 2008 was also a mystery month. Almost as soon as I arrived in South Korea, Paul Kim, a major player in getting me to Woosong had alerted the American Chamber of Commerce about my new position and background and asked if I would be willing to give a speech. This was his way of "welcoming me" to Korea, and I couldn't have agreed more. I set off preparing a talk that could be delivered to a group of businessmen and women who would be quite sophisticated about the goings and comings of the international system, especially as it concerned or related to Korea, as well as Northeast Asia. Finally, I produced a title and dedicated some time to producing a text supported by appropriate PPTs. The title was "Beyond Nuclear Disablement: Assuring Stability in Northeast Asia after the DPRK Fulfills its Non-Proliferation Pledges." Well, there is a lesson right there; the title was too long and deals with a very fuzzy topic. (Unfortunately, we are still nowhere close to closure on this issue.)

The price to attend was a reasonable $50.00, as it was scheduled to be held at the Lotte Hotel, a very upscale meeting place on the 36th floor in the Berkeley Room. The date was great, too—March 20. That was the day in 1958 when I graduated from (the) Ohio State University and was commissioned in the Air Force; it was also when Mitchie graduated from Jissen Woman's College in Tokyo. So, as far as I was concerned, it was a very good date to speak before the American Chamber of Commerce.

The day before the lecture, I received a note from Wade Caldwell, a friend visiting from Atlanta, that the lecture had been canceled. Boy, what a surprise! Of course, even more, surprising was that I heard it from my friend and not someone from the Chamber of Commerce. I never did find out why it was canceled. Perhaps not enough people wished to have their lunch spoiled listening to ways to make North Korea behave. As for me, it was conduct unbecoming of a major organization not to have the decency or the respect to notify me

---

[30] In November 2017, I found myself preparing to take part in another Georgia Tech Alumni Gala, but this time it will be in Shanghai; the President will attend—as well as the Chancellor of the entire State of Georgia University System of 33 institutions, and, as a major attraction, the Georgia Tech basketball season opened with a game against UCLA right in Shanghai. I can see Georgia Tech took in the lessons of our meeting.

personally. Nine years later, I still have not addressed the American Chamber of Commerce; needless to say, no one has asked me.

(I have come to the conviction over the course of almost 13 years that being outside of Seoul is not easy. The close ties of those working in Seoul and their assumptions that individuals outside have the same access to all information can disrupt regional colleagues. They just don't understand, and those in the hinterland find themselves always at a disadvantage. It becomes something we must live with and try constantly to overcome.)

Anyway, my talk was canceled. Maybe it was a good thing, but in the years that followed, North Korea would defy the rest of the world and continue its pursuit of WMDs, including the 2017 test of a 100kt hydrogen device. I look back and am grateful I did not give that speech as the assumption that we had to look past disarmament was ill-timed. Sometimes we are lucky and don't know it at the time. Besides, the title was too long.

While I nursed my wounds over this non-event, I now turned my attention to something that would soon become one of our enduring traditions of SolBridge: the holding of our National Costume Day (which later evolved into our highly successful and exciting Culture Day). In fact, only three weeks after the fiasco of the alumni meeting, we had our first Costume Day on April 7, 2008. You must realize that my mother's maiden name was Campbell, and that is as Scottish as they get. There is another long story here, but let me just say that there is still some deep ill feelings against the Campbell's in Scotland and what they did to the MacDonald's at Glen Coe in 1692. In fact, some 38 MacDonald's were killed in the deep of the night all over the glen, but it has not been forgotten, and when Mom, Dad, and I visited Edinburgh in 1950 we saw "Campbells need not apply" signs on help wanted signs on more than one store we visited. I was told that Scots have long memories, and when I was happily attending a conference at St. Andrews University in the early 2000s, I was booed proudly when I mentioned my mother's maiden name. At that time, I became so determined to uphold the pride of the clan that I went out and bought an entire Campbell Clan kilt and assorted attachments. I looked the part, but never quite mastered the accent.

So, borrowing on the National Tartan Day theme that is annually observed on April 6 in the U.S. to honor the role that Scottish

Americans played in the founding of the United States of America, we started National Costume Day at SolBridge when we asked all students (and faculty and staff) to dress in their national costumes. While the kilt is not exactly the national costume of America, I decided to wear it. After all, what is the American national costume? An Indian headdress? Pilgrim attire? Cowboy outfit? A kilt, in my mother's honor, seemed like a good option.[31]

With that as background and a kilt hanging in my closet, I urged our student leaders to have a day when we would celebrate the national costumes of all the nations present at SolBridge. Then, as an even better idea, the students suggested we also feature food and classic dishes from all of the various nations. Thus was born what is now National Culture Day, which we celebrate now in the fall semester (November) as opposed to National Tartan Day in April. The students decided that one, and that was just fine with me.

* * *

As the spring semester progressed, I was asked to put in a concise form, what I thought was my vision for both Woosong University and our new SolBridge International School of Business. Even now, as I look back, I am still satisfied with what I put on paper in April 2008:

President's Statement for Woosong University and
SolBridge International School of Business
Toward a "Neighborhood Asia"

I wish to welcome each and every student, faculty member, and staff to Woosong University and SolBridge International School of Business. In the case of Woosong, generally, we have an established institution with a well-deserved reputation for educational innovation and creativity. I consider it a great honor and will strive to continue the course already clearly established in the academic world. As for SolBridge International School of Business, we have individually decided to join together to begin a journey into the 21st Century that

---

[31] In 2017 when I couldn't attend our Culture Day because I was on a business trip in Shanghai, I made a five minute video wearing the outfit to welcome everyone and not let them forget their President can also wear a skirt!

will be exciting, productive, and academically rewarding. While the faculty and staff of both institutions will bring our collective experiences and skills together to focus on student career preparation, the students will take these offerings and from the many different perspectives present, mold them into individual career patterns—that we hope will be rewarding in themselves, and to society as well.

We are all here at the creation! I am humbled to be given the opportunity to lead SolBridge International as it begins its first year and stands on the shoulders of the accomplishments of the Woosong Education Foundation. Created in 1954, the foundation has sponsored educational programs and experiences at all levels of instruction. Since 1995 when Woosong University was founded, it has earned a reputation for excellence, which is justly earned. The creation of a college of international business that will include a Bachelor's of Business, a Master's of Business Administration and a Master's of International Business is a natural extension of the academic activism we see here, not only on the Woosong campuses but in the city of Daejeon, as well.

With your assistance and wholehearted support, I intend to use the uniquely different aspect of SolBridge International to gain worldwide attention for our faculty and provide students with rewarding experiences that come from participating in and supporting international activities that will help in the creation of a new "Neighborhood Asia." The innovative satellite model that envisages SolBridge campuses in other parts of Asia will bring reality to the concept of cooperative security. In this sense, we talk of a common security that all mankind seeks to assure the opportunities for a good and productive life. This progressive and highly integrated business education program will demonstrate what can be done as we strive for an even more prosperous Asia-Pacific Region based on integrity, excellence, creativity, diversity, flexibility, and innovation.

As you can see, I firmly believe in the SolBridge mission of applied education and training for international business. We sit at the hub of Asia in this dynamic and energetic nation that stands as an example for all the world to emulate. Our mission will be to jointly bring applied education to the eyes of the rest of Korea, Asia, and the world. Our message is that here in Daejeon, there is a new institution dedicated to producing the best participants possible for the global economy. I desire to ensure that each and every graduate will be well-rounded and ready to accept the challenges that the future will offer.

It is my utmost pleasure to welcome you to Woosong University and SolBridge International School of Business, where we will work together for a better world.

* * *

Early on, we looked at the vast student market that could be found in India. We strove to make good contacts with industry leaders and their representatives as well as explore the possibilities of making partnering arrangements with British schools to facilitate a plan that would have Indian students at SolBridge for two years after which they would go to a partner in the U.K.

With that goal in mind, I traveled to India with an Indian associate, Ms. Neeru Biswas in late April 2008. It became clear that there was no enthusiasm on the part of Indian students (and their parents) to go to South Korea to an American style school and speak English in order, after two years, to go on to a British school. They could do that all themselves and while there might be much to gain being exposed to the Korean miracle, who had even heard of SolBridge? It was a useful exercise, but the number of Indian students at SolBridge has remained below the horizon. The British of late, have done us a favor as they now require any foreign student obtaining a degree from a school in the U.K to return home—without a chance to stay and work. That being the objective most of the time drove down the number of Indian students going to the U.K. but opened to us a variant on the original scheme that involved another Commonwealth nation, Canada.

In 2016, we formed an alliance with Carleton University in Ottawa, which has a business school that is also AACSB accredited. Their programs end with a six-month internship with some business enterprise after which they can stay and work and possibly apply for citizenship. The program has been well received by our SolBridge students, but sad to say, we are still working on the Indian issue.

Another useful organization that has helped quite a bit in getting to know Korea better in these early days, especially its academics, was the Fletcher Alumni Organization in Seoul. As you recall, I received two Master's Degrees and my Doctorate from Fletcher that is run by

Tufts University with some collaboration with Harvard. Friends such as Kim Dal-choong who predated me at Fletcher, Professor Suh Chang-rok of the School of International Studies, and General Kim Jae-chang were there to call on when I needed some advice. It would probably have been easier if I used them more often, but just the regular meetings led to opportunities to meet the daughter of the revolutionary leader Kim Koo who oversees the Kim Koo Museum in Seoul, and the two deans of the Fletcher School in the office while I worked here in Korea. These kinds of organizations act as a very informal network but can be extremely valuable. In truth, if I look back, the Fletcher connection helped me tremendously as I worked on my Ph.D. dissertation, "Japan's Nuclear Option." During my interview program in Japan, I visited many Fletcher grads and was then handed off to another. Sometimes it is called the Fletcher Mafia; in the sense that the Mafia is a network that works as a team, the word is well used. Thanks, Fletcher!

From the earliest days of 2008, we had been preparing for the 12th Plenary Session of the Limited Nuclear Weapons' Free Zone to be held at SolBridge in October. In May, for example, we had contacted the former President of South Africa, His Excellency Frederik Willem de Klerk about the possibility of being our keynote speaker. You may recall that President de Klerk and I had addressed a major international conference held in Hiroshima in conjunction with the annual observance of the August 6, 1945 bombing of Hiroshima. He spoke on the South African decision to reverse its decision of possessing nuclear weapons, and I spoke on the need to create a viable limited nuclear weapons' free zone in Northeast Asia.

His presentation as I recall was far more popular than mine as I was calling for a limitation on nuclear weapons whereas the people associated with the event desired the abolition of all weapons. As a pragmatist, I called for a step-by-step approach and attempt to do the "doable" not reach for the sky. I can fully understand their position, but as a world, we have come down from approximately 65,000 nuclear warheads in 1987 to a figure in 2017 that approaches 15,000. That is a reduction of 50,000 or so and gets us on our way. Are we better off? I would say yes.

Unfortunately, President de Klerk was not available, but we did obtain the participation of another acquaintance, the American diplomat who negotiated the 1994 Agreed Framework with North Korea, Ambassador (Ret.) Robert Gallucci, then the Dean of the Edmund A. Walsh School of Foreign Service, Georgetown University. In addition to Ambassador Gallucci, we probably put on one of the most meaningful meetings of the 13 we have done to-date. It was a veritable "who's who" of experts in the field.

Just to give you a feel for our meeting let me list some of our speakers:

Dr. Lee Hun-gun, President, Korea Institute of Nuclear Nonproliferation and Control (KINAC); Ambassador Ret., Robert Gallucci, Keynote; Dr. Chang Soon-heung, Provost, KAIST; Dr. Ham Hyung-pil, Korea Institute of Defense Analysis; Dr. Hong Lim-chae, Wonkwang University; Dr. Kwan Kyoo-choe, President, KINAC; Minister Oh Joon, Deputy Foreign Minister for Multilateral, Legal and Policy Affairs; Dr. Kang Kyung-ho, President, KORAIL (Keynote); Mr. Chang In-soo, Director KORAIL Research Institute; General Moon Seong-mook, Deputy Director-General for Arms Control, Policy Planning Bureau; Dr. Osamu Terasaki, President Musashino University; Minister Ha Young-je, Korea Forest Service; Minister Lee Kwan, Chairman, Korean Academy of Science and Technology; Professor Moon Woo-sik, Seoul National University; Professor Ken Quinones, Akita International University; Mr. Don Kirk, Foreign Correspondent—*Christian Science Monitor*; and the members of the LNWFZ-NEA You can see, it involved many of the top officials and academics in Korea, and the message delivered, again and again, was that such a concept would benefit the region and North Korea specifically.

As was customary, at the conclusion of the meeting, a declaration was issued:

2008 Daejeon Declaration

Interim Secretariat, Limited Nuclear Weapons' Free Zone for Northeast Asia (LNWFZ-NEA)

12th Full Plenary Session Of The Expanded Senior Panel of Limited Nuclear Weapons' Free Zone for Northeast Asia (LNWFZ-NEA

The Asia Institute
SolBridge International School of Business
Woosong University Daejeon, Republic of Korea—October 8,
2008

Hosts:

SolBridge International School of Business,
KINAC (Korea Institute of Nuclear Nonproliferation and
Control)
Woosong University

Sponsors:

Council on Korea-U.S. Security Studies (COKUSS)
Daejeon Metropolitan City
KORAIL (Korea Railroad Corporation)

The 12th Plenary Session of the Limited Nuclear Weapons'
Free Zone for Northeast Asia (LNWFZ-NEA) was held in
Daejeon, Republic of Korea, from October 5-8, 2008. It was co-
hosted by SolBridge International School of Business, the Korea
Institute of Nuclear Nonproliferation and Control (KINAC), and
Woosong University, all of Daejeon, Republic of Korea.

Diplomatic, military, and academic specialists from
Argentina, China, Finland, France, Japan, Mongolia, South Korea,
the Russian Federation, and the United States met to continue in-
depth discussions on the concept of the LNWFZ-NEA. This
forum is a means to build confidence in Northeast Asia and to
support and reinforce the Six-Party Talks aimed at settling the
nuclear crisis on the Korean Peninsula. The attendance and active
participation of all delegates ensured that a lively and candid
exchange of views was held on a wide range of security and
economic issues.

The meeting was held in the SolBridge International School
of Business building and on the first day concentrated on the
progress of the Six-Party Talks, the current situation about the

DPRK nuclear program, discussions regarding the institutionalization of the LNWFZ-NEA process, and the adequacy of inspection techniques to ensure adequate verification and assurance regimes. Discussions on the second day focused on ways to develop confidence and security-building measures (CSBMs) for the region, and economic incentives for the DPRK. The conference, because of the unique conditions of Daejeon, was able to examine the role of railroads in building regional cooperation, advantages of a possible reforestation program for the DPRK, and higher education as a valuable element in creating regional understanding. The status of the DPRK economy was reviewed, as well as the impact the Kaesong Special Economic Zone is having on that economy. The status of the South-North military talks was also considered and put in the context of the overall current situation.

All attendees of this Track II or unofficial meeting acted in a personal capacity. Some of the participants traced their involvement in this process back to March of 1992 when the idea of a Nuclear Weapons Free Zone for Northeast Asia was first presented.

This conference, involving over 65 participants took place in the midst of government transition in Japan, South Korea, Mongolia, the Russian Federation and an election campaign in the United States, questions about the health of the leader of North Korea, Kim Jong-il, and concerns over a reversal of DPRK dismantlement efforts. All participants of the 12th Plenary emphasized the need to embrace comprehensive verification techniques in any agreement reached with the DPRK and the need to recognize the continuing importance of CSBMs in Northeast Asia to help build an integrated community and advance the peace, prosperity, and security of the Northeast Asia region and the global community.

Among the ideas advanced by participants of the plenary session are the following:

–Complete dismantlement of the DPRK nuclear program and facilities to maintain peace and prosperity in the region is essential for the LNWFZ-NEA.

–Comprehensive verification techniques need to be incorporated into any agreement related to DPRK nuclear programs.

–Current military-to-military agreements need to be implemented in place in the South-North context and encouraged in the region as an effective means of improving mutual understanding.

–Efforts to move from Track II (unofficial) to Track I (official) status for the LNWFZ-NEA program itself should be strongly pursued by the Interim Secretariat using working groups made up of members of the Expanded Senior Panel. Specific near-term objectives include:

> •Draft recommendations to the 2009 NPT PrepCom will be addressed by a working group of the expanded senior panel.
>
> •The subsequent plenary session will address the progress of recommendations for the 2010 NPT Review Conference for changing the accepted definitions of NWFZs.
>
> •Related efforts to gain official NGO status for the organization and possible official sponsorship by a sovereign entity of the LNWFZ-NEA concept.

–CSBMs are needed among all the countries of the region on bilateral and multilateral levels to further peace and stability in Northeast Asia. The possibilities represented by the Trans Asia Railroad, proposals to restore the railway infrastructure in the DPRK, and efforts to help the DPRK with reforestation were particularly noteworthy. Multilateral organizations connected with such programs need to be supported to further needed CSBMs.

–Efforts should be encouraged to establish a joint South-North panel of military, technical and political experts to create a northern corridor for railway traffic on the Peninsula.

–An agreement between South and North Korea is needed regarding transit procedures for expanded railroad service.

–Efforts to embark on a "Green Korea" Program involving carbon credits that might contribute to a reduction in the costs of unification should be encouraged.

–To facilitate assistance to the DPRK, the government of the Republic of Korea might consider closer cooperation with NGOs outside of the Republic of Korea.

–An agreement should be sought with the DPRK to admit the ROK to the OSJD (Organization for Railway Cooperation) thereby expediting multilateral cooperation in NEA railroad development.

–Support for positive exchanges and dialogue between South and North Korea should be encouraged.

–Further development of special economic ventures with the DPRK, both public and private, are useful, but they must be undertaken to adhere to the principle of reciprocity within the context of active engagement.

–Continuation of humanitarian aid should be encouraged.

The 12th Plenary was made possible through the generosity of its hosts: SolBridge International School of Business, Woosong University, and KINAC, as well as its sponsors: the Council on Korea-U.S. Security Studies, Daejeon Metropolitan City, and KORAIL. Candidate cities for the next plenary session were discussed, but further funding requirements will need to be resolved before a decision is made.

John E. Endicott, PhD
Chairman, Interim Secretariat
LNWFZ-NEA
Daejeon, Republic of Korea
October 8, 2008

(Source: personal e-mail files for 2008.)

* * *

You can imagine everyone connected with this meeting was exhausted by the time it was over. I was particularly pleased with the number of constructive suggestions that were made that came from officials in positions to see that suggestions became a reality. Of course, we were unable to have North Korean representatives present, but I felt assured that what we discussed clearly made its way north via official channels. It was a true demonstration of the support that would be made available to North Korea in the event they actually made an effort to denuclearize—a high mark toward resolving the North Korean nuclear issue.

Rounding out this very eventful year, on November 27, 2008, we held our first formal meeting of our Corporate Advisory Council (CAC). We assembled a group of 14 first-class individuals who represented Korean business enterprises, multinational corporations, research institutes, and business academics. We had representatives from firms like Estee Lauder, AIG, Bank of New York-Mellon, Tata Services, Reliance, DHL, Campbell's Soup, LaFarge, and Samsung. First, about our curriculum and the student body, we asked them to review our curriculum and provide advice about most relevant course topics and areas of concentration from their own experience so SolBridge graduates would be ready to grow professionally in the workplace. We asked them to sit down with our students and provide some practical operating experiences and advice about career paths and be available to teach or offer EMBA or certificate programs. Finally, we asked for their help in finding great faculty.

We also stated that we would meet quarterly and hope they could attend regularly, give one annual lecture on a subject useful for SolBridge students, and be available for career advice sessions—possibly involving one hour per month.

In return for asking quite a bit from these busy executives, we offered networking opportunities, priority access to the faculty and students for special projects/consultations, access to our executive meeting facilities for their own meetings, and unlimited use of the Sol-Sporex, the health club located in the school's basement. Since most of the members were in Seoul or even further away, this last benefit really involved their time here in Daejeon. That, of course, was not too much in any year.

Even with these rather limited "benefits," we gathered a very impressive body for advice. Later, we would expand the advantages of membership to the nomination of one student per year at a full scholarship. This was received extremely well by the members, but only once was a nominee actually recommended.

Our experience with the Advisory Board has been very positive and to make attendance even easier, we made arrangements to have every other meeting in Seoul at a centrally located hotel. That makes it more costly for SolBridge but does result in greater involvement by very busy people.

As 2008 came to its end, I was informed that I would be promoted from Co-President of Woosong University to President with the inauguration set for January 6, 2009. The year ended with Mitchie and I taking our home leave in Atlanta for the Christmas and welcoming the New Year. Although we both looked forward to coming home for the holidays, looking ahead to 2009, we both knew that it was going to be an exciting and eventful one back at SolBridge.

NINETEEN

Staying the Course

The New Year started out with a first for me; I had never married a soul during my life, but on January 3rd, I married one of our junior Woosong/SolBridge staff in a beautiful ceremony that started me on a career that I never expected. To get ready for this event, Mitchie and I met with the groom-to-be and his fiancée in a restaurant near the Daejeon Expo site which took place in 1993. Facilities associated with the Expo were still standing in 2009 (before many were demolished starting in 2014), but the place we met in 2009 was still quite nice and just right to talk to the prospective groom and his lovely wife to be.

Because I was expected to say something that had relevance to their life and the courtship, I needed information that was not all that easy to get, but the couple opened up and really let me know why the "love switch" turned on and when. Those are the things the witnesses on both sides of the aisle like to hear, and I did my best as a reporter trying to get the facts to write a good story. The story, in this case, was the congratulatory message I would give after they were married. I must say, Mitchie was a Godsend in putting all at ease. (I can see why we celebrated our 60th wedding anniversary in October 2019!)

A Korean wedding is very beautiful, and all the ceremonies I've been asked to perform were in wedding halls, not churches. I can understand that. If the couple is Christian and has a minister or priest, that is that. Those in the business, so to speak, take care of their flock.

However, about 35% of Koreans do not profess any religion and are agnostics. I will not try to psychoanalyze those who I married, but they exchange vows, and often rings, kiss each other at the end and cry at any time—just like the weddings in a church. The only thing different is that the word god is seldom heard.

Now the Christian weddings I have attended, and actually quite a few, have ministers who seem to have a major gift for elocution. I try to make my services short and meaningful to draw the witnesses into a full commitment to assist the couple in life.

Starting off the year by presiding over a wedding was just the beginning. Shortly after that, Mitchie and I were invited to participate in another great Korean tradition called *Tol Jan Chi* or first-year birthday celebration. Friends are invited, and at some point during the ceremony, the baby is placed in front of several objects: a pen or pencil, a ball, some money, a small book, etc. The baby is allowed to show his or her interest in one of these items, and the one picked becomes the predictor for a life of writing, sports, financier, etc. It is great fun, and on the occasions, Mitchie and I have participated, the babies seem to enjoy the event as well.

While these two meaningful events are an aside to my busy life at Woosong and SolBridge, there is a deeper meaning to them, which is the importance of knowing a little about Korean culture if one is going to be in South Korea for any length of time. Without question, it really helps, if one does stay for a while in Korea, to embrace these wonderful cultural treasures which are opened to the sojourner one by one, and can take several years.

Of course, January 6 for me was a moment that I had dreamed of since walking across the Quadrangle at Ohio State one late snowy evening and seeing our President Howard Landis Bevis who came from northern Cincinnati (actually Bevis, Ohio) who was a true product of Cincinnati (remember my roots?). For some reason, as we passed, we exchanged greetings, and I noted, "Boy, I'd like to be president of a university one day, too." Or something close. Believe me, I did not set out with a plan to get his job or set my eyes on any one institution, but the notion of being a university president captured my interests in education and I suppose reflected somewhat of my dad's influence as a teacher.

The day of investiture was certainly a grand day with invited guests, my wife, Korean friends I had made over my career, local university authorities, and the faculty and student body of Woosong University and the Woosong Foundation. My special friend Dan Papp, who was President of Kennesaw State University in Georgia and had been put in charge of bringing me to Georgia Tech by President Pat Crecine, came to give a speech that I will always remember with the words of a true friend. I was particularly thrilled when I did not cry as I made my acceptance speech. Since Vietnam, I had been known to recall too many things for my own good and would have to stop for a moment to gain composure, often saying "Sorry Mitchie," as I would search her out for eye contact.

As I recall, this speech was my attempt to indicate to the university and community as a whole, that I was grateful for the opportunity to take Woosong into the globalized world of education with the hope that not only Woosong but the region as a whole would benefit from active and meaningful interaction.

I will comment that while the investiture ceremony was lovely with banners proclaiming the new era and faculty in splendid academic regalia from universities the world over, the carrying of the mace, probably by a provost, and the wearing of the university medallion by the president were absent from the Woosong ceremony. Of course, those are traditions of the Middle Ages in Germany specifically and Europe generally; it seems only the gowns made it to this area of the world.

The mace is a symbol of the university's authority and power to grant degrees while the medallion represents the transfer of that authority to the president. Thus, individual medallions could be designed for each president, while the mace would stay the same and represent the university throughout history. Admittedly, these are European traditions, but perhaps we in Korea could adapt the concepts to Asian traditions. I could see a grand university seal crafted by an artisan that would represent the university as seals are still vital for the conduct of official business with the Ministry of Education, for example. (However, AI may take care of that in the future.) A traditional symbol of authority in Asia, especially China and Korea, was worn on the chest as an indication of rank—much like a vest with a specific embroidered design. These could be added for a bit more pageantry in the investiture ceremony.

(You can see, I am thinking of the ceremony for the next president; I hope it is not too soon, but I am 84—in Korean age, which starts counting a person's age when they are in the womb—which means I just turned 83. I'm no "spring chicken" as the saying goes, but there's still a lot of "spring" in my step.)

Looking back on the investiture ceremony, waves of emotion flowed all over me as it has remained one of the most memorable days of my life. However, once it was over, the press of keeping SolBridge on course, and learning about the other colleges and their particular contributions kept me focused on work. So, one week to the day after the pomp and circumstances of January 6, I had a meeting with the Director of the CIA. Now, if you paid attention in the early sections of the book, you remember that I had quite a career in and around the security community of the U.S. One of the most famous agencies in this community is the CIA. So when I met with the Director, I sent e-mails to many of my friends and let them know. Of course, dear reader, if there's one thing that you have learned about me while reading this story of my life is that I enjoy a good joke now and then. Well, this Director was indeed the head of the CIA, but not the CIA you might be thinking about. Instead, the meeting I had was with the Director of the Culinary Institute of America—another CIA!

Master Chef Ferdinand E. Metz, former President of the Culinary Institute of America, paid a visit to mark the tenth year since Woosong began its culinary program in earnest. In fact, he had been the consultant that Woosong employed to make sure our program would meet international standards when we began, and he was invited back to discuss where we were and where we should go in the future. I really don't need to say that during the time he was at Woosong, we all ate at the highest standards of the culinary world. Now you know why I have this problem with my weight. I've tried to stay at 75 kilos, but the challenge is endless.

On February 20, 2009, I officiated at my first graduation as President of Woosong. I don't think it made much difference as far as the graduates were concerned, but I can recall, even then, that I was having trouble keeping up with the communication gadgets that were becoming omnipresent. I do remember trying to make a point of the speed of technology change, and for effect, I held my "flip phone" up high and asked how many students were still using this kind of phone.

No one was the answer; the graduates I am sure questioned the president's actions but were confirmed in their belief that he was not of their generation. I wanted to stress how fast things were changing, and obviously, I did, but that proved I was the one behind and not our kids. As an aside, that phone got me into more trouble when I was having lunch with a Samsung official and had to answer an incoming call. I thought he was having a heart attack when he saw what I was using; the following Monday, I found a Samsung Note Three smartphone on my desk. It was before the legislation introduced that keeps gifts at a $50.00 level, as I am sure this model was at the top of the line. Since then, I have tried to stay up-to-date as much as I can, but in this ever-changing world, it's not always easy.

Not long after graduation, the real start of the school year begins in early March with a Convocation Ceremony. This particular year it fell on March 2 and was full of pageantry with an entry procession resplendent with the gowns of many universities the world over. To give you a feel for the ceremony marking the beginning of the school year, let me describe what we do. We use the Woosong Arts Center, which has the largest auditorium at Woosong. It holds roughly 3000. All freshmen are expected to attend, and others who like a good ceremony are invited. The place is filled to capacity, and the MC announces the entrance of the President and Chairman of the Foundation, plus other "high officials"—a nice term to include the vice presidents and senior deans.

(These days, with an ROTC attachment at Woosong, we have "upgraded" the ceremony. As the MC announces that the procession is about to begin, the ROTC Detachment, with sabers and in their dress uniforms form an honor guard bearing the Korean flag and the official flag of Woosong University. Bam! The jackboots that are being worn by the honor guard come down in unison and hard enough to reverberate throughout the hall. Other cadets already positioned along the walkway come to attention and raise their sabers as the President moves down the aisle heading for the stage that is draped with Woosong celebratory banners.)

Once the official party reaches the stage, it breaks into two parts with the President going right and the Chairman going left. Other officials find their designated seats on the stage as the President and Chairman take their seats on either side of the stage. After sitting and getting adjusted, the MC calls the audience to attention and the pledge of allegiance, national anthem, and moment of silence for fallen colleagues are observed making the real opening of the ceremony. All sit down as the President takes his place behind the podium to formally announce the admittance of all students to study at Woosong. Once that is done, usually identifying the exact numbers admitted to the various colleges, representatives of the new students come to the stage and swear an oath to be diligent and truthful as they study at Woosong. To me, this is one of the most meaningful moments of the entire ceremony. As the representatives recite the oath, their assembled colleagues also repeat the oath. I hold my right hand up, they follow and swear in unison. It is so striking.

The President then welcomes the students and covers the theme he wishes to resonate especially with the students and then is followed by the Chairman of the Foundation who also talks for five to ten minutes on his subject. After the speeches, some formal entertainment is offered to the students. Usually, we bring out our Woosong Opera Singers who perform popular opera to the unbelievable cheers of the students. Classical music is alive and well in South Korea, which as a French horn player, tickles my heart.

After three or four pieces are performed, the ceremony is declared over and all head home. It is a ceremony that I like so much, and wish we had some form of it in the U.S. I am sure some schools have similar practices to open the school year, but it marks that point when students are to get serious once again. The breaks are over, and now long term and career planning interests take over.

You noticed that we did that in March, not September. In America, the school year starts in September; here it starts in March. The reason why is that most things academic were put in place by the Japanese who took their cue from the British. Thus, the first semester is from March to mid-June, and the second semester is from late August to mid-December. We also have two six week sessions in the winter and summer. We go to school 42 weeks in the year leaving ten weeks for vacation or research. It is a system we put in place so languages we teach would not be forgotten in the long breaks between spring and fall semesters. If the students take advantage of those time offerings, a four-year program can be completed in three-and-a-half years, and a two-year master can be finished in 16 months. We called it the *"Il yan sa ha ki"* Program, which roughly translates into "Four terms in one year." That actually provides the student with more class time than any other university in South Korea and was one of the changes implemented in 2009.

On the SolBridge side of things, by March 16, we were starting to see "light at the end of the tunnel" in our negotiations with Georgia Tech to begin a 2+2 Program with their business school. Right from the beginning, I knew we were going to have to provide some specialized courses for students wishing to attend what was once respectfully called the "North Avenue Trade School." As I have already indicated elsewhere in this narrative, that name was only used by University of Georgia fans during the annual Georgia Tech-Georgia football game held the weekend after Thanksgiving annually. The reforms by President Pat Crecine who took over in 1988, changed Tech completely with the addition of an international studies school, a computer college, and ultimately the formation of a college of arts and science named after one of the more progressive mayors of Atlanta, Ivan Allen.

These advances, plus being the Olympic Village for the 1996 Atlanta Olympics, were key in the reformation of Georgia Tech and its emergence as a national, even world-class university. So, we knew that many Korean students would be attracted to SolBridge if it could serve as the gateway to Tech. To have that happen, we had to develop at least six courses that would turn our grads into active candidates for admittance to Tech. We ended up designing a "Georgia Tech Track" that consisted of calculus, chemistry, physics, American history, and two courses in honors English. Of course, those who took the track made themselves eligible for many other fine schools as a result of this special prep.

All this background is to say that by mid-March 2009, we were making really good progress with Tech. It still took another eight months before we signed an MOU, on November 10, 2009, as Chuck Parsons, who ran the undergraduate programs for the business school visited SolBridge and "signed on the dotted line." Having that relationship allowed us to talk about it in our brochures and helped in such a big way to give us legs on which we could really stand. Now, this little school in Daejeon had a big brother on the playground that could really make a difference.

By the middle of March, we also had our second CAC meeting where we went over our curriculum and discussed their ideas about moving forward and differencing ourselves from the established business schools who stood on the high ground. Increasingly in meetings with the faculty, we turned to consider methods to gain academic recognition. Especially our Vice Dean, Pat Leonard, suggested going forward with general regional accreditation or business school accreditation with such a respected organization as AACSB, the Association to Advance Collegiate Schools of Business. Several members of our small faculty were very familiar with the AACSB process, and increasingly it became the consensus that looking seriously into AACSB accreditation should be the option to increase our visibility and respect in the very competitive world of business education. The problem, however, was the limited public awareness of AACSB and what it means in assuring high standards of excellence in business school education. Thus, while its impact was judged problematic for recruiting students, people in the know, i.e., prospective faculty, would be aware of the value of such endorsement.

Also, in early spring we began one of the most enjoyable phases of life at SolBridge; it was the initiation of the Ballroom Dance Classes run by one of the most multi-talented faculty members we ever had, Professor Rudd Johnson. Rudd came to us with a Ph.D. from the University of Kentucky in agricultural economics. He also held a Master's in Physics from Georgia Tech, so could offer math and other subjects including his business-oriented ones. Well, he could dance like a swan can swim; absolutely flowing. With a talented partner, he put us all to shame, but he also helped those who are challenged in this field, and all enjoyed the course. When Rudd left us, he left a void that has yet to be filled, and my dancing has retrogressed and is now limited to repeating the simple waltz square, and hoping no one is watching. While he was here, we all advanced as dancers.

By the middle of June 2009, Mitchie and I welcomed our son and his family for their first visit to South Korea. We took them around to see Seoul as well as the great attractions of the Paekche Kingdom here in Daejeon. The Paekche Kingdom basically ended in 660 C.E. with Shilla's victory over an inept king and a general who was so devoted to his king that he with his wife's agreement killed their children and his wife so not to be distracted as he fought overwhelming odds against him. General Gyebaek is known to history as one devoted subordinate who fought extremely hard to make up the imbalance between offense and defense, only to lose in the end. Our son (John II) and his son (John Charles) are all history buffs, so the time passed incredibly fast.

When our time to tour South Korea was over, we all headed to Japan so John could see the country he left when only five, and reintroduce him and family to relatives he once played with in the mid-1960s. We actually spent six days in Japan, where he and his family met Mitchie's brother and family. Virginia and John Charles enjoyed meeting Mitchie's surviving family members, and we toured Tokyo and Kyoto to give all a great taste of the international part of our family.

Soon after returning to South Korea, Mitchie and I left for Atlanta to spend our annual home leave there. It was 2009, and that made it 50 years since 1959, the year of our marriage. Since August 9 was my birthday and August 25 the date of our civil wedding in the Ward Office in Tokyo, Charlene, and Virginia did some major planning and presented us with a magnificent 50th Wedding Anniversary party on August 8, which was attended by relatives from Kentucky (opposite Cincinnati), thus, Greater Cincinnati, and friends and neighbors from Marietta and Atlanta. My sister, Alice, and her daughters and son came down from the Cincinnati area with their families, and the walls to our Brittany Lane home were bursting. It was wonderful. Of course, Bob Marmer and his family were there as there would have been no 50th anniversary without him (remember, he was the one who had saved my life). They presented us with a beautiful glass-encased frame that included an original wedding invitation, and pictures of the beautiful bride and the very smiling groom sporting a mustache and, according to my mom, looking very much like Poncho Villa. That collage is now hanging in the dining room of our home in Marietta, a reminder of a very happy day that honored 50 happy years for Mitchie and me.

Back to Daejeon by the middle of August, and we began meetings of the faculty and staff to ready ourselves for the arrival of international students and orientation week. Remember the academic year begins in March in South Korea, so the fall semester did not involve new Korean students but new international students coming in August. Since I have always taught one course to keep in touch with students, I was also getting ready to offer a course titled "Peace Dividend on the Korean Peninsula." It was the last time we offered that particular course, as peace was certainly not breaking out on the Peninsula. But in addition to the course, we were getting ready as a college to host the 13th Plenary of the Limited Nuclear Weapons' Free Zone for Northeast Asia some ten months ahead.

As October approached, it became clear that a massive celebration would be taking place on the first in Beijing to mark the 60th Anniversary of the founding of the PRC. In anticipation of the worldwide television coverage that would take place, we hurried to set our 4th-floor auditorium into a grand reception hall to celebrate with all our students. When the parades began, we were ready and glad we were, as it meant so much to our Chinese students who were marking this day away from home and far from family. I observed plenty of tears of joy among the Chinese students and the young men stood a bit taller that day, as it was an impressive moment. The observance clearly announced to the world as dramatically as Mao's announcement on October 1, 1949, that China had arrived, and the world, and especially East Asia, should take notice.

October for us at SolBridge was very important as we received our first visit from an official of AACSB, the business school accreditation organization that looms so large in the world of business schools. It is much like the "Good Housekeeping Seal of Approval," which was prominently displayed on products and goods that were sold in the markets of the world. It basically notified the consumer that the product that the seal was on had been reviewed and found worthy of purchasing. Only five percent of the world's business schools have this AACSB "seal" and getting it is no small accomplishment. In a sense, this visit put us in gear to complete the necessary paperwork to begin a very lengthy process. We had developed the concept to apply for AACSB membership under the umbrella of the Woosong Foundation involving SolBridge standing as a unique school with active autonomy. In a sense, we made the decision to develop SolBridge as an almost independent college under the Woosong Foundation umbrella. It would allow us to cut a new course, somewhat apart from the existing university and continue our focus on building an international school, with an American "feel" that would attract not only Korean students but students globally.

By October 16, we sent our application forward to be a member. Now the real work would begin. Two days later, we were told by AACSB that we were in!

At this point, let me just say that being a member only means just that. The process of being reviewed, assessed, and minutely evaluated does not start with membership; it only indicates that sometime in the future, the member may wish to go on and become an accredited member. The difference is like night and day.

Along with becoming a member of the AACSB, by the fall of 2009, we also put into place another aspect of our future growth strategy. On November 10, we signed an MOU with Georgia Tech. These two pillars became the features around which we built SolBridge. The foundation was in, and it was supported by the original vision of the Woosong Foundation. Now we had begun the process to truly turn a grand concept into absolute reality. Actually, by 2009, we had grown to 310 students from 29 countries and were operating in the new and grand facilities of the SolBridge building. All 14 floors above ground and two below ground including the swimming pool, sauna, spa, and exercise facilities were now welcoming students and local residents. The 13th and 14th floors opened as the SolHeim Guest House and consisted of five nice rooms on the 13th floor and three grand quarters on the 14th. We were able to assure our guests that after a long flight from the United States or Europe, and the not so long flights from Asia, a pleasant room, and a good night's sleep were awaiting.

As the year was moving to a close, SolBridge hosted its first play by our Actors Club, *Sometimes Love is Nearby*. As part of SolBridge's mission, to educate the next generation of Asian thought leaders, one area that we focus on is creative management. Over the years, we have offered various classes to help students explore the "creative" side of life. One of the more popular classes—and one that we still offer now—is our drama class. This first play presented by students was a cute and rather short play that caught the pressures of young love in a college environment. The two persons involved finally realized that they were actually in love with each other and to the loud applause of the audience they embraced—I am sure with thoughts that Hollywood was waiting.

Three days later, we were visited by the then Prime Minister of South Korea, the honorable Jung Woon-chan for dinner and discussion about Korean education and the SolBridge example. The evening went extremely well and as we said farewell we had no idea we would meet him the next morning at a breakfast meeting of the seventeen university presidents of the Daejeon area.

To my surprise when the Prime Minister made his opening remarks, he noted that the previous evening he had dined at SolBridge and had seen, so to speak, the future of Korean education. Of course, I was delighted but noticed it did not go well with my university colleagues. Receiving such an endorsement from the Prime Minister was so huge that I could hardly get over it. However, as is often the case, he left the position in a short time over an issue dealing with the new administrative city of Sejong. (While that was the case in 2009, by 2018 the former Prime Minister surfaced once again as the Commissioner of Korean Baseball. Well, if you recall, I am a baseball 'nut" so in 2018, we invited him back to SolBridge!)

TWENTY

2010:
Working Toward AACSB Accreditation

As we entered 2010, we faced many problems and opportunities. We were still working on getting accepted into AACSB for accreditation purposes, beginning our active involvement with the Beijing Foreign Studies University that has trained and still trains a significant number of Chinese diplomats, rounding out our curriculum so it represented a stable range of subjects for our students, and making sure our dormitory situation was ready for increasing numbers of foreign students. The year really marked the period when we began to come to grips with our own self-image as a growing player in business education in South Korea. It also marked the last year that we were able to support a major plenary session of the Limited Nuclear Weapons' Free Zone for Northeast Asia. Of course, Mitchie and I kept the pressure on our Korean colleagues to involve wives in the life of SolBridge. We made dents, but the resilience of traditional culture is strong indeed, possibly more so in Daejeon than the situation in Seoul, but our gains were modest at best and short-lived for sure.

Our first function in 2010 was to open up the institution for the New Year and have a festive luncheon where all staff and faculty present meet the Chairman of the Foundation, the President, and other senior staff. Although it was held on January 4, when most faculty are either on research leave or vacation, it is a time when reflection and a focus on the courses we teach throughout the year are possible.

John E. Endicott

January 2010 was also a time when we first surfaced a new procedure for SolBridge to make our professors more accountable for the work they were supposed to do. A new draft of our Management by Objective Evaluation Form was completed. To some, it seemed like an invasion of the sanctity of the classroom, but it was designed to make our expectations for certain work objectives clear cut for all parties. The professor involved was expected to make his reflections on the work assigned clear also, and a mutual expectation would result. We put a mid-year "course correction" in the form, so at a meeting later in the year, both sides could again reflect on the objectives and modify them as necessary. Some professors, especially from non-American colleges were not too happy, but we made clear expectations in teaching, research, and service, and after several cycles, it became clear that expectations for salary increases could be backed up by documented work and the positives were seen. Certainly, I had more hair when we began this process, but it helped immensely in the overall governance of our small school.

I have not mentioned the great role Dr. Tridib Biswas played as we were getting SolBridge off the ground. He became our first Interim Dean during this period but left in January 2010 to enter service with the Mauritius Government to take a presidential appointment, but after leaving SolBridge, developed some medical conditions that prevented him from actually taking up the new posting. I am happy to say he lives happily with his wife in India and is still a strong supporter of the SolBridge experiment.

Toward the end of January, we received a bombshell from the Pre-Accreditation Committee of AACSB. In reply to our first letter of application, they noted it would have to be revised and resubmitted. What exactly we had to do was not clear, and we were told to wait for the formal report of that committee. As it turned out, it was nothing to worry about. I guess there's always bound to be some hiccoughs along the way when you're reaching for new heights.

In early February, we began our Beijing Foreign Studies University relationship and sent one of our premium professors, Dr. Thomas Grisham, to teach on campus in Beijing. This relationship proved to be a most valuable one, but it was not one made easy by several different cultures, languages, and personalities interacting in an academic environment. For us, as well as our Chinese counterpart, it was a pioneering experience. It has endured to this day (2019) and all have benefitted. In fact, BFSU itself is now engaged in the AACSB accreditation process, and all that surrounds it. In a sense, one of the best outcomes of AACSB membership is the long and demanding road to accreditation. Their requirements are in all cases the most stringent of all the accreditation standards that exist in the business education field and all members "float" higher as a result of the specific standards that must be met. You will see, that in 2010 we were still at the beginning of our struggle to even obtain membership, but as we as a faculty generally recognized that it was going to be extremely difficult, we gained in meeting the challenge with one united vision. The petty differences that can exist among colleagues were gradually being put aside as a larger, more important goal loomed ahead. We had no tenured faculty at that time, and have only one now after 12 years, so there were no "crusty old inhabitants of an ivory tower" to denounce efforts to reach standards required by AACSB. In a sense, the challenge we faced brought us all together, and all together, we did work for accreditation.

One of the complications that the BFSU relationship presented was our eligibility for AACSB. There had to be a "firewall" between the two schools so that they would be judged separately by AACSB and not at the same time. Eventually, it was easy to demonstrate that such a wall did exist between the two schools, as it was easy to demonstrate that each school had a different national Ministry of Education ultimately calling the shots. There is no doubt that SolBridge is under Korean control, and BFSU under Beijing's. These were the kinds of situations that had to be made clear as we inched forward on our way to AACSB membership.

Now is also an appropriate moment to give public recognition to the fellow who led the march toward AACSB membership and ultimately accreditation: Dr. Patrick Leonard. He joined SolBridge from the earliest days and was key in so many of the steps taken on the way to the development of the college, including the provisions and regulations needed to provide "take off" for our new and struggling institution. Pat stayed with us until well past the standard age limit within the Korean personnel system. Professors can work up to age 65 and are covered by retirement and medical insurance programs. After 65, however, they go "off the books" so to speak. As an institution you can elect to keep individuals over 65, but they do not count when it comes to establishing faculty to student ratios, and the government requires a certain ratio be maintained, nor do their research contributions count—another major measure of a schools' qualifications. If the faculty/student ratio is not maintained, drastic action is taken to dis-enroll all students who were in the cohort that included the aged faculty member. Because of his superb contributions, we were able to have his assistance until he was 73, but at that point, he decided to seek new challenges. Pat left in 2016 but left his mark as one of the key founding members of SolBridge. My thanks for his counsel and friendship are unlimited.

Then came the revolution. In early March 2010, SolBridge received its first officially designated Dean. Dr. Jun Yong-wook (Woody) joined us after presenting a lecture in our 4th-floor auditorium to the student body. "Woody," as we instantly called him, took the audience by storm, not to mention the rest of us! It was clear, he was the person we had been looking for to take SolBridge to the next level—as we all say. Well, he truly did. And, he did not look like a Korean dean, forgive me all my friends who happen to be Korean and deans, but you do have similar characteristics: conservatively dressed in a dark suit and tie, inaccessible for the most part, with students having contact in only the most controlled of conditions, and, finally, leadership from the rear. Woody, by his very nickname, was rejecting all the standard behavior patterns and interacted freely with the students and led from the front a faculty that could not believe its luck.

Thus began, a wonderful time of expansion, new initiatives, and a positive, can-do attitude that was just what I and SolBridge needed. Woody opened his first faculty meeting by renaming it to the "Faculty Advisory Council" and presented an outline of his intended objectives: "Revisiting the 'Big Picture' of SolBridge;" "New Organizational Initiatives;" "Teach Hard Culture;" "Study Hard Culture;" "Major Changes;" and "Request." Of all these, it was his idea regarding new organizational initiatives that revealed his activist goals. He defined four major forces that would guide SolBridge: the Curriculum Committee, the AACSB Committee, the Activity Committee, and the New Horizon Team. Each group had clearly defined objectives such as: "Develop courses to fit our strategic focus" for Curriculum; "Set milestones for the whole process" for the AACSB Committee; "School-wide events" for the Activity Committee; and "Case writing/teaching workshop" for the Faculty Committee. Finally, he outlined five specific topics for the New Horizon Team: "Long-term plan for SolBridge," "HBS Benchmarking," "Establishment of a Case Clearinghouse," "New Budgeting Program," and "New Library Plan."

Here was the leader I was hoping for. When I met with Woody to discuss our relationship, I basically said, "Woody, where have you been? I will turn my attention to the other five colleges and see what I can do for Woosong University. Oh, and only call me in emergencies."

Now the above rendition of our meeting may be affected by my 83-year-old memory, but it was not far from what happened. Two weeks later, I was in Beijing at the formal opening of the SolBridge-BFSU relationship. While I was there, I gave a short speech, had an interview with the *Chinese Economic Net*, and attended many meetings involving our Director and now Vice President Isabella Kam, who built the Woosong-China network. I was off on my new trajectory and, meanwhile, back home, SolBridge was in good hands with Woody at the helm.

Also in February was a wonderful experience to lecture on the Limited Nuclear Weapons' Free Zone to a very influential body in Tokyo. The Ozaki Foundation, with its headquarters adjacent to the Diet Building in Tokyo, invited me to present the status of our work in NEA. It was a pleasure as many Diet members involve themselves in the work of this foundation that honors Ozaki Yukio who served in the Diet from 1890 to 1953. He is still considered the "God of constitutional politics," and as such his fans are numerous. I received an invitation from his granddaughter to lecture on a panel that was considering nuclear issues and Japan's policy response. It was a case where my contribution was well-received, but interest in any follow-up initiative was not to be seen. Not to matter! Keeping the concept before the public is always time well spent, and when an opportunity presents itself to get close to the "corridors of power," I'll take it.

About this time, actually early March of 2010, we received word from the Ministry of Education that Woosong University was receiving $3,000,000 for innovative programs across our campus. Good news, as the ideas of the Chairman of the Woosong Foundation, Dr. Kim Sung-kyung were starting to pay off. It was our Chairman and

Vice President Jung Sang-jik who had prepared the foundation for my arrival at SolBridge back in 2007, and now they could breathe a little easier about the future of this institution. (I could also.) Certainly, we had a long way still to go, but this recognition marked a turning point in the program to internationalize Woosong University and use SolBridge as one of the primary engines to do so.

Our rather happy and tranquil life came to a sudden jolt on March 26 when the Korean naval ship, the *Cheonan* was blown out of the water with the loss of 46 of its sailors. It is something that inhabitants of the southern half of the Korean Peninsula have become accustomed to since July of 1953 with the signing of the Korean War Armistice, but not a true peace, as both countries are still technically at war. Let me continue telling this story by using the article I wrote for the *Korea Herald* appearing on May 11, 2010:

The Cheonan Tragedy Right Here at Woosong

As a born optimist, I like to share pleasant experiences with my friends. Today, sadly, the story I tell is about life and death as it is in the real world. As you can see from the title, it deals with the sinking of the South Korean corvette, the *Cheonan* on March 26 in the sea off the west coast of South Korea in the dark of night.

Like most of you, I read with horror the initial accounts of the explosion and the desperate struggle to rescue as many as humanly possible. (Of course, we recall that even the rescue was fraught with tragedy as a courageous deep-sea diver and helpful fishermen died in their individual efforts to save the *Cheonan* crew.) When all was finished, of the 104 onboard all but 46 had been accounted for. I was, of course, aghast at the event and I need not hide the fact that it brought back many similar instances from my 28-year career in the U.S. Air Force. In most of those cases, the cause was easily related to enemy fire; once, however, a very dear colleague was taken by "pilot error." Putting on an impromptu air show for a Boy Scout encampment at the air base we worked at in Vietnam, he attempted a difficult maneuver and lacked the altitude to complete it. Still, enemy action or mistake, lives were lost, and we as comrades grieve for our friends and their families left behind.

Thus, we paused, as you paused, and hoped for word on the cause of the sinking. We all went back to work as we must to ensure that goals set today can be attained for those coming behind us. Then, several days after the explosion we received word that two of the missing were Woosong University students who had completed one year of school—their majors were computer science and railroad engineering—had taken a leave of absence to complete their military service and planned one day to return to finish their formal education. To Korean readers, of course, this is a natural sequence of events for many young men. I must say, in my now almost three years of observing the practice, the men who return after military service are focused and ready for success, and normally, they do just that.

Our two students, Sergeant First Class Im Che-yob and Private First Class Chang Chol-hee, will not be returning, however. We held a memorial service on April 21 for them, and faculty, staff, and fellow students gave touching statements about the 26-year-old computer science major and the 19-year-old signals department major of railroad engineering. As president, I was asked to be the concluding speaker, and my comments concentrated on the unfortunate and disproportionate burden that is placed on the youth of a nation to ensure our national security. Their brave sacrifice and that of all the other personnel of the *Cheonan* underlined the inherent danger in answering the call to arms. It also underlined the fact that we in Northeast Asia have miles to go before achieving the peace and stability we all desire.

One week later, I found that I was being invited to the national ceremony to honor the entire crew of the *Cheonan* to be held in Pyongtaek. I have just returned and am still in the sense of bereavement that I know is only a microcosm of the pain and grief felt by family members and close friends. To be close to the altar where 46 pictures of the honored fallen were mounted and to witness the families approach the altar with incense smoke blowing and solemn music playing will be a picture I take with me the rest of my life. But, it was the touching, quiet weeping that soon grew to sounds of disconsolate despair and wanting that will be the sounds that I will never forget.

After this very solemn ceremony, I was fortunate to meet the parents of our two fallen student heroes. One, Private 1st Class Chang Chol-hee was the youngest man serving and listed as Number 46 on the roster of sailors. I hope all of us do not need to repeat such a day. However, I will treasure that day in the years I have left. It will remind me that not all souls on this earth are here to do good and some perish in the cause of liberty. That eternal vigilance is the price of liberty. I am reminded of the saying attributed to a great American patriot, that eternal vigilance is the price of liberty. I am afraid it is still true in the 21st century.

*   *   *

Now into April in this very active year, we did something that we have not really said too much about during my tenure at Woosong. We gave an honorary degree to the former (at that time) Prime Minister of Japan, Abe Shinzo, and the yet to be Minister for Education, Shimomura Hakubun who at that time was Vice Chief Cabinet Secretary—a very powerful position in itself. This all came about, not because I was a friend or even acquaintance of either of the gentlemen, but one of our Japanese professors, Nakamura Toraaki had worked for Shimomura when he was a Diet Member. Both the Abes and Shimomuras came as couples, and we had several engaging meals together during their short stay. Little did we realize that Abe Shinzo would make the "comeback of the century" and become Prime Minister once again after a uniformly recognized failure during his first term as PM. That tenure was short and marked by his apparent ill health and indisposition toward the job. Later, of course, Prime Minister Abe during his "second chance" began to set records for success and is still in position as I write this note. Many say it was extremely prescient to see his return to power, but this is just one of those cases where luck was our handmaiden. You know, "If you can't be smart, at least be lucky!" This was a case of luck.

In this narrative, I have concentrated on the professional aspects of our stay in South Korea, but I would really be remiss not to include some of the typical kinds of social activities that we had with our colleagues both Korean and international. May 2010 seems to be a good month to indicate the kinds of activities we took time to do. For example, my wife and I are great fans of Sumo, the distinctly Japanese style of wrestling where often giants of 300 pounds plus crash in the middle of a circle and try to force each other out of the ring or on to the ground. Sumo tournaments occur six times a year about every two months for exactly two weeks. At the last bout, number 15, a winner emerges. If there is a tie, a runoff is conducted until one person remains. Good health and no injuries play a major role in determining the winner. Just imagine bones built to take a frame possibly of 150 pounds is expected to weather through crashes involving 600 pounds colliding at kinetic energy force. Wham!

These bouts became wonderful opportunities to invite colleagues over to see something most do not see regularly. Since we had satellite TV and NHK the Japan Broadcasting System, we served as ambassadors for Sumo and teachers in the basics of the sport. We invited folks up to our apartment, ate good food, and watched Sumo. It was really great fun, as they often appreciated the sport, but to my knowledge no one ever invested in a satellite system after our orientation sessions.

On many occasions, especially in the first five to six years, the Woosong Arts Center, part of the Woosong Complex, sponsored opera troupes or symphonies for concerts where all the Woosong Faculty was invited and gave us a feeling of "big city class." It was just lovely to hear good classical music, and as I have said before in this text, classical music in South Korea is performed to the very highest standards of the industry.

In addition, field trips and outings to various areas in South Korea—even once to the Island of Tsushima, were taken by large members of the faculty. One trip in June 2010 that Mitchie took part in was to Paju, very close to the DMZ, where an artist community has developed within sight of North Korea. She, in fact, went to the Mount Odu Unification Observatory on the 60th Anniversary of the outbreak of the Korean War, June 25, 2010.

I also should mention the great, but often overlooked role Mitchie played in bringing the wives of the international faculty into play and contact with each other. At least once a semester, and at times more so, she would hold Friday Morning Coffees where all the women—

both spouses and faculty—were invited to meet and greet each other. As Mrs. President, she did a wonderful job in not only teaching her frequent classes in advanced Japanese but keeping the wives in touch with each other so our little group of ladies could feel socially engaged. Truly it was an important function, and I need to recognize and thank her for a task not as easy as it might seem from the pages of this text. Thanks, Mitchie!

Another diversion that I will never forget was the first time I was asked to throw the first pitch for the Hanwha Eagles, Daejeon's professional baseball team. The Eagles are one of the professional teams that make up Korean baseball, and they play at Hanbat Stadium in Daejeon. *Hanbat* is Korean for Daejeon before it became Daejeon. On September 4, 2010, Woosong University had a Woosong Baseball Day at Hanbat Stadium, having already bought around 2000 tickets and provided them to Woosong students. So, you can see, there was some reason for inviting me to throw the first pitch. In fact, it probably was an agreement between both organizations: "You buy 2000 tickets, and Endicott gets to live out his lifelong dream of playing baseball." (Remember that is all I wanted to do, back in the early pages of this story?) Again, I really do not know if that is what happened, but I am a big boy now and understand how the world turns. Nonetheless, I still got my chance to "play" baseball—even if it was only throwing out the first pitch.

Anyway, it was my day on the mound, if only a little bit off so I would not ruin it for the real pitcher who was warming up as I prepared to pitch. I knew of this appointment a good three weeks before and had practiced almost every day, throwing at the standard 60 feet distance to the plate. I really had worked pretty hard to get my 74-year old body for the task at hand. Ready I was, and when the umpire said: "Let's get on with it!" (Or something in Korean quite close.) I let go with a fastball that made a nice pop when it hit the catcher's glove that magical 60 feet away. No bouncing lob from me and I was in heaven. I heard later that when the radio/television announcers saw the pitch, they observed: "Now this is a real 'first pitch,' and it comes from a guy almost 75!" You have to understand my sources for the story were friends, very dear friends, who knew the old guy would like to hear something like that, but I will go with the story. To me, it seemed quite reasonable. Being in a stadium with a partisan crowd and a bevy of international cheerleaders from SolBridge can do wonders for the moment and the memory. I don't have to tell you, I enjoyed that moment immensely.

A significant achievement for our Railroad College came in early May with an MOU between ourselves and the Korea Railroad Corporation to conduct classes in their new headquarters located only minutes from the Woosong Campus. Offering undergraduate and graduate programs that could be completed by the employees of the organizations that run and oversee the railroads of South Korea was a matter that benefitted all concerned. In 2018, Ph.D.'s in railroad technology from Woosong are being pursued by four to five railroad executives.

Overseeing Woosong's Railroad College has been very near and dear to me because I've been a railroad enthusiast my entire life. I was even given a chance to be an Honorary Station Master where I ran into many Woosong graduates who were so pleased to see their president in a railroad uniform taking it all in!

(I only wish the railroads in the United States ran better than they do now. As much as Americans take pride in owning a car, or another vehicle, and taking to the roads as it were, it's too bad that we have let our railroad infrastructure decline, and in some cases, missed the chance to have the kind of high-speed rail systems that are the marvel of countries like France, Japan, and South Korea. At the same time, my heart breaks every time the railroad system in America has another accident; it happens all too often.)

May closed with a visit to South Korea and Daejeon by my former secretary at Georgia Tech Angie Levin and her husband, Jay. Mitchie and I were delighted to "pay back" years of faithful service and enjoyed her visit so much. We all were particularly close as I had called 911 back in 2007 when Angie was bent over double and holding her head; literally, the first responders said it was a lifesaving call, and we all were grateful for the additional seven years that Angie graced the earth. She worked tirelessly to bring people from far off lands together in peace. Sometimes she could not understand why I had stayed in the Air Force so long, but we agreed to work for peace in our own ways, and she did.

Sadly, she passed away in 2017 all too soon.

Another visitor that I must mention if I truly wish this to be a book that captures the meaningful people and things in my life, and that would be Professor Robert Scalapino's visit to Seoul on June 22, 2010. Dr. Scalapino was considered a *guru* by practically all students of East Asia, and in June of 2010, he came to Seoul to announce the publication of the Korean translation of one of the 39 books that he authored in his career. Mitchie and I traveled to Seoul to see this giant in his field (and mine) and had what turned out to be our last time together. He died in November 2011 at 92 years of age. I met him first when I attended a conference at the National War College while teaching at the U.S. Air Force Academy in the 1970s. Later, when I introduced the concept for a Limited Nuclear Weapons' Free Zone for Northeast Asia, he joined 24 other experts in Washington as I described the concept in 1991.

In a room full of individuals who certainly respected Scalapino more than Endicott, he came out for full support and helped turn critics into skeptical supporters. I also admired Robert for his love of his wife, who he brought to every conference he attended—even if in faraway Mongolia, as he led the field in normalizing relations with Mongolia after the fall of the Berlin Wall. This I know as he involved me in all of those early meetings when we could hardly hear the Mongol participants as they still had not become accustomed to public speaking. Most of these meetings took place in Gers, a portable round tent covered with animal skins or felt and used by nomads in the Central Asian Steppes and the conversations were normally held at a whisper to keep prying ears from listening from outside.

Behind all the activity depicted above, the months leading up to October 2010 were very busy with the preliminaries to the 13th Plenary Meeting of the Limited Nuclear Weapons' Free Zone for Northeast Asia that was held from October 7-9 with the help of The University of Toulouse 1 Capitole's Research Group on Security and Governance, and SolBridge International School of Business of Woosong University. This meeting was, in a sense, highly successful, but it also had some very unfortunate consequences. The territorial issues still facing the states of Northeast Asia today raised their disruptive heads at this meeting and marked an end to our regular meetings. We, of course, stand ready to continue under better circumstances, but it will take a moment in time when all realize the imperative of solving the nuclear issue in NEA trumps all else. (No pun intended.)

The 2010 Toulouse Declaration came to reflect the positives that were achieved and should be celebrated. Perhaps in the charged political atmosphere, we find ourselves in 2018-2019, the value of our concept will be recognized once again:

2010 Toulouse Declaration

Interim Secretariat, Limited Nuclear Weapons' Free Zone for Northeast Asia (LNWFZ-NEA)

13th Full Plenary Session Of The Expanded Senior Panel of the Limited Nuclear Weapons' Free Zone for Northeast Asia (LNWFZ-NEA)

Research Group on Security & Governance (GRSG)
Toulouse 1 Capitole University
France

Woosong University
SolBridge International School of Business
Republic of Korea

Toulouse—October 8, 2010

The 13th Plenary Session of the Limited Nuclear Weapons' Free Zone for Northeast Asia (LNWFZ-NEA) was held in Toulouse, France, on October 7-9 2010. It was co-hosted by the Research Group on Security & Governance of the University of Toulouse 1 Capitole (France) and SolBridge International School of Business, Woosong University at Daejeon (Republic of Korea).

Diplomatic, military, and academic specialists from Argentina, the People's Republic of China, Finland, France, Japan, Mongolia, Republic of Korea, the Russian Federation, and the United States met to continue in-depth discussions on the concept of the LNWFZ-NEA. This forum is a means to build confidence in Northeast Asia and to support and reinforce the Six-Party Talks aimed at settling the nuclear problem on the Korean Peninsula.

John E. Endicott

The attendance and active participation of all delegates ensured that a lively and candid exchange of views was held on a wide range of security and economic issues.

The meeting was held in the Toulouse 1 University Conference room and concentrated on the progress of the Six-Party Talks, the current situation with regard to the Democratic People's Republic of Korea nuclear program, discussions regarding the institutionalization of the LNWFZ-NEA, and the complicated situation in NEA that was witness to several serious territorial incidents. Discussions also focused on ways to develop confidence and security-building measures (CSBMs) for the region. The conference, because of the unique conditions of Toulouse, was able to examine the role of higher education as a valuable element in creating regional understanding. The status of the South-North Korean military talks was also considered and put in the context of the overall current situation.

All attendees of this Track II or unofficial meeting acted in a personal capacity. Some of the participants traced their involvement in this process back to March of 1992 when the idea of a Nuclear Weapons Free Zone for Northeast Asia was first presented.

This conference involving over 55 participants took place in the midst of government transition in Japan, North Korea, Mongolia, and an election campaign in the United States, questions about the health of the leader of North Korea, Kim Jong-il, and concerns over a reversal of DPRK nuclear dismantlement efforts. All participants of the Plenary emphasized the need to embrace comprehensive verification techniques in any agreement reached with the DPRK and the need to recognize the continuing importance of CSBMs in Northeast Asia to help build an integrated community and advance the peace, prosperity, and security of the Northeast Asia region and the global community.

Among the ideas advanced by the plenary session are the following:

1. In view of the Nuclear Security Summit (NSS) in 2012 in Seoul to seek gaining official NGO status for the LNWFZ-NEA organization and possible official sponsorship by the

preparatory committee to prepare and endorse at the 14th meeting a special report on NWFZ in NEA for NSS.

2. Considering European experience of community building which started from joint economic projects to recommend both Koreas and neighboring powers to identify and pursue multilateral economic projects which are capable of contributing to the promotion of CSBMs on the Korean peninsula and in NEA as a whole. The possibility to consider the ABACC experience in South America for the denuclearization of the Korean Peninsula was proposed.

3. Start advance discussion within the organization on the Republic of Korea intention to seek inclusion in any future nuclear cooperation agreement with the USA (the current one expired in 2014) an authority to reprocess nuclear fuel transferred under the agreement. Analyze the possible influence of such developments for the NPT regime, and resolution of North Korean and Iran nuclear problems.

4. Participants widely supported Mongolia's concept of NWFZ status and appreciated that the current development of nuclear weapons' free zone status contributes to international effort toward establishing a Northeast Asian regional collective Security system. Also noted the importance of Mongolian single nuclear weapons' free zone status as the internationally accepted model.

5. All were reassured that Japan will be keeping its "non-nuclear policy."

6. The conference discussed the sensitive issue of Sea Lines of Communications (SLOCs) surrounding the Eurasian continent. Recommend the need to cooperate to establish effective governance of sea traffic.

7. The conference noted that the DPRK should return to the six-party talks but realizes the need for adequate recognition of the need for security guarantees for the DPRK.

8. Noted that the status of conventional weapons and the necessity of achieving an eventual settlement of NEA regional security.

9. The conference took great interest in the manner in which Europe dealt with the reconciliation and conflict resolution since the end of World War II.

10. Noted the concept of using DPRK natural uranium resources as a means to enhance their economic situation by possibly concluding a contract with Russia to make low enriched uranium available for the international nuclear fuel market.

11. There was consideration about educational and technical exchanges to help DPRK specialists' master energy, water, and other environmental issues, as well as various fields of the social sciences, in particular, International Relations.

12. A research group composed of scholars as well as students, members of the senior panel and private experts should propose confidence-building measures for North-East Asia regarding the following issues:

13. Sustainable development, responsible economics, management, health, food, water, energy, education (training, research, double diplomas on "global security"), and infrastructures.

The group should meet regularly twice a year to deliver a report by October 2012. The report should state regional priorities and set up a precise agenda to identify and select relevant problems and solutions. The implementation of the adopted proposals should take place within the year following the next plenary session.

* * *

Looking at the recommendations made some nine years ago, I regret not being able to make them all come to pass. However, as I have mentioned, the grand consensus that had existed among our group came to reflect the geopolitical situation in Northeast Asia, and the meeting in Toulouse stands as the high water mark for our work. May I say we are waiting for an opportunity to re-energize the program, and as an optimist, I know it will come.

On October 8, 2010, I had the distinct honor of receiving an honorary doctorate from the University of Toulouse that was given in recognition of the many years spent in attempting to bring some degree of common security and peace to the states of Northeast Asia. Coming one day after Mitchie and I marked our 51st anniversary among the friends and colleagues working for the limited nuclear weapons' free zone, it was an absolute honor. Furthermore, coming from a university that has been in existence since 1229, I felt extremely humbled by the award actually suggested and facilitated by one of our most productive colleagues of the LNWFZ-NEA project, Mr. Michel Dusclaud. It is indeed one of my most precious memories, as I was never able to attend my earned Ph.D. ceremony at Tufts, as Air Force requirements precluded attendance, but one cannot complain, after all, they paid for my Fletcher adventure and wanted me back at work. Also, Toulouse University itself does not award such degrees on a whim; I thank all who initiated the award, reviewed it, and presented it. My wife was joined by our daughter Charlene and our son John to observe the ceremony. It was beautiful, and as usual, my tears flowed as soon as I made eye contact with Mitchie. She was embarrassed also as usual, but they flowed in tribute to her never-ending love and support.

Closing out 2010 in Daejeon was the good news that AACSB had accepted SolBridge as a member of AACSB. Now we could start the process of obtaining accreditation. The letter dated November 23, was signed by the Chair of the PreAccreditation committee, Bob O'Keefe. It would take until May 9, 2014, to achieve this precious goal and plenty of hours of intense work by a great faculty and staff team.

I had taught "Peace Dividend on the Korean Peninsula" during the Fall Semester, but there was no peace nor any dividend to be seen. In fact, on the same day as the good news from AACSB, the Korean island of Yeonpyeong-do was shelled by North Korea, causing significant damage and killing several South Korean soldiers and civilians. This was as bad as or worse than any incident on Korean soil since the 1953 Armistice which ended the Korean War. (Interestingly, South Korea did not sign the Armistice, which means technically, the two Koreas are still at war.) It reminded all that the situation on this peninsula can change overnight, and could be the start of a far more general war than before.

Mitchie and I headed home for our Christmas break, a break we all needed and looked forward to so much. The stress of pushing a startup organization further up the hill was put on hold, and we headed back to Marietta, Georgia. But just like the situation in the Korean Peninsula can change overnight, so can one's health. Therefore, it was time for a friendly visit to my cardiologist. He listened to my heart, put me on a treadmill, and put me in the hospital. You see, you never can tell. We had met him before Christmas, and he scheduled an operation for a stent insertion on December 28. Well, I cleared Christmas and Boxing Day, and I hoped to see the New Year. It turned out to be a "standard stent insertion," and I was out the next day. I was told it is so "routine" that most folks don't even need to stay overnight. However, given my previous bouts with circulation, they let me enjoy the hospital overnight. I wondered if a 14-hour flight on the day after New Year's would be a bit much, but all agreed, it was time to get back to work.

The fact that I had dodged another bullet did not hit home until I officiated over the beginning of the school year early March. I calmly made a reference to the number of years since I started college and there it went—more tears—and Mitchie was not even in the room.

TWENTY-ONE

Going Strong

Once the New Year was rung in by popping the Champagne and singing "Auld Lang Syne," it was time to follow up on the medical procedures I had done in the States. Upon returning to South Korea after the holidays, my New Year started out with several follow-up appointments with my Korean doctors who needed to check my condition after the angioplasty in Atlanta. The Korean health program is certainly excellent, but like all programs that are government-controlled, extreme pressure is put on the individual doctors to see as many patients in a day as they can. Thus, one really never waits a long time to see a doctor and begin your appointment, but don't count on having a long chat about your condition and that of your dogs or cats. I mean it is a production line affair—in and out in minutes if not less. However, having said that, Korea's healthcare is world-class. Unlike in the U.S., when someone goes to the hospital, a person is expected to be with them. Yes, all night, and at meals, as well. I suppose eliminating relatives or close friends from experience would place increased pressure on the system to hire more nurses or nurse's assistants—which means money. Luckily, in these follow-up appointments, we did not need to stay overnight.

Thus, January passed rather quickly with everyone focused on the upcoming Lunar New Year and the vacation entailed. Mitchie and I headed for Japan and had a delightful time visiting relatives and staying in the New Sanno Hotel that is used by the U.S. military as an R & R

(Rest and Relaxation) facility in the center of Tokyo. Again, because I had 28 years in the active Air Force, I have access to the New Sanno and its wonderful facilities as a retired officer. So that first week of February was spent very much in a vacation mode. The entire month became a time to catch up on letter writing, lesson planning, and planning for the soon to start semester in early March.

It was at this time that I met a colleague who would play a major role in my life, Jeffrey Miller. He became my partner in teaching two principal courses, American History and Politics of East Asia from a Regional Viewpoint. (Because I often have to take business trips, instead of canceling the classes I teach, my co-teacher would "fill in" for me during those trips; however, Jeffrey and I end up "team-teaching" on the days I am here. As we often like to joke with our students, "two professors for the price of one.) These courses are ones extremely useful to our foreign students as they progress through SolBridge, as well as Korean students. The level of knowledge about both subjects is astonishingly low, a very fruitful area for teachers to make a difference. Now, I am not picking on students from Asia; believe me, American students are found wanting as well, as our collective appreciation of history is one of our major shortcomings in America. I have seen it throughout my career in government; individuals making policy who had no foundation in history from which to build. Forgive me that is the subject for my next book; let me get this one done first,

Anyway, Jeffrey and I formed a partnership—a one-two punch, as it were—that I believe our students enjoyed. Our American history course used Robert Remini's *A Short History of the United States* as our basic text, and we branched out from there, and the East Asian course actually spent half the semester on Korean history since 1945 and used Don Oberdorfer's superb tome, *The Two Koreas* as our primary text before we went on to the policies of Korea's neighbors. I knew Don well and felt the loss when he passed away, but he never left our classroom, and never will.

(Initially, we used Kent Calder's *The Making of Northeast Asia* as our main textbook, but with things always changing so fast in Northeast Asia, the book was dated. It is still an excellent book. Since then, we have relied on several outsides sources, specifically the annual publications from the Korean Economic Institute of America, which have adapted well to our course.)

Both Jeffrey and I served in the Air Force and share many of the same faults, but our dear students appreciated our mid-western accents—slow with plenty of extra "R"s— and I think we imparted a good introduction to America. The impetus for the course was the Georgia Tech requirement that all first-year students had to have a course on American history if they want to go to Tech. Since it was a great attraction, we had sufficient enrollment and some wonderful minds to work with. Of course, what makes teaching in an environment where students from 61 nations could take your course is the fantastic range of worldviews held by the students. You just can't say this is this—remember it! Our friends from China, Russia, Japan, Korea—you name it—will have a different take on so many issues. Thus, really, we learn from them, and they learn from us. Exams, in this case, cannot be based on subjective reality but must be based on the way the student presents his or her defense of the position taken. There are certainly some things that can be black or white, but consider the U.S. dropping the atomic bomb on Hiroshima and Nagasaki, thus ending World War II (you see my bias showing through?). The grade must reflect the information presented and the method of presentation. It makes for an enriching experience.

Let me give just one more example that comes to mind. For the final in one of our Asian Politics course, we asked a question to take a stand on the period in South Korea when Park Chung-hee was the president. I will never forget one of our bright Chinese students, who responded in part with, "Park Chung-hee was the source of the economic miracle for Korea, but he was a dictator. There is no place in this modern world for dictators!" (Best as I can recall the argument.) Well, my world view was rocked, as if she came from a country with an elected liberal democrat as a leader. You can see the rich nature of such an interchange.

But before I leave this subject, let me note that Jeffrey is also a very successful novelist and a bastion of the English language. English here is most important, and Jeffrey has contributed to the life and success of SolBridge and thus Woosong in so many ways.

(If you ever get the chance, I highly recommend his first novel, *War Remains*, a novel about the Korean War and the recovery of the remains of service members listed as MIA. I read it on a flight back to the States, and I have to tell you, the old Colonel couldn't hold back the tears by the time I got to the end of the book. In fact, one of the flight attendants, who noticed that I was crying, came to my seat and asked if I was okay. Of course, I was okay, I told her, but this book moved and touched me deeply. I think you will be just as moved.)

Along the way, SolBridge celebrated the signing of a new MOU with the Drucker Institute's representatives in South Korea and prepared to reserve a small section of the library to house publications describing Drucker Institute programs and publications. I particularly enjoy this organization as Peter Drucker, its founder, focused on the need for a positive work environment and worker involvement and dedication in meeting customer expectations. Treating employees as members of a team to ensure quality was a trademark of Drucker's, and his impact on the business world was revolutionary. To have Drucker associated with SolBridge was a welcomed partnership and another step forward in building our own institution.

School had started in early March, and we were still welcoming new faculty and spouses to our school on the 11th. We invited the entire SolBridge faculty with spouses to enjoy an evening of social sharing—we did so at our new and improved SolBistro a multi-cuisine restaurant that is on SolBridge's main floor.

On that same day, however, in the afternoon, a huge earthquake had rocked Japan. The quake off the coast of Tohoku was a 9.1 level which was incredible in itself, but it caused a tsunami that reached over 30 meters high in some areas along the eastern coast of Japan. Then the waters overpowered the tsunami defenses at the Fukushima nuclear reactors causing a meltdown of one of the reactors and increasing nuclear fallout as efforts were taken to once again cool the reactors. Some 15,894 people died in this disaster.

When the full scale of the human tragedy was realized, the SolBridge community, led by the Student Council, arranged a fundraising campaign and a "healing flash mob." Now most of us are accustomed to fundraising, but even here the method reflected a unique way of personal sacrifice. For example, a list of items was drawn up with prices, and faculty and students were asked not to purchase the item, but give the money to the Japan Donation Campaign.

Let me show you the list—which one(s) would you have selected?

Items not to buy to help Japan:

Cola – 1000 Won
Coffee – 2000 Won
Cigarettes—2500 Won
Meal – 3500 Won
Taxi to Dorm – 4000 Won
Beer – 5000 Won
McDonald's 6000 Won
Sauna and Pool – 7000 Won
Gasoline – 8000 Won

* * *

The campaign for contributions ran from March 22-24 with tables outside the Library on our 2nd floor.

In addition to the fundraising campaign, a more personal and caring method to indicate support for Japan and the Japanese was the "Healing Flash Mob" approach that I admit would not have been on my radar screen, but was carried out on the 23rd on the first three floors of our building. Its stated purpose was to "add on to the concern and respect for the lives of people in Japan along with the donation campaign."

Instructions to all students noted that it would be held on March 23 and last for six minutes. At 2:23, students would leave their classrooms and go to the balconies on the first three floors. There they would greet their classmates, hold hands on both sides, listen for the bell, and bow their heads in two minutes of silence. Then, they would listen to the bell again, lift their heads, and walk away in silence, knowing that they sent their thoughts and hopes to Japan.

The money raised was sent to the Japanese Embassy in Seoul to use at their own discretion. The total amount of money was not as significant as the involvement of the student body focusing their concerns away from self to fellow mankind.

About this same time, we learned that one of our members of the American team for the Limited Nuclear Weapons' Free Zone had a serious health condition. Ambassador John Kelly who was now heading the American Team was in a fight with cancer. He had been

Ambassador to Finland as well as to Lebanon when the Marine Barracks was bombed with great loss of life in 1983. Once he retired from the State Department, he became an active member of our Center at Georgia Tech. His condition was listed as "grave" which was not a word we wished to hear, knowing it is only used in his circles to describe the most severe situation. We went on prayer alert and hoped for the best.

By the end of the month, George Peterson, Vice President at SolBridge, exited with a ceremony held in conjunction with a CAC Meeting on March 24. George had joined the school in 2008 and had contributed in many exciting ways—bringing his experience as a senior businessman to aid SolBridge to keep its focus on business and the applied lessons needed for young professionals. We appreciated his contributions so much that we asked and he accepted a continuing role as an emeritus member of the CAC. He has been faithful in that capacity since 2011 often coming to us from all over the world via Skype and providing advice that is always welcome.

It was good to say goodbye to March that year, and in early April, I was asked to be a keynote speaker at a SAUPO Conference sponsored by Kennesaw State University and held in downtown Atlanta. It was a wonderful time to showcase SolBridge to a large group of business-oriented executives interested in doing business in Asia. The presentation about SolBridge and what we hope to accomplish was so well received that one executive in the audience volunteered to join our Corporate Advisory Council. While in Atlanta I took the opportunity to visit KIA and Hyundai in Georgia and Alabama again. One thing that stood out most from this visit to the plants was what one of the executives in charge of operations and development told me. He explained that the plant had plans to go from 1,000 workers on one shift per day to many more on a second or night shift. Business was good, and the company was still reaping goodwill from American consumers after allowing cars to be returned during the economic crisis in 2008-2009. All in all, I was impressed by a company that was doing all the right things.

My trip to Montgomery was also pleasant, but the person I had hoped to meet was out of town, and my immersion was not as great as while at KIA. But, I left to drive back to Atlanta with a feeling we were all better off after some 5 billion dollars were invested by Korean companies in the U.S. Of course, it was done with the expectation of making money, but one could see a win-win story here.

After the week in Atlanta, I traveled north to Virginia to attend meetings at the Pentagon and George Mason University. This became one of the longest overseas business trips I have done in all my time in South Korea. In the Pentagon, I met with a Deputy Assistant Secretary of the Army to discuss opportunities for military spouses living in Korea to work at Woosong and SolBridge. It seemed like a good idea as military spouses often have advanced degrees and great administrative abilities. It turned out our location is just too far from U.S. bases. Commuting time or commuting costs have resulted in only one person being employed, but we were able to employ the male dependent of a female officer. This was another twist that I did not anticipate, but he was a great addition to our Digital Media College.

My meetings at George Mason University were aimed at building a bridge to the university my wife attended and received two degrees. It is a university that has developed very fast as a very substantial addition to the higher education opportunities in Northern Virginia. We now have excellent relations with its sister organization, the George Mason University, South Korea, located in the Song-do area near Seoul. I now serve as an advisor to its president, Dr. Steven Lee.

Returning to South Korea put me right in the middle of preparations for a big application to the Ministry of Education for what was called an ACE grant or award. ACE stood for Advancement in College Education and was the premium award granted to exceptional schools within the Korean higher education system. At any one time, 22 to 23 universities out of the 202 in Korea receive sizeable grants for usually three year periods.

On April 14, a delegation from the Ministry of Education arrived to review our application. This I remember as if it happened yesterday. Of course, we wanted to show them our best foot, and we completely rearranged the auditorium, so it became a huge "hearing room" almost in Congressional style. Very nice desks were arranged in a U-shape with the chairman of the delegation seated in the center. Only a few presenters were permitted to represent SolBridge, and they were aligned facing the delegation with a screen in the center for the briefing to be seen.

Dean "Woody" Jun carried most of the heavy water, but I delivered an introductory message after the panel chairman provided his "guidance" as to what would be permitted and what would not. To everyone's surprise, he immediately criticized the fact that we had enlisted members of our student ambassadors' corps to greet them at the main entrance to lead them to the 4th-floor auditorium. "Using students for such a purpose is taking them away from the classroom where they should be!"

So, after that wonderful start, it was Endicott up front to hopefully change the atmosphere and begin the formal presentation. Basically, I welcomed them and told them why a foreigner was greeting them— who just so happened to be the president of Woosong and Vice Chancellor of SolBridge. Even in my presentation was a picture of young John Endicott in his early days in Cincinnati. By the time I ended, I could see positive eye contact had been made with most of the members, but I had no idea how what I said was received.

"Woody" took over and presented the bulk of the information to them in Korean. You have to understand that Woody was at that time and remains so today, more western than Korean. As a dean, he joined together all the positive aspects of leadership that our school needed. He wonderfully had one foot in Korean culture and his other solidly in the West. Well, I would call his presentation brilliant, and you could see at question time that the members had listened and had good questions. The atmospherics had shifted from cold and stiff to warm and friendly.

As you can probably guess, when we received the results in May, the news was great. Woosong University was awarded one of the 11 ACE Awards that the Ministry handed out. Of the 204 universities at that time, 168 competed, and 42 had made the first cut. (Making the first cut made one eligible for the review visit described above.) Only 11 universities received ten million dollars each, but Woosong was awarded an additional $2.5 million for innovative education. (I think the delegation had seen innovative SolBridge and was impressed, even though we were told not to use our ambassadors in such a non-academic manner.)

Woosong Sports Day was held from May 12-13 of that year, and we used that occasion to announce dramatically that Woosong had won an ACE Award. As I recall, sitting in the reviewing stand overlooking the assembled athletes, pretty powerful fireworks rockets were launched from the rear of the stands and came screeching out over our heads and smacked decisively on the other side of the football field with much smoke and explosive effect. I am sure that was a little over the top as far as announcing a Ministry award, but you also must appreciate, it announced the new Woosong, now recognized as a pacemaker and on its way to academic excellence endorsed by the Ministry of Education. That was worth celebrating; thank goodness no one was hurt.

In addition to almost getting another combat award, May 12, was also Teachers' Day, and I am always impressed by the way Korean students honor and celebrate their teachers. With the students assembled on the field below the stands, at a signal from the Master of Ceremonies, selected students ran from the field into the stands and gave flowers to their appointed target. Then, in unison, all the students sang a song that honors teachers. It is a lovely tradition and needs to be cherished as the year progresses. Sometimes I feel that the system puts too much pressure on students in South Korea, but then, here is a moment that I would like to see developed in the States.

As the semester raced to its conclusion, all of SolBridge stopped on May 27 to once again celebrate Culture Day. All classes were canceled after 1600 hours, and all turned toward preparations for the rest of the day. To set the stage, I had worn my kilt from the morning, and as I walked through the halls, it was a walking reminder that tonight was set for enjoying many dishes from many countries and seeing a grand variety show featuring acts done with students in their own countries' costumes. I can only say that this is still one of the biggest events every year. Now I believe it has become so good we could actually open it up to the public and charge admission, or better still, make it free and advertise SolBridge. You see, I am now thinking like an administrator. Sorry students let's keep it for you and for your memories of SolBridge.

In June, we received good news about our debating team that was engaged in the China Open debate finals. For a program that only began in 2009, the students were certainly carrying the SolBridge banner and actually winning. In the Beijing case, we did not win but made it to the Grand Finals. Other universities were taking note.

John E. Endicott

On the Korean home front, Mitchie and I also received the bad news that our landlord decided to sell his property, which also meant our apartment. His father had passed away, and there was no need for keeping it for him. We took it in good form and looked for a place in the area we had been living for four years. The area called Taepyongdong is a nice residential area with many twenty to thirty-story apartment buildings. Most have three to five bedrooms, and ours had had five—very spacious for two folks, but we had what we considered necessary in light of the many visitors we hosted. This was found in the same housing complex we had been living. (In South Korea, clusters of apartments form various housing complexes; during Korea's rapid economic growth of the 1970s, there was also a "boom" in the housing industry with blocks and blocks of apartments rising up all over Korea. Critics often called the unaesthetic style of these dwellings as "cookie-cutter" because of how fast they were built. These days, it's not the case with beautiful, towering apartment buildings dotting the skylines of Korea's cities.) It was perhaps five to seven minutes' walk from our first place and had higher ceilings and a good view of the river running nearby. It provided us with a nice four bedroom place that was still close to the stores that we loved and people we enjoyed. However, in good military style, forgive me Mitchie, we moved on one day, and I went overseas on the next. That just happens in life, but I think I have probably pulled that one on my wife just about enough. Sorry again, Mitchie.

On July 6, I was invited to be the keynote speaker at a Model United Nations involving all of South Korea at the Yongin Campus of Hankuk University of Foreign Studies (HUFS). It was a real treat for me for you may recall I had served for the United Nations Security Council's Military Staff Committee as the Deputy Air Force Representative for two years during the period when the Soviet Union invaded Afghanistan. So, I made some observations about the role of the UN in peacekeeping and its importance for the coming era. It was enjoyable, but it also set up the possibility that Woosong could host a similar conference the following year. I returned to Daejeon with a great proposal for our university, but it would cost more than anticipated. However, from my point of view, this was another moment when Woosong began to emerge and reflect its ability to reach out and contribute to an awareness of globalization in Korea. Before the end of the year, we were visited by officials of the Korean UN Association to assess our ability to host the national Model UN the following year. An invitation to do so was in the future.

Also in July, normally a very calm time around the campus with only summer termers about and much of our faculty on research leave or just regular leave, a major development happened on July 7. (This date in 1937, is known in Asia as the day Japanese troops opened fire at the Marco Polo Bridge on the outskirts of Beijing starting the second Sino-Japanese War that did not end until August 15, 1945.) Well, July 7, 2011, brought much better news: Pyeongchang City was chosen to host the 2018 Winter Olympic Games. Our Academic Affairs and Student Services Office put out a flyer which reflected the excitement. (As I write this portion of my life's story, we are into the fifth day of the Pyeongchang Winter Olympics. From my vantage point in Daejeon, it seems South Korea is doing a fine job and enjoying a thaw in relations with its northern brother, the DPRK.)

By September, we were into the fall semester and had a visit that still shakes some of the support beams of our auditorium. Our 10th Platinum Lecturer was General John D. Johnson, Commander of the U.S. 8th Army who spoke on "Leadership for the Future. The Strategic Importance of Korea and the Strength of the Alliance." When we were told he would come and make a speech and stay for lunch, we were all thrilled as I had met the general and knew that he was not your ordinary "Camp Swampy" general. Our main question was transportation; how would the general and staff travel to Daejeon. We all hoped he would use the express train the KTX, but word came down he would arrive by helicopter. Great, but where would he land?

Over the next several weeks we suggested several places a helicopter could land, and finally one of our football fields was chosen; however, it had artificial turf, and all were concerned that in the draft of the rotor blades some chunks of the turf might blow up into the body of the vehicle. So our other football field that is dirt only was picked. We would wet it down before the aircraft arrived and it would be fine.

On the day of the visit, September 22, early in the morning one of our ground crews did in fact water down the field. We were ready when about 0930 in came the thump, thump, thump of a helicopter as it arrived. We had formed a convoy of all the executive cars that we have at Woosong so the general and his party could be swiftly moved to SolBridge about five minutes away.

Down came the helicopter and up went the dirt. While indeed the top had been hosed down, the strength of the rotor blast just picked up the upper layer and exposed the dirt. Like sand in a desert storm, the blast turned all the cars into something out of Rommel's last campaign in Africa. The cars and the people were sandblasted as we waited for the helicopter to set down and release its VIP passengers. Finally, we were on our way to SolBridge, but only the general and his party looked like they were ready for an event. The rest of us were smiling, but gritting our teeth as when you get a cleaning.

The reception for General Johnson was unbelievable. We had about 30 different nations present in 2011 (61 in 2019), and many were from China, Russia, and other places not really keen on listening to American generals. Well, General Johnson had them all in a state of highest excitement; I have never seen someone so effective in making his point and having an entire audience moved to his position. Truly, if we had set up a table for volunteers into the U.S. Army we would have run out of forms, I am sure. He is such a natural leader and charismatic speaker. By the time we said good bye and were sandblasted for a second time that day, we were exhausted. Even to this day, we keep pictures from his visit to our lobby, and we wait for someone to equal his appeal.

On the 20th of August we marked our 4th year in Korea, and on the 24th we celebrated our 52nd Wedding Anniversary; actually, it wasn't until 2017 that we—perhaps I should say I—realized that our actual anniversary is on the 25th of August, not the 24th. Somewhere over the years, the international dateline got involved—in my mind anyway—and we had been celebrating on the wrong day. I'll save that story until 2017, but it has some great irony.

In early September we took a major step forward in our quest for AACSB accreditation. Our mentor, Dr. Craig McAllaster visited from the 8th to the 9th to see SolBridge firsthand and make an assessment of our needs for the future. We are deeply indebted to Craig for his caring and insightful recommendations concerning our unique situation and the preparations we should embark on to ensure accreditation. This is one of the great reasons for schools to seek international accreditation as when it is over, it turns earned credits here into almost universally accepted credits anywhere in the world. Thus, the student gains, the faculty gains, the university gains, and in the end, the nation and the international business system gains. The accreditation comes at some cost, but I am fully committed to its value.

By the end of September, I was participating in my first ACE Conference where other ACE universities exchange information on innovative projects undertaken with the funding of the ACE awards. This meeting was held at Catholic University on the outskirts of Seoul. The month also ended with Woosong opening Sol Hospital in its Health and Human Services College. It was just another significant step forward as it provided our Nursing School with a complete emergency room "mock-up" that had mannequins to work on, but everything as in a real hospital. So, it was not a real hospital, but a place very much like the operating room I remember from my triple bypass. As you might expect, I really don't like to visit this fine facility; it is too much like what I remember.

Our Culinary Arts College also won recognition by being selected by the Korean Government to run a Star Chef Program, and the formal opening was held on October 9. This was a government supported program to take individuals who are already chefs and make them into Star Chefs or chefs who could present Korean cuisine to the world and thereby increasing the restaurant business as another profit generating area for Korea. This program was funded for approximately three years and did graduate many talented chefs ready to take Korean cuisine to the world. Sadly, it fell short of the expectations many thought that program would bring.

Besides the Star Chef initiative, October brought two more exciting events, one for our search for a limited nuclear weapons free zone in Northeast Asia, and the other regarding obtaining an ROTC detachment for Woosong University. From the 10th to the 16th my wife and I joined our French and Finnish colleagues to see if it would be possible to build on the 13th Plenary Conference held in Toulouse in 2010. We visited officials in Paris, and academics in Toulouse and Bordeaux in search of a magic combination that would repair the damage done to our group at the last meeting. Many heads nodded in agreement, but we returned to South Korea feeling that the right time had moved on. In early November 2011 at a meeting of the Korean LNWFZ Team in Seoul, I reported our lack of progress as we needed to reinvigorate the concept for a system of cooperative security on the Peninsula. Then, only nine days later, came news of the death of Kim Jong-il.

The year ended with the Endicott's enjoying Atlanta once again at Christmas time, but aware that the death of Kim Jong-il brought with it the succession of an unknown to power in North Korea, his son, Kim Jong-un, not the oldest, but one who had received some of his education in Switzerland. Was this good or bad? No one knew. Only time would tell.

PHOTO GALLERY FOUR

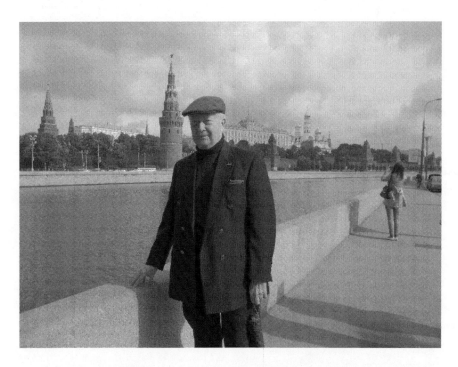

Pausing in front of the Kremlin in September 2012 while attending the conference marking the 50th anniversary of the Cuban Missile Crisis.

AACSB panel members and SolBridge leadership in front of Woosong Kwan, the Woosong University headquarters building. Dr. Linda Hadley of Columbus State University, Georgia, led the team. She is second from the front, left side.

My office at Woosong Kwan explaining to Dr. R.C. Natarajan, a member of the AACSB review team, the significance of the picture of the SS *Washington*, the ship I took to Southampton, England, in August 1950. (The review is over, so I am relaxed.)

2014 Endicott Christmas, Marietta, Georgia

A visit by our son-in-law Greg Noble and his son, Nick standing in the entrance hall of SolBridge International School of Business; from the left, Mitchie, Greg, Nick, myself and Chairman Kim of the Woosong Foundation.

Formal ceremony for the Naming Day for the Endicott College of International Studies. I am speaking, and distinguished international VIPs, leading faculty members, and Mitchie are in attendance. The audience faces the stage, and MC and interpreter stand on stage to my left.

Ribbon-cutting ceremony for the Endicott Building with me in the hat, our son John II to my left, Mitchie next, and Woosong VIPs.

Signing an MOU of cooperation between Endicott College of International Studies and Pittsburg State University of Pittsburg, Kansas, where my father graduated. Professor Lee Sang-heui of Pittsburg state represents his university.

Receiving an Honorary Doctorate in Political Science from Pres. Chang Ho-sung of Dankook University in February 2019. It was given in recognition of the almost three decades of work for a Limited Nuclear Weapons' Free Zone in Northeast Asia.

Receiving flowers from Chairman Kim at Dankook University during the ceremony when I received an Honorary Doctorate in Political Science; Mitchie with flowers stands to my left.

With Mitchie at the annual USO Gala in Seoul. (Photo courtesy, USO)

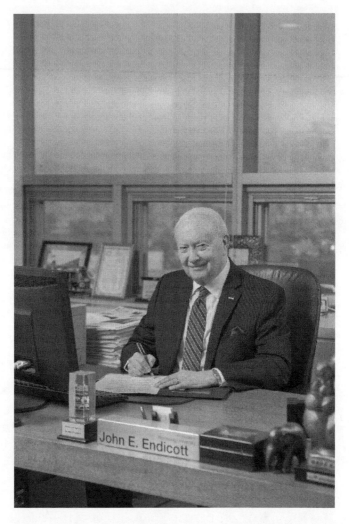

In my office on the 12th floor in SolBridge.

TWENTY-TWO

What Comes Around; Goes Around

As we entered 2012, Mitchie and I sent New Year's Greetings to our friends and colleagues, and in reviewing it, permit me to place it here in the record. It captures 2011 in one page and does reflect our feelings about the rising nature of Woosong University:

Mitchie and John Endicott's
NEW YEAR'S GREETING
2012

Dear Friends and Colleagues from Around the World,

This has been a very eventful and blessed year for us. As you know, we have been in South Korea since August 2007—now some 53 months. Three years ago in December, I became President of Woosong University, as opposed to Co-President. It has been a great year; the number of applicants—critically important in the Korean system—continues to place us first in the province for private universities. Mitchie's role as "Madam President" and Visiting Lecturer of Japanese Language continues to be enjoyable, and she is increasingly called on by the Culinary Arts College to help in assessing new tastes for traditional Korean dishes. Woosong was selected among the "Best 11" Universities of Korea in a competition for eleven 10 million dollar Ministry of Education grants. We also placed first in a nation-wide competition for new ROTC Programs. Six universities were authorized to begin programs, and five were ordered to disband existing programs. The four-terms per year curriculum begun last year continues with a major improvement in student acceptance. This features two 15-week semesters and two "mini-semesters" of six weeks each. The objective is to end the traditional long vacation periods in winter and spring (about three months each) that only serve to detract from the learning process—especially foreign language study. This is a first for Korea, so when the 200 university presidents meet, it is clear they are "benchmarking" Woosong. Mitchie and I are both as busy as we have ever wanted. Daejeon, South Korea, where we live, is about 50 minutes by express train from Seoul. So, we work and live in one of the most comfortable cities in Korea. It is also the science and technology center of Korea, with over 7,000 Ph.D.'s in the region. In fact, Daejeon was just designated as the hub for the new Science and Business Zone in Korea.

The two big events of this past year were moving from the quarters we had enjoyed for the past four years to a close-by, but more modern apartment and a return visit by both of us to Paris and Toulouse, France where we celebrated our 52nd Anniversary. While in Paris, we were able to continue discussions with government leaders on the Limited Nuclear Weapons' Free Zone for Northeast Asia. There was significant interest, but with recent events, an even greater relevance should be realized. We also had wonderful home leave visits to Tokyo and Atlanta, which allowed us to catch up with Mitchie's family and Charlene's and John II's families now both living in Atlanta.

We now look forward to visiting partner universities in China, Japan, Kazakhstan, Russia, Uzbekistan, and Taiwan in the coming Year of the Black Dragon.

Mitchie and I wish you a Joyous New Year.
Fondly, the Endicott's

I hope it was received well by those we sent it to, but it did sum up a year that was hard to beat. Let's see.

* * *

Our Vice Dean, Patrick Leonard also shared the good news that our application for AACSB accreditation was progressing. It seems that the required Standards Alignment Plan we submitted was accepted and moved forward to the Pre-Accreditation Committee and its review in mid-March. (I am sorry to include such seemingly minuscule administrative information, but it brightened our day—believe me.)

By early February, in fact the 14th, we received a certificate from the United Nations that read "The United Nations Welcomes Woosong University as a member of the United Nations Academic Impact and values its commitment to the following ten principles: "Commitment to the United Nations Charter, Human rights, Educational opportunity for all, Higher Education Opportunity for every Interested Individual, Capacity-Building in Higher Education Systems, Global citizenship, Peace and Conflict Resolution, Addressing poverty, and Sustainability—the 'Unlearning' of Intolerance." When that arrived, I realized that our hosting of the 2012 Model UN required such a certificate. Okay, we were now ready to begin the serious planning for an event that might involve as many as 600 college students from all over South Korea and as many as 65 colleges. At this point, we knew it would happen in June or July. Well, in February, I suppose that was what we might call an "alert warning." I was enthusiastic as in one major conference we would be putting Woosong on the map, just where I wanted it to be.

By the end of June, we were reaching top speed at exactly the time that most academics were going on vacation or doing their research. From June 25-26, we hosted the Global Entrepreneurship Forum at SolBridge. Fifty-three participants from 6 countries: Indonesia, Vietnam, Thailand, Singapore, South Korea, and Japan, came to discuss their experiences in entrepreneurship under the guidance of Professor Sang Lee of the University of Nebraska. Discussions, presentations, and exchanges between participants were done at warp speed. I have never seen such enthusiasm and dedication as I saw in the delegates who began talking about their involvement with start-up enterprises. They were "true believers" without a doubt. Unlike other academic meetings, they talked openly and freely about failure, as that was part of the package. From failure came success was their motto. It was very clear that we were witness to a different brand of academics. They were doing something and using their business skills to turn theory into a thriving business.

Their presence at SolBridge was useful for all to see this particular field, and I am sure contributed later to our adding a specialization in this area to our curriculum and our relationship with Babson University.

Another adventure that marked a major accomplishment for the university was our hosting of the 18th Model United Nations Conference in the summer of 2012.

I have long been interested in the United Nations, and you may recall my references to parades or festivals where the support of the UN was one of the prime features. I was one of those who supported the organization from the very beginning—at first, through the prompting of my 5th-grade teacher, but later as a specialist in international relations. My association with the UN in South Korea began in 2011 when I was asked to be the keynote speaker for the 17th Model UN held at Hankuk University of Foreign Studies (HUFS). I was impressed that such an opportunity was offered to the students of Korea each year and was delighted to participate. In fact, I was so delighted by that opportunity that I offered to host the meeting in 2012. (I think a university had already been selected, but for some reason backed out and the offer was quickly acted on favorably by the Korea UN Association.)

After asking for the 2012 conference, I realized that inviting perhaps 600 students from 60 or so universities was going to require significant buy-in by our own faculty, staff, and most of our students. In the latter category, we would need student participants and student support; it would be big indeed. And then there were conference room facilities and dorms not to mention food services. Everyone smiled when I returned from the HUFS conference when I told them that I sold the cow for a hand full of beans. They gave me the Korean equivalent of the Japanese expression *Arigato meiwaku* which might be translated as "thanks, for nothing."

John E. Endicott

After a lot of preparation, we opened the conference to 458 students from 66 universities on July 4, 2012. I greeted them with the following:

Opening Remarks for the Model UN

July 4, 2012

Vice president of United Nations Association of Korea, Ambassador Sun, Ambassador Moon, Vice president of UN R.O.K. Cho, Ambassador Kim, and Chairman Kim, and Distinguished Colleagues, and delegates to the 18th National Model United Nations Conference here at Woosong University. One year ago at the Yongin Campus of Hankuk University of Foreign Studies—it was my pleasure to address the 17th National Model UN. To be hosting the conference this year is Woosong's greatest honor and we look forward to an event so exciting that it will be one of those moments you will carry forever as one of your fondest memories. As the Founding Director of the Center for International Strategy, Technology, and Policy at Georgia Tech in Atlanta, Georgia, I used the format you will be following several times, as I invited outstanding students from around the City of Atlanta and the State of Georgia to help me gain insights into several international issues I believed needed input from intelligent college-aged students. Of course, that included several sessions dealing with the nuclear issues, both power and weapons-related.

We are so fortunate to be here in the presence of a former Korean Ambassador to the UN, Ambassador Sun Joun-yung. Ambassador Sun now represents the Korea United Nations Association and is deeply involved in assuring that the Model UN Program continues as an integral part of Korean colligate education. We are also indebted to Ambassador Hayong David Moon Deputy Minister and Ambassador for Overseas Koreans, Consular Affairs, and International Counter-Terrorism

Cooperation. Deputy Minister Moon will be our keynote speaker, and I welcome him sincerely.

I too had some time at the United Nations Headquarters in New York as the Deputy Air Force Representative to the Military Staff Committee. Originally that organization was to be the prime coordinator of the use of force by the UN, but Cold War competition between the Soviet Union and the U.S. intervened. Every two weeks we met but only continued our impasse. The only thing we were able to agree on was who would pay for lunch—we rotated. That very predictable format continued until the Soviet invasion of Afghanistan in 1979, then the Military Staff Committee became one of only two avenues through which the U.S. and Soviet military could talk. From famine to feast overnight. In a sense, the mission of the UN is to be ready when needed, and then attempt as much as possible to preserve or enable a return to peace.

May I encourage you to explore the four questions you will address with all the power and intellect you can bring to these issues: Global efforts to counter nuclear terrorism and nuclear security; protecting basic human rights of migrant workers; addressing the challenges and threats of cyberspace and going beyond the Millennium Development Goals. These are all questions worthy of careful and thoughtful assessment and ones that will be dependent on your generation to solve successfully.

Besides welcoming you today, may I interject one aspect of my own background that may be of interest to all participants, but especially to you in the 1st Committee examining aspects of the nuclear issue? This year in October is the 50th Anniversary of the moment when the U.S. and the Soviet Union came face to face and held the fate of the world literally in their hands. In 1962, I was an Air Force Captain and assigned to SAC Headquarters—the Strategic Air Command—located in Omaha, Nebraska, in the very center of the country. There I participated in the October Cuban Missile Crisis from the vantage point of the Nuclear Planning War Room three stories below ground in a concrete reinforced bunker. As the confrontation evolved at one point, my boss, a three-star general, told us he believed only minutes remained until execution. You must understand the situation;

SAC bombers were on airborne alert—flying just outside Soviet territory with nuclear bombs only awaiting the "go" code. Our ICBMs, IRBMs, and SRMBs were on alert the world over—if they were launched, they could not come back. Submarines also stood ready at their positions at sea. From that point on I became a firm advocate of arms control, arms reduction, and finally nuclear arms removal.

To show you how far we have come, I have been invited to Moscow to take part in a conference commemorating that moment. I will be paired with Col-General Yesin who also at that time was a Captain and in command of a unit armed with short-range nuclear missiles ready to be used against American troops who might land on the beaches of Cuba. We will start the conference with an exchange of our stories.

Before turning the conference over to those who have really been working day and night to realize today, may I recognize some of them for you and state my profound thanks for their efforts: Our Secretary-General Yoon Dan-bi of the Department of Nursing Science; Dep. Sect. General Kim Hee-chul of SolBridge International School of Business and the Undersecretary Lee Seo-jin, also of the Department of Nursing. Also Yook Eun-ah, Yun Tae-su, and Kim Do-hwan, plus 22 staff members of the Secretariat and 49 volunteers. I wish to thank them all as well as their faculty advisors: Professors Lee Yong-sang, and Kang, Lee, and Shin. As in almost all worthwhile endeavors in life, teamwork is at the center of success. My thanks again.

Finally, on behalf of our Chairman Kim of the Woosong Education Foundation, may I officially welcome all 328 delegates and 130 observers from 66 universities throughout Korea. We are excited to welcome you and wish you well as you begin your deliberations over the next three days.

Welcome to Woosong!

* * *

After I spoke, our keynote speaker was Ambassador David Moon, Deputy Minister and Ambassador for Overseas Korean, Consular Affairs, and International Counter-Terrorism Cooperation. He came from the Ministry of Foreign Affairs and Trade out of Seoul. Once he was finished, it was a totally student-run affair. As in all these projects that are run by students, the best of everything is accomplished. They are in charge, make decisions—some good, some not so good—but it is their show. As I toured the conference rooms where all debated the four issues mentioned above, it was very clear we had with us some great new leaders for Korea.

After it was all over, we received a letter from Ambassador Sun Joun-yung, the President of the Korea United Nations Association letting us know that Woosong University had "...set a standard of new heights for the Model UN."[32] Of course, we were pleased and could finally relax as it was summer after all.

Relax we could not do, however, as the invitation to Moscow required a bit of attention. On July 4, during the Model UN, I sent a letter to the U.S. Air Force Attaché in Seoul, Colonel Hank Shin that transmitted my proposed speech for the September 6 Moscow conference. Why would I do that as a retired officer? Well, it turns out if you are what is called a Regular Officer and not a Reserve Officer, you really never leave the service. I had served on active duty for 28 years, but I still had to observe the pledges I had made when working on very sensitive issues in government. I needed the Air Force to okay my text before standing in front of an assembly of Russian nuclear experts. Below is what was approved:

Talk for Cuban Missile Crisis Anniversary

Thank you, Anton, and I am most pleased to meet Col. General Yesin. I look forward to your comments, and it does my heart good to see that we are both working to bring the nuclear genie completely under control. I am sure we both now have grandchildren, and we live in a time when hope is really an option.

Let me set the stage for my comments and go back to 1962. As the year opened, I was stationed at Pacific Headquarters in the Targeting Directorate and awaiting orders for my next assignment. I had started an Air Force career—

---

[32] Letter from Ambassador Sun Joun-yung, July 21, 2012.

after initial training—by being assigned to Japan, and to Tokyo—actually the area that is now the Olympic grounds for the 1964 Tokyo Olympics. As a 2nd Lt. with a political science degree and a certificate saying I had completed the Basic Intelligence Officer Course, I threw myself into learning Japanese and following international events in Northeast Asia. I am still following international events in Northeast Asia, but as an academic, not a practitioner.

Now Hawaii is not a bad place to be stationed, and I was assigned to the Headquarters of the Intelligence unit I worked with. Very importantly, when that organization was deactivated because new technology was going to give us all the information we needed. I was assigned to PACAF Headquarters in the Targeting Directorate. That began a concentration on targeting that lasted well into my Air Force career.

When the time came for reassignment, everyone in the Directorate waited eagerly to see where I would end up. When word finally came through that I would be assigned to Headquarters SAC—the Strategic Air Command—in Omaha, Nebraska, it was clear that Mitchie and I had made the right decision to stay in the Air Force; it was a wonderful opportunity to expand my professional competence.

Arriving mid-year at Offutt Air Force Base, I entered a world that was unique. SAC was famous or notorious for security and the Commander of the Air Force at that time, General Curtis LeMay, was well known for unannounced inspections when his plane would land on some SAC base and all hell would break loose.

To give you an understanding of the degree of security, let me tell the story of a friend of mine, a Lieutenant, who failed to have his ID photo changed when he shaved off his mustache. On entering the tunnel to approach the underground command post at SAC Headquarters, he was stopped by the guards for his ID which still had the photo of him with a mustache. When I walked by, he was naked, spread eagle against the wall with two guards holding weapons at the ready. There was no room for error in those days. When he finally reported to work, he had a new ID card and was fully dressed.

When I reported to SAC, I was immediately detailed as a SAC Augmentee to the Joint Strategic Target Planning Staff (JSTPS) that actually made the master nuclear war plan. My desk was immediately adjacent to the War Room/Command Post where the total plan could be displayed using the latest state-of-the-art computer assistance. In retrospect, we were driving a Model T Ford but of course, didn't know it. A violent thunderstorm hitting the surface three stories above could play havoc with the stored data, but several Colonels who had memorized the entire plan would save the day and rebuild the entire file in a matter of hours. Back then, we used punch cards which were still looked upon as being very modern.

My job was to insure that all critical targets were "covered," in other words, that each target had several weapons assigned against them within three days to meet the guidelines of 75% assurance of destruction. And in that sense, I worked closely with the Intelligence Directorate. As they identified new targets or known targets that for some reason now had a higher priority, it was my job to check the coordinates, make sure that they were in our data base resource files and pass the information with a proper priority assignment to the folks in the War Room where the actual assignments were made.

The environment of the entire operation was one that did not appreciate error. I remember as a Captain accompanying on occasion "my" Colonel to weekly meetings with the Commander of SAC (General Thomas S. Power) where he met with his staff. As a Captain I was seated next to the wall; only the "principals" were invited to sit around the rather large table.

As General Power presided over the individual briefings, the situation could become very tense if the briefer was asked a question and was found wanting. Often, the exchange with the General, if faulty or incomplete, would end with an invitation to find new employment. In fact in those days "Off my base by sundown!" was heard not infrequently throughout the SAC base system. Thus, when that happened, the access to base housing would be immediately terminated, and families would be relocated as the Colonel looked for a new assignment.

I realized that people thought very highly of my work when on one Saturday morning when I reached the first Guard Post, I was told to immediately report to the War Room. When I entered the room besides the normal haze of cigar smoke (General LeMay liked cigars and set the standard throughout the Air Force) a number of chairs had been arranged in a circle in the center of the room. In these chairs were seated Generals and Colonels evidently waiting for me. My immediate boss said, "John, would you stand in the center." Then from around this 360 degree "firing zone" came one question after another using English not normally taught in our Learn English Academies. Maybe that was why I only weighed 145 pounds in those days, but it was an experience I will never forget.

I had missed one of those extremely high priority targets, and the ranking officer present finally said, "John, that was one, there will never again be two, right?" I realized at that point that they really thought I was doing a good job because if I hadn't, myself, Mitchie, and our two-year-old daughter, Charlene, would have been on the road to who knows where Air Base—by sundown.

The guidance for compiling the SIOP came from the Pentagon and the joint planning staff crafted an overall plan that would incorporate that guidance to provide the President with as much leeway as possible in choosing his response. As I now understand it, President Kennedy was not all that pleased with the SIOP as it did not provide the flexibility he required. The staff had been working for some time to give this flexibility by the time I got to Offutt, and the record shows that it was briefed to the President on September 14, 1962. While I was not present at the briefing—only very select principals—I do recall that a special rocking chair with a high back was obtained so that President Kennedy could take the briefing and be as comfortable as possible in light of his back problems. I remember that so clearly as when President Johnson visited sometime later to take the SIOP briefing he requested that the same chair be provided for him. I am not sure the chair was provided, but knowing the tenor of the times, I am sure all possible efforts were expended to have it there.

As the situation in Cuba came to the attention of the U.S. Intelligence Community, being in the Underground at SAC Headquarters and working on the SIOP did not necessarily make me privy to developing events in Cuba. In essence, in those days I was a customer of intelligence output, and material covering Cuba was out of my area of responsibility—it was something special and would have to be handled in a special way.

However, when President Kennedy spoke to the nation on television, and the Defense Establishment went to DEFCON 3, our attention was focused. The next day, October 23, General Power put SAC at DEFCON 2, and many SAC aircraft were launched in a status of Airborne Alert. Thus, they launched with weapons, went to prescribed loiter points, and waited for the necessary codes for an actual attack. Of course, the orbiting in race track fashion was not new. A friend of mine who also worked at SAC often relayed accounts of when he would be on airborne alert, and well into the flight he would be greeted by a charming voice that welcomed him to his duty station and asked how his wife and family were— and they used his real name. We were closer to each other than was commonly realized.

General Power's reaction to the increased tension was reflective of Air Force doctrine at the time and probably still is today. As a result of the devastating raids at Pearl Harbor and Manila at the opening of World War II, the Air Force learned the hard way some lessons about the vulnerability of aircraft in such situations. I am sure. General Power was reflecting these lessons and was determined to get as many aircraft in the air as possible to permit a systematic relay of aircraft in the air, aircraft ready to take to the air, and aircraft returning for rest and refueling.

As the operational force got itself up to peak readiness something absolutely unusual began to happen. I will call it the raid on the "Hanger Queens." Hanger Queens was the term picked by the operators to describe aircraft that loved to be in hangers being repaired and not on the flight line ready for combat. Now, most of these "birds" were capable of flying. It was a matter of some system within the aircraft that needed to be repaired for it to be 100% combat ready. All of a sudden, we received a flood of additional aircraft available for combat and target assignments. Aircraft were being declared "mission ready," even though the altimeter might be down, or something else. Anyway, additional aircraft became available requiring additional aircrews.

To obtain these crews, a call was made for volunteers for rated pilots and support crews now working at desk jobs in SAC Headquarters and the units around the States. These individuals were fully trained as pilots and support personnel, but working as administrators as part of their continuing careers. Soon, the word was that enough aircraft and crews were generated to equal 120% of the requirements of the plan. So while the SIOP equaled 100%, SIOP plus Hanger Queens equaled 120%. That is my recollection, but I would question the actual number. A flurry of target assignments were made; however, that in some cases brought the percentage of success to the required 75%, in others, it exceeded requested norms. Nonetheless, it was clear we were ready.

Then, on one day of the crisis, the entire U.S. Defense establishment went to DEFCON 2, (it might have been the 27th a day when all hell broke loose with a missing U-2 and an errant U-2, but I cannot remember for certain). However, things were very hot, and tensions were extremely high. One of my bosses, a Lt. General, came down from the Intelligence Directorate and gathered several of us who were working in the ante-room, just outside the War Room, and said, to the best of my memory, "Well men, I believe we have about 20 or 30 minutes until execution, why don't you call your spouses and say goodbye." I am sorry I don't remember the exact time nor date, but I do remember making the call and asking some non-descript question like, "What are we having for dinner?" I think it was Wednesday the 24th as it was in the morning. At that time, the folks on the surface had a better idea of what was going on than we did in the Underground. Rather like the frog in the well, I called and spoke to Mitchie. She remembers the call like it was yesterday; but like most human beings who tend to suppress extremely bad memories and look for the sunshine, I don't think she can put an exact time on the call either.

I can remember some years later being on an expert's panel with Secretary of Defense Robert McNamara, and the subject of airborne alert came up. I said something very close to "Mr. Secretary, do you remember when we launched the fleet to avoid a Pearl Harbor during the Cuban Missile Crisis?" He turned to me and said that he had never approved of such a move. I responded that he didn't need to approve a protective launching of the fleet as that was authority designated to the SAC Commander in the protocols for emergency response. The color went out of his face, and he stared at me in disbelief. Well, that is what I remember; we were very conscious that the aircraft in the air should be extremely well managed and returned for fueling or some aircraft would have to attack with enough fuel only to go one way and seek an emergency or "safe" landing area. One of us is wrong, but at my age now, I can appreciate the unreliability of memory.

As we look back on this very dark era of U.S.-Soviet relations, we all realize how close we came to the unbelievable. In the *History of Knowledge*, the author points out that the most important finding of the 20th Century was the fact that we could indeed destroy our world. Not a very pleasant contribution to the development of knowledge, but one that General Yesin and myself have been trying to moderate. Since 1991, but especially since 1995, a group of former senior military officers from China, Japan, South Korea, Mongolia, Russia, and the United States, with great help from official observers from Argentina, Finland, and France, have been working to popularize the concept for a Limited Nuclear Weapons' Free Zone for Northeast Asia. Starting from the premise that maybe the only thing we can agree on is the need to reduce—possibly eliminate nuclear weapons from

Northeast Asia, we have spent over twenty years paddling upstream. We have had great interaction with the individuals who became involved in the Six-Party Talks, and we stand ready to share our experiences with those interested in looking at cooperative security as a way to enhance peace and security in the world, but especially NEA.

Along the way, our group has become close friends and stand witness to the fact that former foes can come together in the name of peace. And we have not given up on the LNWFZ-NEA, but will keep a close eye on the negotiations to return North Korea to its non-weapons possessing status. However, with the DPRK inserting its status as a nuclear-armed nation into their Constitution, we may have continuing difficulty. We think we can build a prosperous Neighborhood Asia involving all the nations of the region that integrates the concept for a limited nuclear weapons-free zone. For those who think that will never happen, I direct their attention to the Cuban Missile Crisis and how it started the process that helped make friends out of former foes.

* * *

Toward the middle of summer actually the middle of July, Woosong announced the addition of an "Honorary President" to our university leadership. The person chosen was Nam K. Woo who had been a very senior executive in the LG industrial/business conglomerate. He had served in the United States, China, and Europe, and in his own words was "present at the creation." He was promoting Korean made goods when it was a hard sell. But his determination and the fact that Korean products were, in fact, becoming better led to his success in the competitive international marketplace. By the time he retired from LG, he had a Korean award for exceptional service to the nation and even became a Fellow at one of Columbia University's programs for international business executives. What was really exceptional about the appointment was my earlier acquaintance with Mr. Woo. In 2005 he had given a speech to one of my programs at the Sam Nunn School at Georgia Tech when he was at Columbia.

When we met in 2012, Nam said that he knew me, and I, unfortunately, could not remember the occasion. Two days later, he returned to my office and said: "John, take a look at this." In his hand was my name card from the Sam Nunn School at Georgia Tech. "And how do you think I got this?" he asked. Well, I realized that older folks meet so many interesting people—sometimes many times over. Nam was a super partner and helped set up so many contacts for the university with our Korean colleagues. Even though he stepped down in 2017, he is now in California still on the lookout for great students and new opportunities for university to university cooperation. One of his last accomplishments was establishing a wonderful program with the University of California at Irvine that involves sending as many as six SolBridge students a year to that fine institution.

As July picked up speed, I did as well in a very unexpected way. The Public Relations Office of Woosong came up with the idea that Woosong should have its own day at Hanbat Stadium (again), the home of the Hanwha Eagles one of the professional baseball teams in South Korea and based in Daejeon. And, guess what? I was invited to throw out the first ceremonial pitch. Again.

I am sure in the commentary you have picked up the fact that I am a real baseball "nut." Perhaps in this venue, I should use "enthusiast;" anyway I really love the game. I am sure the way that came about is Woosong University bought a block of seats—a sizable amount and I was invited to throw the first ball.

One afternoon a representative from the team called and asked all about my size as they were making my own full uniform. As we concluded our conversation, he said, "What number do you wish on your uniform?"

I thought for a moment and replied, "Please, number 14."

"Okay, but why did you pick that?"

"Why, it was Pete Rose's number, and I would like to honor him."

(Pete and I graduated from Western Hills High School in Cincinnati—about five or six years apart. He went on the have one of the most spectacular careers in baseball and would today be in the Baseball Hall of Fame, but he bet on baseball and was separated forever from the sport. There are many fans, mostly in Cincinnati I presume, who would like to see him honored for what he accomplished in baseball, not banned for life.)

Over the next several weeks at about 4:00 pm I would change into shorts and a tee shirt, go to the gym or out in the parking lot and practice. My driver at the time, Kang Tae-won, a tall fellow with very long arms was my battery mate. In fact, he should have thrown the opening pitch as he is a natural pitcher with speed and accuracy that could be heard every time he returned the pitch I threw.

Finally, July 25 came and the 75-year-old reported in for his day in history. It was my fantasy for certain. So in front of about 2000 Woosong students screaming wildly, I stepped on the mound and threw a pitch that was around 60-70 miles per hour—or was that kilometers per hour? The announcers in the radio booth, stopped their unrelated chatter and said something to the effect: "Hey where did this guy come from? He can really throw! He obviously played serious ball before."

Of course, I did not hear that, but many folks came up to me with the account. Was I ten feet tall that night? Well, I certainly filled out all five feet, seven inches that I am. I do not even remember the score. I do recall that the Eagles won and for that year that was really unusual and one of the reasons we got such a deal in buying the tickets. I just sat there eating my hot dogs and reliving the moment on the mound.

As the month advanced, plans for the Moscow trip became firm and a side trip to St. Petersburg was added. It would be our first chance to visit this historic and cultural city built to show the world that Russia had entered Europe as a full-fledged member. And, of course, it was Peter the Great who led that charge. We wanted to see this star of the Imperial era to show our respect for the accomplishments of Peter the Great, but also observe its darker history as it heroically withstood the 900-day siege by Nazi forces in the early days of World War II.

July also sadly ended the story of a good friend of mine, the President of KAIST, (the Korea Advanced Institute of Science and Technology) the Georgia Tech/MIT of Korea. He had tried to reform KAIST and free it of the bureaucratic structures it had, and also advance its internationalization by requiring all courses to be taught and taken in English. He was able to accomplish much in his seven years, but the pushback regarding English was too much. As he left, I sent him a message with my parting thoughts. He had been a trailblazer doing much of the same kind of things we were doing at SolBridge. However, rather than convert to English, we started with English as the language of instruction. Both students and professors understood; there were no surprises.

By the first week of August, our plans for St. Petersburg were getting more complete. Our initial schedule included the Artillery Museum, Peter and Paul Fortress, and the Peter and Paul Cathedral and the Summer Garden. Then we would visit Peterhof, the Lower Park, the Grand Palace, and the entire visit would be facilitated by a guide, a driver and an E Class Mercedes. You might think we paid quite a bit for this side tour to St. Petersburg and yes, we did. But this was one of those times that we knew we would not be coming back. It took us 75 years to visit it for the first time, and certainly, we did not plan on being around for the second.

The old adage, when it rains, it pours certainly seemed appropriate all of a sudden. While we were doing all the paperwork for the Moscow visit, I received an invitation to participate in the 45th Anniversary of the Vladivostok State University of Economics and Science—in Vladivostok (one of our partner universities) in the same month that I would be visiting Moscow (September 20-23). Here was another chance to use my rusty Russian language that I took at the Ohio State University from 1954 to 1958. I was thrilled but scared to death at the thought of making congratulatory comments in Russian. Nonetheless, challenge accepted!

As August reached the mid-point, we received a note offering us the opportunity to recognize an Austrian Member of Parliament with an Honorary Degree from Woosong University. Honorary degrees are a way of saying in public that someone has contributed to society in a manner quite significant. Usually, a university will give them to graduates as that is a win-win operation. In this case, Mr. Werner Amon was not our graduate but had contributed significantly to Korean-Austrian relations. We looked at this as an opportunity to further good relations between the two nations and put Woosong University in front of a population far from ones normally reached. We responded that we were very interested and would be inviting the Member of Parliament to deliver a lecture and receive his honorary degree at a convenient time in November.

I think it is appropriate to include a note here about honorary degrees. Normally in the academic world, we use the terms "earned degree" and "honorary degree" to distinguish between work done in the academic sense and work done as a result of life's experience. Normally, an honorary degree does not qualify as meeting the criteria for an academic position at a university—only earned degrees would count. I am sure there are exceptions when the need arises.

After digesting the Russia-bound travel for September, I learned that from September 25-29 I would be in China, as well. Well, why not I confided to myself, might as well get all the travel in before winter weather becomes a factor. The reader might be somewhat bemused by a president's travel schedule being decided by others than himself. It just demonstrates that many departments and offices are running at full speed all year long and at times need to call on the Office of the President to attend some important function. Often we know of these well in advance, but just as often—it seems to me—we are "invited" at the last moment and to say "no" would be disruptive to many parties, including Woosong. So, you can understand, I build my own schedule with as much information as possible, but then additional requests flow in, as often as not, they must be accommodated somehow. One of my mentors and best friends here at Woosong, President Jung Sang-jik of the Woosong College, laughs and notes that such a schedule makes me younger each year. I always respond, "How do you reckon that?" and he replies, "You are too busy to age." It seems to work.

The end of August always brings the rush of business that is associated with a new semester about to begin. Inevitably the Fall Semester will start during the last days of August or the first days of September. During this time we welcome back faculty who have been on vacation or research, as well as totally new faculty who are joining us for the first time. Thus, the orientation of new faculty, the Fall Semester retreat and workshop, and the simultaneous programs to provide orientation to new students are engaging us all. It truly is one of the busiest times of the year since we have many foreign faculty and students, so in addition to regular programs for starting the new academic semester, there are countless trips to the Immigration Office and coordination across campus.

In the midst of this activity, on the 31st of August, I received the draft agenda for the Moscow nonproliferation conference. Certainly, it was going to happen and right on the first page was the information about the first plenary session: "Remembering the Cuban Missile

Crisis: 50 Years On. A Talk with Crisis Insiders." Both Col-General Victor Yesin (Ret.)," and John Endicott, "SES-4 (Maj./Lt.-Gen)," were listed, as well as Konstantin Von Eggert, a political analyst, who was listed as the Chair.[33]

And it did happen. In retrospect, this was one of those moments in life when you have a chance to reflect on an experience that was very much part of those moments in the 20th Century that set the framework for the entire century. Thus, I would place it on a list that would include the assassination of Arch Duke Ferdinand and the beginning of World War I, the bombing of Pearl Harbor and the beginning of World War II (for America), the bombing of Hiroshima and the end of World War II and the beginning of the nuclear Era, and the launching of Sputnik in October 1957. To complete that list, I would add the assassination of President John F. Kennedy, the fall of the Berlin Wall, and ultimately the collapse of the Soviet Union on December 25, 1991.

My role as explained in the paper presented earlier in this text, was primarily as an observer—close by, if I may say so. But now, let me tell you the story of the conference itself and the interaction that occurred between General Yesin and myself. It is awful, but I do not remember who went first. I do believe it was me, but it does not matter that much as the interaction between the two of us I remember like yesterday.

I presented the story largely drawing from the paper I had already submitted to the Pentagon for clearance. I brought out in detail, however, the moment when my boss had come down to the War Room and opined that only 20 or so minutes remained until execution, so we had better call our spouses and say goodbye. That was so dramatic to the audience that the chair called on my wife who was sitting in the front row of the audience to relate her own side of the call that I made. This too was an emotional moment as Mitchie noted how I called and asked, "What was for supper?" Well, she said she felt extremely odd getting such a question at that time of the day and my voice was not normal. She said she felt something extremely odd and has remembered that moment clearly for the 50 years that had

---

[33] Center for energy and Security Studies, "The Moscow Nonproliferation Conference 2012," August 31, 2012

transpired since. Remember those folks on the surface knew quite well we were in a crisis situation with the Soviets.

When General Yesin began his story, it was one of extreme hardship describing the departure from a port in Crimea and having to stay below deck during the day and only getting out on the deck during the cool of the night. It was chokingly hot in the hole of the ship were most were staying below deck and the closer they got to Cuba the more they worried about being discovered by U.S. air reconnaissance. When he finally got to Sagua La Grande in Santa Clara Province, it was even hotter with extreme humidity.

All work was done at night in conditions with heavy thorns all around. Uniforms and work attire were shredded by the thorns, and often one's skin was also torn. Working only nights, the work progressed so that they had reached operational readiness for their SS-4 Sandal Missile Regiment. People were falling from heat exhaustion and lack of proper food. It was a scene where dedication to duty had produced results, and according to the General, this was done before the first U.S. recognition of work that was underway in other areas.

It was at that point in the narrative that my Russian colleague became quite angry, but he was not angry with me, or the Americans; he was enraged at what Soviet officials, namely First Secretary of the Communist Party and Premier Nikita Khrushchev did with the knowledge that his forces had achieved nuclear capability. He held onto this knowledge so it could be released on November 7, 1962, the 45th Anniversary of the Great October Socialist Revolution. Khrushchev thought it would be impressive indeed to reveal that during the gala celebration of the October revolution that now takes place in November because of the adoption of a new calendar.

Of course, it was too late then. It was like carrying a concealed pistol and not mentioning it in an argument. However, as soon as the foe sees the gun, the atmosphere changes and deterrence begins to have a chance to work its magic.

Our interchange stressed the importance of nuclear arms reduction and nonproliferation there was no doubt. It also pointed out how lucky we were and the importance of good intelligence in any crisis. General Yesin and I have only exchanged correspondence once since then. After Mitchie and I returned to Daejeon, I sent a message saying it was an honor to have our conversation for the benefit of scholars and policymakers. He responded with a very kind note noting how fortunate he felt to have the exchange. I hope he is enjoying life with his grandchildren and waiting for his first great-grandchild. Certainly, I am most grateful to Dr. Anton Khlopkov for arranging this exchange.

That, happily, is not the end of the story, as the next morning Mitchie and I got up early and made an exciting trip to the Moscow Railroad Station to start our trip to St. Petersburg. The station was teaming with people and security lines at several of the major checkpoints. We had our share of baggage and looked somewhat bewildered seeing all the crowds and not knowing the way. Then all of the sudden a middle-aged Asian looking fellow emerged from the mass and said, "Going to the express train to St. Petersburg?" Oh, wonderful fellow! I put one of our bags in his outreached hand and off we went—really running through the station. At every checkpoint at which hundreds of people waited, he waved at the guards, pointed at us and we continued our best to keep up with him.

Soon we reached the modern express to St. Petersburg, mounted our car and found our designated seats in first class and sighed a big sigh of relief. At that point, our wonderful friend from Central Asia held out his hand! He didn't move until I "paid for his services" which amounted to around ninety dollars in Russian Rubles. He smiled, and then I smiled. I said *spacibo Bolshoi* or thanks a lot, shook his hand, and he was off the train. Now, was I taken or not? I would imagine he had to pay off at least three other individuals and we really had just made it. Well, I always say you are willing to pay for good service. This was good and with a smile. I don't regret it, but you can see, I still remember it clearly.

I would also like to say something about the train. It was first class, and we paid, I am sure, enough for the seats, but we have never had such good and complete service on a train—in Japan, South Korea, France, Germany, or China. Shortly after we sat down and the train started to move, the attendant came, arranged our table for eating, and served us one of the best breakfasts I have ever eaten. Of course, we were really tired from getting on the train, but it was truly first class service and almost like I remember from the dining cars on trains in the 1950s in the United States.

After checking in at the hotel, we immediately started our tour of this fabled city. Our first stop was the Peter and Paul Fortress where they were observing a very solemn moment marking the beginning of the 900-day siege by the Nazis. Boom, a cannon fired at noon, and about two hundred new recruits for the Russian Army were sworn into the Service at that moment. As a retired colonel, it was very touching to see these young men take an oath to prevent the recurrence of the tragedy of World War II.

I will not go into the details of our visit. Let it be enough to say it was one of the most marvelous visits to another country that we ever had. Having struggled with the Russian language for four years as a college minor, I really felt I had seen much of what was taught to us by Professor Justina Epp in those years of the Cold War when nothing good was supposed to be found in the Soviet Union. It just makes the point that we must guard against considering all in absolute terms.

Back in South Korea, it was only several weeks, and I was off for Russia again. This time I was not spared having to use the Russian language. But let me tell you the story as I saw it immediately after returning in September 2012. Here is an article I wrote for the *Chungdo Ilbo*, a Korean daily:

Chungdo Ilbo October 13, 2012[34]
A VISIT TO A NEAR NEIGHBOR

Well, you might be asking, which neighbor is he talking about? In truth, I went to Vladivostok, what some call the San Francisco of Russia. Certainly, it was an exciting trip, as my last visit to "Vlad" was in October 1994 when the skies were overcast and gloomy, just as the people—at that time.

First, let me tell you why I was there and then let me share my pleasant experience. I arrived just two weeks after APEC held its Fall 2012 Summit in Vladivostok, so perhaps it was the best time to arrive. The summit was over; people could relax and enjoy the advent of an "Indian Summer" which was really warm, almost hot. (By the way, in America we call a return to warm weather after fall has begun an Indian summer; in Russia, it is called a Grandmother Summer.)

---

[34] Find exact source in the *Chungdo Ilbo*, October 2012.

We were there to take part in the 45th Anniversary Celebration of the Vladivostok State University of Economics and Science. The university has grown to over 20,000 students and marks many important graduates who now have leadership positions in not only the Premorskii Kray area of Russia but European Russia, as well.

Once we arrived and the formal program began—leading up to the grand celebratory meeting to officially mark the 45th Anniversary at 1500 hours that afternoon—the first changes came to light. We were scheduled to tour the downtown area of Vladivostok, but word arrived by the omnipresent cell phones that the head of the Russian Orthodox Church, the Patriarch, was arriving to offer a special religious service in the Old Town City Center. That meant that all streets in and around the City Center would be blocked. (It is a rather common occurrence when a VIP is in a certain district of a city; all roads are closed for security throughout Russia.) The happy alternative was to go to Russia Island, newly joined by a beautiful suspension bridge, and visit the new facilities made for hosting the APEC Summit.

In a sense, this gave us a grand opportunity to see the new Vladivostok, which boasted new roads, new bridges, and a new hotel and conference facilities. And, as an added bonus to our travels, on the way out of town, we were able to see new housing that included multifamily apartment buildings as well as beautiful individual homes. Truly, I was amazed. Still, the infrastructure is not sufficient to meet the insatiable desire for automobiles, but as cars become plentiful, pressure grows from these many car owners for better roads and the entire infrastructure that goes with a more mobile society.

(As an aside, Korean cars are extremely popular in Vladivostok. They are fast replacing Japanese cars. The reason? The Russians drive on the right side of the road—like South Korea—and the tax structure favors cars that are left-hand drive.)

Once we returned from Russia Island, we prepared for the ceremonial meeting to celebrate the anniversary. It was now my time to sweat and breathe deeply because I was going to give quite a bit of my speech in Russian. Was I up to the task? You bet I was! Actually, the story is rather long, but back in history from 1954 to 1958, I studied the Russian language at the Ohio State University where I received my BA in political science. That should not be so difficult if you used your Russian in the interim, but here I was 54 years since I took Russian and never had a real chance to use it. One of my Russian-speaking staff members took me under her wing and helped me prepare in the weeks before this approaching hour. A true angel indeed!

Once I got up on the stage, the lights were so strong that I could not see a soul of the more than 500 officials, faculty, students, and alumni who were there. Actually, that helped. It was like presenting to a light bulb—not hard at all. The audience, not expecting to hear Russian coming from the American president of a Korean university, was taken by surprise and the talk was so well received that afterwards I ended up on TV with the university rector for an interview. Well, it just goes to show you how far a little foreign language use will get you in today's world. The more you use of a nations' language, the better it is.

I would like to close with a comment or two on the comparison of my visit in 1994 and my 2012 visit. First, as you looked into people's eyes, there was a vision of the future. In 1994, as I walked the streets of this famous naval port, I would see sailor after sailor who had only blank stares. The situation was so acute that the Navy could not pay the rent nor the cost of electric and gas for sailors and their families. I had actually seen ships of the Russian Pacific Fleet serving as housing for the families complete with clotheslines hanging from cannons like railings of apartment buildings.

Today those scenes are only memories. The dock area is clean, and the city and port are focused on the future. After the ceremony, the next day we went by modern catamaran ship on a cruise around the port. Everywhere were new buildings and homes and most of the old homes were now reconditioned to bring back the elegance of the long past.

So, if you have an opportunity, a visit to our near neighbor could be quite enjoyable. But don't worry, they speak good English, and the food features abundant seafood. Just remember how to say thank you (*spacibo*) that helps in any language.

* * *

On October 24, in the late afternoon, we held a beautiful ceremony for the honorable Amon Werner, MBA and member of the Austrian Parliament to present him with an honorary degree and cite his major contributions to education within the Austrian context. He was a member of the Austrian People's Party and served as its spokesman for education for many years. One of the things that drew us close to him was his role as President of the Austrian Korean Society and the President of the Austrian Korean Parliamentary Friendship Group. After receiving the honorary doctorate, he spoke to the assembled faculty and students of "One Hundred and Twenty Years—Austria and Korea: A Retrospective Outlook." Of course, while he was in Korea, he spent a good deal of time in Seoul, but we had the honor of hosting him for the degree ceremony and a fine dinner following. Today, we can say a member of the Austrian Parliament carries the Woosong colors and can speak with authority about our school among Austrian academic circles. It was a win-win moment for us all.

One day after the ceremony for Hon. Dr. Werner, I received a note from General Victor Yesin. It means so much to me as you might recall, our conversation at the Moscow conference was sometimes easy to hear without an interpreter. Let me introduce it below in total:

> Dear John and Mitchie,
>
> First of all, let me thank you for your kind letter that touched me deeply.
> As for our joint presentation, it was a great honor for me as well to recollect with you, John, the events of 50 years ago in front of a live audience. I believe we had a wonderful conversation.
> I also hope that we will have the opportunity to meet and talk again. In the meantime, I wish you all the best in your endeavors.
> With the deepest respect and in friendship.
>
> Sincerely,
>
> Gen. Victor Yesin[35]

* * *

Such a warm letter said so much more than was written, and represents once again the importance of face-to-face communication and the ideas underlining such international outreach programs as

---

[35] In my private e-mail file dated October 25, 2012.

Eisenhower's People to People Program. When basic humanity has a chance to break through layers of indoctrination, we can see how the human condition can benefit. I hope this is not the end of the story, but let's see at the end of this commentary.

November and December quietly passed into someone else's account, and we found us welcoming 2013, the Year of the Snake or in Chinese folklore, Year of the Little Dragon.

TWENTY-THREE

The Man of Many Hats

This Year of the Little Dragon started off with a bang that for me created a third hat that I would be wearing for the next year-and-a-half. Our Dean, Jun Yong-wook, who had been the fire and drive for all sorts of things at SolBridge cited "personal reasons" for submitting his letter of resignation. We were all "laid low" by the announcement, as all loved this energetic, outgoing, and free-spirited academic who brought to life everything he touched. It meant that I would be assuming his roles and become "Acting Dean." The problem was, I would not be "acting." It would be for real.

However, as he left SolBridge, he was immediately picked up by King Sejong University in Seoul as their Vice President. We were all proud that we had produced a new vice president and happy it was for a very fine university in the capital. "Woody" as he was called by all, had been with SolBridge for three years and truly had put his stamp on a place that he called "interesting, stimulating, and ultimately rewarding." From the first day that he addressed the students, he took them by the hand and charged up the hill, so to speak, that resulted in a level of energy that permeated the entire institution.

The same response came from the faculty, as well. So, from my standpoint, I was determined to keep the momentum going with both students and faculty and just not be run over in the process. I knew I had giant shoes to fill. Writing now six years later, I am still indebted to this great person who genuinely loves life and can make that trait infectious.

Then, another shoe dropped. That was the news that our Vice President of SolBridge, Dr. Jung Sang-jik after seven years with SolBridge was going to return to the faculty of Woosong University. Of course, it was a move that he so rightly deserved. Dr. Jung had been given the job of getting ready the necessary infrastructure at SolBridge in 2006, so he had been working on the SolBridge experiment since that time. The immediate needs were to start a global search for a new dean and find Dr. Jung's replacement soon. In a sense I was beginning to feel rather exposed—but I had not panicked yet.

To give these two wonderful gentlemen a proper send-off, I sat to compose emails that I would share with them as well as the SolBridge faculty, staff, and student body. News of the departure of these "two giants" was sad, to say the least:

Dear Woody, Faculty, Staff, and Students,

I would like to be the first to publicly and repeatedly thank Dean Jun, our "Woody" for his fabulous three years with us at SolBridge. He put us into high gear, and the entire SolBridge Community got his infectious message and took off running. Thank you, Dean, for inspiring us all to a higher level of commitment and activity. It will be up to all of us to continue the development of SolBridge and the realization of its full potential.

So, while we search for a replacement for Dean Jun over the next months—not an easy task—it will be up to all of us to keep up our high level of involvement and dedication to our missions of teaching, research, and service and ensure our students continue to receive the highest level of education available on this peninsula. Just days ago, we did receive some good news— Woosong and SolBridge were identified by the Ministry of Education as one of 28 universities in all of South Korea to serve as role models for educating foreign students. As you all know, we can do better, and it will be our resolve to do just that and provide the model not only for Korea, but for all of Asia.

As we say "good-bye" to Woody, it is time to put on your thinking caps, scan the horizon, and prepare for the coming semesters. Once again, Dean Jun, thank you from the bottom of my heart for a job well done. May your future at King Sejong University be as successful as your past at SolBridge.

In closing, I added, "With the utmost of our professional respect and in eternal friendship." His time at SolBridge might have been short, but he definitely made a difference that I would like to believe still resonates to this day.

* * *

And then only three days later, I composed another email in response to the news that Vice President Jung was also leaving SolBridge:

Dear Colleagues and Friends of Dr. Jung,

As we read this beautiful message from Dr. Jung to all his friends and associates here at SolBridge, it requires an endorsement that reflects the six years of close interaction with this wonderful gentleman. Permit me to give a little background: When we began negotiating for our move to Daejeon in the spring and summer of 2007, the person who wrote me e-mails and called on the phone was Dr. Jung. When we got off the plane, the person who met us and escorted us to Daejeon was Dr. Jung, and the person who was at our side during all the formative years of SolBridge was Dr. Jung. As he mentions in his note, he began creating the foundation for our school in 2006 and had already established much of the infrastructure when the first faculty arrived in August 2007. To Dr. Jung, we owe so much. It is a debt that we can never repay fully, but it is a debt that we shall try to pay back, not only to Dr. Jung, but to all of South Korea, Korean students, and now, students from around the world.

The good news is Dr. Jung will be only a phone call away—continuing his work in SolAsia, and I hope a chance to work somewhat less than 24/7 365 days a year.

I am sure all who know Dr. Jung and his commitment to SolBridge specifically and education generally, will join with me in thanking him for his service thus far and wish him all the best in the years ahead.

With the utmost respect and in friendship, Dr. Jung, "Thank you."

* * *

So, on the 10th of January, I called a staff and faculty meeting to go over the situation and let them know I would assume the "acting" Dean's role, and that I would need their help and their prayers. They laughed, but I was dead serious. Remember, my academic background is international and security affairs, and now I was going to be back in the vanguard of business education; at 76 would I still be a "fast learner?"

The realization that "acting" is a lot more serious than it looks came only five days later when the new POC or point of contact letter was sent to AACSB headquarters in Florida. Very simply it said that I would be serving as Acting Dean and that I would be attending the "Deans' Conference" in San Antonio the next week and would become the member of record, allowing me to vote on AACSB issues for SolBridge—once we became accredited. Already the "third hat" I was wearing was being put to good use.

Just before leaving for San Antonio, we received the significant news that the Initial Accreditation Committee had accepted our progress report and considered it now appropriate to begin the initial accreditation process. That meant that the "heavy lifting" was about to begin. AACSB would appoint a Peer Review Team Chair to help us develop our Self-Evaluation Report and prepare for a site visit. Actually, it was a great letter, as it gave me the chance while at the Dean's Conference to indicate to AACSB officials and colleagues that SolBridge had not arrived, but was starting the car.

In a sense, it gave me an opportunity to talk with our AACSB Mentor, Dean Craig McAllaster, as well as the Director of AACSB's Asian headquarters, Dr. Elaine Peacock. I also met with "over fifty Deans, and brought back continuing contacts for 26 who were interested in SolBridge." That meeting certainly put "action" into Acting; we were off to the races and as the date became certain for the AACSB team to visit the pace just got faster.

One thing to moderate the pace was put in place by our wonderful student services manager, Ms. Deborah Bang who was always coming up with ideas to bring together our students, as well as our faculty and staff. This time her idea was "Cake Time" to bring together those having birthdays in the same month together to celebrate and have some moments of light-hearted conversation on the last day of the month. Later, we changed it to the first day, but the result was the same. Good cake and conversation. Anyone could come who had a friend who was having a birthday that month; it became so popular that eventually, we had to charge 1000 won roughly a dollar to help somewhat with the cost. We had a simple format, Deborah would introduce me, we all would introduce those with birthdays, and we ate the cake. About fifteen minutes later everyone went their own way or went to the coffee shop to continue discussions that had come up having cake. I must admit, when we stopped being around 700 students and generally crept up to almost 1200, we discontinued the practice.

Another thing that crept up was my weight. I was sorry to see this social function discontinued, but it was fun while it lasted. Who said you can't have your cake and eat it too?

Also in early February, we received the good news that three of our professors were asked by the Foreign Ministry to become "Honorary Envoys." They would serve as informal advisors to the government, possibly serve as a sounding board for various international initiatives. Why was this such a big deal to SolBridge? Only 16 appointments were made. Hankuk University of Foreign Studies (HUFS) was first with four appointments, but SolBridge was second. The list of universities with only one appointment is impressive: Seoul National, Yonsei, Korea, KAIST, Dong-A, Konkook, Ewha, UINIST, and Pukyong. The new guy on the block was coming through, and I could not have been more pleased.

Soon after, I received a letter from a former Korean Ambassador who was starting a discussion group to encourage dialog across gender, age, and national background. His new organization was appropriately named the Korea *Sarang Bang*, roughly the Korea Discussion Society. The name has a very historic precedence as in the later years of the Choson dynasty a special room was set aside for high-ranking guests often from overseas, to meet and discuss matters in a westernized social setting with Korean counterparts. *Sarang* in Korean means love, as well, so it had an auspicious name. I met some wonderful people from many walks of life in Korea, but it was a very good example of how difficult it can be to bridge the differences in age groups. This was one of those times, and after two years of sometimes unbelievable exchanges between members, it was disbanded. It brought to mind the *Doctor Strangelove* moment when the U.S. President shouts, "There is no fighting in the War Room!" In this case, it was more like, "There is no fighting in the Love Room" (*Sarang Bang*).

As the year got well underway, I received an invitation to visit the National University of Tainan on March 18. Now, I had been at SolBridge for going on five years and had received many invitations to visit schools all over Asia, so why was this invitation different? I had served on an Inspector General Inspection trip to 13th Air Force at Clark Air Base in the Philippines and went to see its forward-deployed aircraft sitting alert on an airbase in Taiwan which was located in Tainan. We are getting into ancient history at this point, but it was after I was assigned to PACAF headquarters and had become a targeting office, so perhaps 1961 or 1962. It was after the Taiwan Straits Crisis, but near enough to be able to feel the real tension that still remained. I remember doing my inspection and having great interaction with the detachment officers, who despite our inspection mission, were happy to have a visit from Hawaii, the headquarters. I must say in 2013, I found little trace of former times, in fact, I did not even step foot on the base. But what I could see was that the area had prospered, a major museum was under construction, and the city looked to the west with a little less concern than before, but was known as a hotbed of support for the PPT—the political advocates of an independent Taiwan.

During the middle of March 2013, we received an alert that my wife and I were going to be invited to visit the Kanda University of International Studies (KUIS) in the Makuhari region of Tokyo. One of our staff, Tomonari Takachi who graduated from KUIS was setting up the meeting which would include a tree planting ceremony, a special lecture by me for the students, and, of course, plenty of good food for the old Colonel. It was hard to say no. In fact, never for a moment did I think that that hill was too hard to climb. I set myself to preparing a lecture that I thought all would have an interest in. Of course, I started writing about the Limited Nuclear Weapon's Free Zone for Northeast

Asia—always an appropriate topic for a Japanese audience—I would hope, all audiences.

By the end of March, I received another surprise from Deborah Bang that Woosong University Sport's Day would feature the "Dr. Endicott's Cup." Well, I was quite taken with the idea as I had played the right back position when I went to school in London in 1950. And I really enjoyed watching our SolBridge team take on the teams of the more established colleges. It's another rewarding part of my job to preside over such events with our students. And I'm sure it's just as much a treat for our students as it is for me. Of course, the Sports Management Department usually won at the end of the day, but sometimes over the years, our Uzbek students can surprise everyone. But Sports Day is such a wonderful tradition, and here in South Korea, it is maintained with vigor. My only problem is the kick I have to do for the championship game on the final day of Sports Day (always two days long). It seems to get more uninspiring each year.

(As I write at 83, I dread the next kick as it only serves to announce to all how old I am.)

April brought the good news that we had two professors who were promoted to full professor. As you might guess that is a very tough rank to attain and in our system takes about six years at assistant professor, six or seven as associate professor and then four or so to full, It really takes about ten years to make full, and then there are several more to full tenured professor. Professors Rao Kowtha and Chia Hsing Huang were our two, and we feted them and spread the news far and wide.

On May 25, 2013, I was invited to Seoul National University, the school that combines Harvard, Princeton, and Yale for most Koreas to participate in a conference—the First International Conference on Human Completion and Education—that was reviewing the human condition and its relation to education. Of course, in South Korea education is accompanied by a regime of stress cycles broken by intensive private school preparation and stress again. It is so intense, some students just decide to opt out of the competition, still worse, some decide to opt out of life.

In this environment, I was asked to speak and address the quest for "happiness" in a world complicated by the need for educational excellence. To answer this call, I prepared the following paper which I include as an example of what academics do in their "free time:"

"Human Completion and Education—the Need for Creative Innovation."

First, may I thank the organizers of today's meeting and the opportunity to think about a subject close to the core of society and its capability to cope with the challenges of the 21st Century. When first asked by Professor Lee to accept this assignment, I was not sure he was asking the right person—I'm still not sure. But I have truly enjoyed turning away for the moment from daily responses dictated by operational necessities to consider what I should be considering in the first place. So today I am calling on you to "Ask the Mind about Happiness and Education in Korea."

Humans, in order to be complete, should be as free from stress as possible, at least that is my proposition. The situation in Korea is complicated by the inordinate stress associated with the current demands imposed by the desire to have the best education possible. Recently, in a report issued by Statistics Korea, the toll on the youth was seen as severe. Suicide as of 2011 was listed as the number one cause of death among the ages 15-24. (*Korea Herald*, May 3, 2013, p.3) While pressures from education cannot be blamed for all these tragedies, we can acknowledge that it is a major component.

Additionally, we see in the recently published study by the McKinsey Global Institute (Beyond Korean Style: Shaping a new growth formula)[36] that the desire for the best education is coming in conflict with the increased cost of housing, fewer "good jobs" and the limitless range of educational goals that can move ever upward: good, better, best elementary, middle and high school pressures; SKY, Princeton, Harvard, Yale, Oxford, Cambridge, etc. All pressed forward with the backdrop being: "happy wife-happy life." Start with a great university, find the perfect job along with the perfect wife, and experience the happy life. That is human completion in the Korean context. Or is it?

---

[36] "Beyond Korean style: Shaping a new growth formula." Retrieved from http://www.mckinsey.com/featured-insights/asia-pacific/beyond-korean-style.

The McKinsey Study and this is not a brief for that company, just that they are relevant, shows that the increase in housing costs along with the increase in education costs act as a gigantic vice squeezing the middle class into greater and greater desperation—as the number of "good jobs" continues to contract. Of course "good jobs" are those that come with National Health Insurance, appear at least to offer long-term employment, and are usually in the large internationally competitive corporations. High costs and scarce "good jobs" are observables—causing young couples to delay marriage or forsake it all together with those who do marry waiting to the ever-so-close 40 years of age when risks of birth defects increase, and female fertility drops considerably. In fact, a poll indicated that more than 60 percent of respondents noted that the burden of education and child care were causing them to delay marriage. (McKinsey, p. 30).

With the advanced economic sector unable to provide good jobs for a productive middle-class life, McKinsey suggests some reforms especially the vitalization of SMEs to offer good job growth. Attitudes toward entrepreneurialship need to change, long-term financing for housing needs to be available and ultimately increased vocational training options as in the Meister Schools need to be adopted.

This last recommendation for vocational training resonates in my mind with the happiness associated with my own childhood memories. My father was a vocational arts teacher in the Cincinnati Public School System. In those days, both vocational training and college prep coexisted within the middle and high schools. In my high school career, besides taking the normal college preparatory classes, I took electric shop, woodworking shop, print shop, and industrial drawing. Can you imagine setting type, inking the press plates, slip sheeting the copies and having a sense of great pride when a beautiful wedding invitation was printed? Dirty hands, sweat, the smell of printer's ink, and the loud noise of the printing presses are there right in front of me, even today. Can you imagine getting the same satisfaction out of a Xerox machine? Please, no offense meant Xerox, but it is the march of progress and inevitable automation of the workforce that we are dealing with, isn't it? My father, again, wrote his

Master's Degree Thesis for the University of Cincinnati on the Coming Era of Automation. That was, I believe, in the early 1950s.

In April, presidents of the Council of Private Universities met in Onyang for our regular meeting to discuss the state of education, especially private education in South Korea today. As part of the agenda, we toured the massive Samsung Complex in that city where the flat-screen panels are manufactured for their products. We saw huge automated and highly sophisticated machines but very few workers. When the working day is over, I wonder about the sense of satisfaction and happiness?

I must insert an aside in my commentary at this point to describe one part of the briefing that all the presidents received while visiting Samsung. The briefer kept referring to the progress being made in SDI. SDI was mentioned many times, and I was totally confused. As you may know, I spent 31-years in the defense community in the United States—28 in the Air Force and three as the Director of the Institute for National Strategic Studies of the National Defense University. For those in the audience who remember the 1980s, SDI was short for the Strategic Defense Initiative—Star Wars as it was commonly called. All I could do was think that Samsung was now going into space, not only space but Star Wars space.

Knowing that I was the only one who did not know what SDI meant in the Samsung context, I had to ask. You can imagine I was much relieved to find out SDI means Samsung Digital Interface.

It was when The McKinsey Study started using some very familiar terminology that I really started to like what they were saying. The study opined that one of the most important things Korea can do is "Curb the Education Arms Race" (McKinsey, p. 47). The study pointed out that South Korea spends more on education than all other OECD members, but one. Although individual households spend 9% of their income on education, the public education system is perceived to fail in preparing students for university entrance exams and employment. Finally, the report claimed that the total cost of a college education makes technical or vocational training a "better lifetime bargain" because "the unemployment rate for college graduates exceed that of vocational school graduates"(McKinsey, pp. 47-48).

To counter all these negatives the study recommends, among other things, a greater use of vocational training, increased investment in vocational training and alternative education tracks. In addition, integrating the Meister high schools into a dual-track system; strengthening the service sector to create more high-quality jobs; and recognizing that health care, social welfare, and tourism will have the highest potential to produce "good jobs" (McKinsey, pp. 50-52).

One of their suggestions for a new growth model for South Korea was to increase the number of two income earners in each household. That means putting both spouses to work. In OECD the average is 57% of households both husband and wife work. In Korea, it is only 44 percent. I am not sure that is on the same "search for happiness" track that we are on or not. (McKinsey, p. 71.)

Against this backdrop that focuses on the pressures of education that thwart the realization of happiness, Woosong University and its all English language colleges have attempted to enter the picture with several initiatives that will reduce the need to travel overseas to get an American-style education. The SolBridge curriculum addresses the development of soft skills leading to the development of critical thinking. Hopefully, these initiatives will moderate the keen completion issue somewhat.

In 2007, we created the SolBridge International School of Business, and we started with 29 students and eight professors— including myself. At this point, SolBridge International School of Business at Woosong University has approximately 700 students from 32 different countries. Slightly over 30% are Korean, 30% are Chinese, roughly 10% each for Russia, Kazakhstan, and Vietnam and lesser percentage figures for the other 27 nations present. The faculty—of roughly 40 full-time professors—comes from 13 different nations. Of course, all instruction is in English except foreign languages (all international students take Korean, and all Korean students take Chinese). That is for our BBA; MBA students are encouraged to take the Korean language but are not required to. Of course, if they wish to stay in South Korea working for an internationally oriented firm, they had better speak Korean. That is a matter of life of which we do make them aware.

At SolBridge we have 2+2 and 1+1 agreements with universities throughout the world. To meet the requirements of possible host universities our first two years are aligned with the first two at Georgia Tech for those in the Georgia Tech track. While we have introduced an international environment right there in Daejeon—potentially saving the strapped middle class the thousands of dollars required to go to the States for higher education, we do face the fact that we are engaged in trying to curb the impassioned education arms race that is endemic to South Korea. We are trying our best.

One of the most successful ingredients in our curriculum is the focus on "soft skills"—the ability to think creatively, be innovative, use case studies, work as a team member, be comfortable in diverse cultural situations, and speak more than one language. Of these soft skills, one is particularly valuable in the Asian context as memorization skills are extremely highly developed. Taking memorized facts and using them in a competitive setting such as a debate has proven to be an extremely successful way to draw students out of their naturally shy nature. Moreover, these skills reinforce team building, enable one to think on their feet and help to build useful self-esteem.

While debate has been a great tool in helping SolBridge students within our college, an even more exciting development has been taking place over the last two years, and it started off as a voluntary activity of one of our young law professors from Harvard, Professor Joshua Park, took his love of debate to the neighboring city of Osan. His enthusiasm resulted in a general infection among the teachers of Osan—that has a total of 25 schools within its system including 2 high schools. In an MOU signed in April, the City of Osan and SolBridge are cooperating with up to 30 students from SolBridge assisting the teachers in integrating debate into their daily lives. Interschool debate competitions are highlighted. It is a healthy joint activity where the City provides internship opportunities and the students get to sell their own product, debate, and serve the community as well.

I personally know debate works: as a 15-year-old sophomore in high school, my debate teacher gave me an assignment which I readily welcomed. My assignment: defend the tactics, methods, and philosophy of the then Senator Joseph McCarthy of the state of Wisconsin.

My parents, God bless them, were strong supports of Senator Robert A. Taft of Ohio another solid right-wing conservative. So being a loyal son, I reflected their opinions completely. I was given two weeks to do the research and build my case in defense. I can still recall working with the Carnegie librarian as we gathered information and worked countless hours. The more we got into the work, the more I realized I was in deep trouble. When the day of the debate came, I lost big. No greater defeat that year than Endicott's defense of Senator McCarthy. But do you know who the real winner was? Yes, John Endicott. I learned to make my opinions by fact and not political emotion. It was one of the most important lessons I ever had.

Let me say one more thing about Osan and our debate experiment: When Professor Joshua Park began the program, it came under some criticism from critics who called this just another program for the elite and well off. I will let Joshua tell this story completely in a forthcoming academic paper, but let me tease you with this story.

A group of disaffected and uninterested students was put together and offered a chance to form a debate team. They accepted, and the change has been remarkable. They are good citizens, their self-esteem has gone up, they are interested in school, studying and doing well in the debates. I'll go no further here, but I am excited as well as Professor Park. Now there is a road to happiness that I can endorse, and it came through innovation in education. If I were to look at Maslow's Hierarchy of Needs, I could see quite a few being met in this experiment. If that can be aligned with human completion, we may be on a very right track. I am hoping this feature will help in the effort to realize human completion even in the educational arena.

I should not ignore two other initiatives done at Woosong in the last several years: the creation of a Nursing School in 2009 and the expansion of SolAsia School of Asian Management—our

Korean language business and management college—to include an Open Degree Program and a feature we call "Education on Demand."

The Nursing School was added after looking at the increased demand for health care associated with the aging of South Korea's population. It was seen as the right time for a new (or additional) Woosong specialization. The first class of 29 students was enrolled in 2009, but the head of the program insisted that this should not be the same nursing curriculum available throughout Korea, but one that set new standards and set expectations extremely high. All students were to study English at the same time as they prepared for a nursing career. The point being, almost limitless career opportunities would be available if the nurses could perform in both Korean and English.

A dedicated dorm was established for nursing students, and the curriculum was designed to require roughly 11 hours a day contact time. Each day featured English classes, as well as more at night. One student was admitted to the program with only a 200 TOEIC score—barely possessing English survival skills. By the end of this intense program, she scored over 800. The entire class in its first year decided not to participate in Sports Day activities, but use that time to study English. Now I do not consider this a stress-free environment, but when graduation came all 29 were placed in excellent hospitals in the Seoul area, all passed their Korean Nursing Certificate, and all are scheduled to take the American Nursing Exam later this year from either Guam or Hong Kong.

Finally, as we look at using the university to meet some of the challenges identified by McKinsey, let me comment about our initiatives in the SolAsia School of Asian Management. In this college, we have 1500 students: 1200 are Korean and 300 Chinese. We have inserted the notion of an "Open Degree." The student studies for two years and then on selecting a major he or she is interested in, takes courses that will fulfill graduation requirements. Built into this program is an "education on demand" feature. Having memos of understanding with various corporate and business interests, students are matched with the needs of industry/business and given necessary training or internship opportunities so upon graduation they can immediately meet the needs of the corporate world. It is a nice blend of a college degree and vocational expertise. We are currently expanding the relationships with the corporate community to realize a full win-win situation. It is a "work in progress."

As a person who spent many of his years in the military, there are a few comments I would like to make that relate to our quest for security both here in South Korea and America and the impact of this effort on the notion of human completion. I entered the Air Force in 1958—and can claim certainly to be an old Cold Warrior. I was in the underground bunker of SAC Headquarters during the 1962 Cuban Missile Crisis as a strategic planner, served in Vietnam and flew on 50 combat missions. As Chief of Target Plans in 5th AF Headquarters (Tokyo) I was very much involved in the U.S. response to the North Korean attack on the Blue House and seizure of the USS *Pueblo* in January 1968. In April 1969, I was at Misawa AB as the Chief of Staff for Intelligence when the EC-121 intelligence plane was shot down by North Korean fighter planes on the birthday of Kim Il-sung, and was the Deputy Air Force Representative to the Military Staff Committee of the United Nations Security Council when the Soviets invaded Afghanistan. It was a busy career that took me to the very end of the Cold War. I ended my 31-year career as the Director of the Institute for National Strategic Studies in Washington, D.C. In 1989 and began my 20-year career at Georgia Tech.

These events are listed as they help demonstrate some of the basic reasons South Korea and the United States are organized the way they are when it comes to security. In Korea, because of the almost constant threat from its neighbor to the north since 1953, we must observe that its impact on human completion is considerable. As a university professor, I can say that some of the influences are positive. For example, a large portion of college-age males choose to start college upon graduation from high school, and after two years take a leave of absence to complete their military obligation.

I am sure many will agree, they go away from school as boys and come back as men. After their time in the service, they become focused students with a professionalism that is impressive. (As the President of Woosong University, I must add, however, there can be tragedy. When the Corvette *Cheonan* was sunk in 2010 two of our students who were on leave were victims. It was and still is a tragedy we can never forget.)

War and the organization imposed on society to deter or prepared for war I would maintain weighs heavily on efforts to reach the highest levels of human completion. With this in mind, I would like to close out my session with you today with some comments on a concept that came out of the ivory towers of university reflection but was based on years of experience. It has very much to do with our collective response to help remove the aspect of "threat" from our peninsula. For many who know me well, you will understand this effort as part of my own human completion effort. It refers to a concept conceived in 1991 aimed to reduce the dangers of nuclear war in Northeast Asia and create a cooperative security system that is beneficial to all participants.

Let me make it clear, the notion of nuclear free zones has existed for some time, in fact, the first one formally was signed on February 14, 1964, at Tlatelolco, in Mexico City, and it covered the nations of Latin America. Such zones have been proposed several times during the Cold War—even for Northeast Asia, but in the case of NEA, such ideas were usually dead on arrival as it is, after all, an area where major nuclear weapons' powers exist or have special interests.

One of the reasons nuclear free zones have had difficulties in NEA is the basic definition of a zone: it must be an area totally free of nuclear weapons, no presence, no storage, no manufacture, no entry, and no transit. In essence, all the prohibitions that one could imagine. Thus, while Latin America, the South Pacific, Southeast Asia, Africa, Antarctica, and Central Asia, plus Mongolia as a declared nuclear weapons free state, have general restrictions, NEA has China, Russia, and the United States as recognized nuclear weapons powers and the DPRK as aspiring. Northeast Asia cannot be a weapons free zone until the big powers agree to a total ban on nuclear weapons and that is not likely in the near future. The answer, as far as this individual is concerned, is to geographically limit the scope of the first stage of such an agreement and work on the other details such as: included weapons, intrusive inspection agreements and procedures, staffing, administrative oversight and ultimately location of a functioning secretariat that eventually could serve as a regional in-being "first responder" and conflict resolution center.

In this sense, this concept could be a natural out-growth or even precursor of a Northeast Asia Peace Initiative as suggested by President Park Geun-hye (*Yonhap News Agency*, April 24, 2013). It could develop as part of the "Seoul process," similar to the Helsinki process which played such a great role in the ultimate termination of the Cold War.

The basic thrust of the LNWFZ-NEA is to bring all states into an arms control dialog which would limit or control nuclear weapons in China, Russia, and the United States and ensure their elimination completely from Japan, the ROK, the DPRK, and the ROC. All parties would benefit as included within the negotiating framework are extensive discussions of economic development programs for all with special economic and developmental incentives for the DPRK to join in the process.

Let me tell you, it is not a new process. It began in 1991, was presented in Washington, D.C., and then Beijing to an international conference in 1992. At the international conference in Beijing, attended by non-official specialists from all the nations of NEA, the concept was well received by all participants except those from the PRC. The head of the Chinese delegation, a Member of the People's Congress basically denounced the concept and all associated with it. However, at our next meeting—a year later at Georgia Tech—during the first week of March 1993 with representatives from China, Japan, and the United States, the same PRC representative who denounced me in Beijing toasted the idea as one now deserving of "positive" review. I was truly pleased, but not until a week later did I realize its real significance.

A week later the DPRK announced its intention to withdraw from the NPT! It was obvious that the Chinese team knew in advance what was about to happen and was sending a distinct signal that they did not welcome a NEA with a nuclear-armed North Korea.

The story since then has been long and has involved numerous retired diplomats, military officers, academics and official observers from Argentina, China, Finland, France, Japan, South Korea, Mongolia, Russia, and the United States. Canada and North Korea participated on a less frequent basis. Basically, North Korea would join or try to join whenever the meeting was in China. It was our practice to meet at the New York DPRK United Nations Mission to de-brief them when they did not attend our plenaries.

I will not go into the details of the 13 plenary meetings as I am only trying to indicate that universities can play innovative roles in contributing to the quest for human completion. But do permit me to say we have had meetings in Buenos Aires, Bordeaux, Moscow, Helsinki, Tokyo, Beijing, Seoul, Ulaanbaatar, Jeju-do, Shanghai, Tokyo, Daejeon, and Toulouse. Several other meetings are of special interest as one got us all really started and another brought us very close to the resolution of U.S.-DPRK issues.

The first meeting of special mention was a five-week session held at Georgia Tech from January to March 1995. At that meeting, a 4-star retired ROK General, a 3-star retired Japanese General, a 2-star retired Russian General, a recognize academic from the PRC and myself met to draft the first set of principles that became the basis of negotiations that survives even to today. It was a very difficult period, but finally, a general agreement was reached which we took to the arms control communities in Boston, New York, San Francisco, and Washington, D.C. We then followed with the 13 plenaries mentioned above. The most recent plenary was held at the University of Toulouse in October 2010.

The second major meeting that was not a plenary occurred in 2000 when we had bilateral meetings with representatives of the DPRK in March and October. One was in Atlanta and the other in New York. In both sessions, it seemed that relations between the DPRK and the U.S. were about to be normalized, but in the end, President Clinton decided not to go to Pyongyang and meet with Kim Jung Il. He turned to work on Middle Eastern issues and assumed his successor, President George W. Bush would resume where he left off. Nothing of the kind occurred, and for two years negotiations lay fallow giving birth, however, to the Axis of Evil.

Of course, I am so involved in this idea that I must step back and take a better look. We all know that the current DPRK leadership has turned away from negotiations and the Kaesong Industrial Complex stands idle with the last of South Korean personnel leaving on May 4th.

Where does this leave us in our search for human completion? I believe a long way from our goal. The overarching impact of our need for security currently stands in the way of reaching our goal of ultimate human completion. But that should not limit our actions as we attempt to deal with the numerous other issues that remain to be resolved.

Let us solve those that we can resolve by actions within this nation. Education as a complicating factor in human completion is something we can handle and solve by ourselves. Things like the security imperative are more difficult as more state actors are involved, and they do not necessarily share our values or our views. That is the nature of the beast. Perhaps we should take heart in the saying by the Chinese scholar, Luo Guanzhong, who wrote the 14th Century *Romance of the 3 Kingdoms*: "It is a general truism of this world that anything long divided will surely unite, and anything long united will surely divide."

While this may indeed be the case, let us take a more active role in helping to solve all the barriers that stand in the way of human completion. Let us dedicate ourselves to alleviate those pressures that we can address whatever the sector, and hope that human completion can be moved forward in our own lifetime.

Thank You.

*   *   *

Having made the above presentation and sat down to observe the rest of the day, it soon became evident that I had completely misunderstood the objective of the meeting. Speaker after speaker (all Korean so they read the memo) rose to present on the effectiveness of meditation and the way to overcome all sorts of stress by using meditation. Well, it was clear that we don't understand everything when we think we do. I should have meditated on my paper perhaps a little bit more before launching into a twenty-minute discussion on all sorts of items that need to be addressed by society to reduce our stress!

The Youth Dream University Survey

I have given this part of my book a subtitle, as this was one of the most important developments for Woosong University since its creation in 1995. The consulting firm, Deloitte, plus the *Dong-A Ilbo*, one of South Korea's leading daily newspapers and a Seoul-based television firm, *Channel A*, teamed up to conduct a nationwide survey to determine the best universities judging their student support, employment rate after graduation and overall education quality. "Woosong received high points overall and ranked 1st in student activities and 3rd for support of various extracurricular activities." In short, Woosong University was ranked among the top ten universities in Korea that included such renowned institutions as Seoul National University, Yonsei University, Korea University, and Sogang University. To say that we were pleased does not come anywhere near the euphoria that we experienced. It was recognition that we were doing some things right, but of course, in line with satisfaction categories new to the ranking systems normally found in the academic world. More significantly, we were the only university outside of Seoul to be in the top ten.

We were so pleased that we held a university festival to celebrate the news, and we had it on May 29, 2013, and I was particularly pleased as that is my son John II's birthday, who was born on this day in 1964. You might be interested to know that a copy of that newspaper report is framed and in my presidential office at Woosong Headquarters. It literally put us on the map.

*   *   *

Early in June, I received a message from the Dean of the Turner College of Business of Columbus State University in Columbus, Georgia, Dr. Linda Hadley, who had agreed to be the chair and leader of the AACSB site visit that would occur in May. She was informing us that she would come to visit us before the team visit for our initial accreditation review.

Almost at the same time that we were discussing a visit from the designated team leader, we were negotiating with two experts of the AACSB process so that we could have a "mock" inspection done by knowledgeable individuals before the actual official team visit. Dr. Randy Boxx and Dr. Jerry Trapnell were getting ready to visit us in mid-June 2013 to put us through a tough practice that would involve all SolBridge participants, faculty, staff, students, and members of our Corporate Advisory Council. Here we were a good 11 months before the official visit getting everyone ready and on board for the final show.

Perhaps we were showing some degree of absolute concern/fear as we were also discussing with another experienced AACSB authority, Dr. Murray Dalziel, of Liverpool University in England about his visit to help us prepare as well. He ended up being the third paid advisor to come to SolBridge which took place finally in August. The reader might think we engaged in over-kill as far as getting ready for our official on-site visit for initial accreditation. Perhaps my military background was showing through my academic gown. (There is a great story in Japanese history when the famous samurai Yoshitsune was fleeing for his life with his faithful assistant Saitō Musashibō Benkei, who was a priest. When they came to a checkpoint, one of the guards had noticed that beneath Yoshitsune's monk's robe, his armor glistened. Benkei realized they were about to be undone and broke into an elaborate dance to distract everyone's attention. In this case, perhaps you can see the old Colonel still holds to certain military practices of caution.)

In early June, my wife and I made an official visit to Kanda Foreign Studies University in Tokyo. It was a fabulous visit which gave me an opportunity to discuss at length with possibly as many as 300 students my involvement in the effort to introduce the Limited Nuclear Weapons' Free Zone concept throughout Asia. We planted a tree that represented the bond between Kanda and Woosong/SolBridge had several meetings with faculty and staff, and then went off on a two day trip to British Hills of Kanda Gaigo. Several hours north of Tokyo and not too far from Fukushima, Kanda University had a campus in the mountains that looked every bit like a small village in England. It was a campus to facilitate English studies and had a great manor house, great regal hall—right out of Harry Potter, a series of dorm buildings that reminded me of the Tudor and other eras famous for British literature, a magnificent pub and a village café for light dining. I felt like I had returned to London and gone on a weekend trip to the Cotswold's. This is not a commercial for the operation, but if I needed to get away and find a place to write my memoirs, that would be the place. Of course, I can always "get away" in my mind; here, I pause in my narrative for two wonderful weeks of fish and chips, bangers for breakfast with oatmeal and spotted dick pudding for dessert—didn't even know I was gone, did you? Although poetic license allows me to embellish here and there, do believe me when I note that all the buildings were constructed in Britain, disassembled, shipped to Japan, reassembled, and now serve as one of the best academic retreats I have ever seen in my life.

Another great visit happened in June, but that was from my son-in-law, Gregory Noble, and his son Nick. They arrived at the end of June and my wife and I dropped everything and became tour guides for the next week. Not only showing them Daejeon and its environs but also hopped over to Japan and did all we could do to visit Tokyo and Kyoto. With their visit, we had completed the first orientation tours for all our extended family. Charlene, our daughter, brought our two granddaughters (twins), John II, our son, brought his wife, Virginia, and their son, John Charles, and now Greg had brought Nicholas. It was wonderful as when we visited Japan—part of all their visits, we were able to introduce them to cousins and uncles and aunts that they had only seen in pictures and the stories told around the dinner table at night.

As we got into August, it is our normal time to return to the States and bond with our family in Atlanta. This particular August while we were on vacation, the Woosong staff in conjunction with a commercial mover, moved us from one apartment to another. This time we moved into an apartment in the Paragon complex, a very nice place on the 16th floor with a pretty good view.

Once our vacation was over, we had the visit from Dean Murray Dalziel who did a very impressive review of our preparations for the coming on-site visit. He gave us a five-page report of things we had to do to set us apart from other similar schools in Asia. A great review, but it only caused a lot of faculty members to burn the midnight oil to meet his recommendations. We all agreed that his assessment was a valuable planning document to help us succeed. His visit took place only several weeks after we received the official notice from AACSB about the date of the initial accreditation visit. It was set from March 23-26, 2014. We now knew the three-member team composition, and we had things to do. All along, our great mentor, Craig McAllaster, was also keeping us on the straight and narrow. He stressed the need to take the Dalziel Report to heart and "move quickly on our journey."

At this point in the narrative, I have to address one of the less successful moments of my tenure in South Korea. I very much wanted to support our faculty who were working on doctorate degrees, and one of our young professors approached me about financial support for his work. I had always wanted to do it but did not have the chance. I talked it over with our financial guys, and we worked out a deal where we would pay for half of his expenses with the expectation that he would stay with us after completion. Alas, it ran afoul of cultural and traditional expectations of a doctoral candidate in Korean schools. Much time was expected of our candidate to help his "mentor" with various projects that his mentor wished done. Considerable criticism came from his mentor about the time away from the Korean college to do Woosong requirements, as in teaching his proper course load—that had been reduced as part of the deal.

Finally, when our junior professor found himself being publicly criticized for spending too much time at Woosong, we all decided that this was a good idea that would not work. Our professor (actually instructor) left and is now pursuing his Ph.D. in Australia. I hope he will come back when finished, as we all miss him tremendously, but there are some things that we must set aside and wait for the appropriate moment in life; this was one of those. I hope he reads our plea.

As the Fall Semester opened, my colleague, Jeffrey Miller, and I, set out again to teach American History together. You will probably realize that team teaching in the case of the president of the university is a good idea. The reason, of course, is the Ministry of Education requirement that if an instructor misses a class, it must be made up by meeting in the evening, on a Saturday, or even on Sunday. I received so many calls for events that conflict with our scheduled class that our students would be forever attending make-up classes. Not a good option—for either students or teacher. So, we took the team approach, and the show goes on, wherever Endicott happens to be.

John E. Endicott

(You might ask, why does Endicott teach at all if that is what is happening? Well, having a regular opportunity to interact with students leads to all sorts of interesting outcomes, most of which are good, all of which are useful. Besides keeping me abreast of what is happening in my field, it allows me to hear things from students that I would never hear from my office on the 12th floor of the SolBridge building; so American History in the Fall and Politics of East Asia in the Spring.)

One of the things we did that was always fun for the instructors and humbling for the students was to pass out an American History Pre-test on the first day of classes. We provided one page of questions about American history—roughly 20—that we felt were things they should know by the end of the 15 weeks. Some of our students who studied in the U.S. at some time in their life usually got two or three correct; they were the stars. It was always a quiet moment when the class realized how much was to be done. As educators, it allowed us to know the entering level of our students, and at the end of the year the final would tell us "the rest of the story." In a sense, it was a fine "assurance of learning" procedure.

In late September, the orientation visit by Dean Linda Hadley of Columbus State University took place. It is AACSB policy that all team leaders should visit the school undergoing an initial accreditation review ahead of that review for a necessary orientation. That was the purpose of her visit, and she had full run of SolBridge from September 28 to October 2. When we received the out brief just before she left, she reviewed what she had seen and set out the items we had best spend a little time on before next spring. In short, it was an extremely valuable visit for the reviewer as well as ourselves.

Not long after Dr. Hadley had returned, my wife called the women of SolBridge together for her regular "coffee talk" sessions that she has every semester to keep the faculty wives and female professors in contact with each other and abreast of what is going on in the school. You probably realize no matter how the dean or I try to get messages sent home to waiting wives, the conduit is not always reliable. This is actually a very vital mission for our school, as we are somewhat like a diplomatic mission that is operating in a foreign land and morale of all hands is something to worry about. At the same time, it reminded me of the great sacrifices my wife had made as an Air Force spouse and the challenges that came with the assignments I took. As always, I am in my wife's debt for not just being there for me, but for the burden she has also had to carry. I am sure you know the ancient truism handed down by wise men of all ages: "A happy wife is a happy life." With Mitchie teaching Japanese and helping out with the "coffee talk" sessions, she was extremely busy and appreciated by her husband.

Another related story involves a small Thanksgiving gathering that Mitchie and I had at our apartment. We sent out invitations to several colleagues to join us for Thanksgiving dinner. For us, it was to be a Thanksgiving lunch, as it is just easier for folks to visit during the day. We had guests from Pakistan, the United States, South Korea, and Japan and took the precaution to avoid foods that were not eaten by Muslims as quite a few of our guests were. Well, we had not purchased food from a *halal* authorized store, and we found out, to our consternation that for these particular guests that was important. However, it turned out that our guests anticipated exactly what we did and brought their own food and enough for all. It was a moment that drove home something faculty, staff, and students do every day at SolBridge—embracing cultural diversity. It turned out to be a wonderful Thanksgiving while at the same time letting us know that in the future to ask guests beforehand if they have any dietary restrictions.

Around this same time, we received the itinerary for the mock inspection visit from our team of Randy Boxx and Jerry Trapnell. They would arrive in mid-January and stay until the 23rd. They sent an exhaustive list of all the things they wanted to see and do. One of the more humorous items on the list was a request to see the Provost/Acting Dean and then the President. I wrote back that one person was currently wearing all those hats. It would be easy.

Shortly after Christmas, we received a further six-page letter containing all the specific questions they had and wanted to answer during their stay. We all were equipped with our collective tasks and prepared for the January visit. Mitchie and I did get back to Marietta to celebrate Christmas and returned to open the school on Friday, January 3, 2014. We were now getting ready for the most challenging year of our existence as a business school, and we were hoping for the best.

TWENTY-FOUR

A Year of Mixed Emotions

Our first month of 2014 was characteristically busy: a visit from the President of Tuft's University, Anthony P. Monaco; a mock team visit from consultants we hired with AACSB experience; and the coordination of a visit to Australia by our Chairman.

The visit by President Monaco was delightful as he met with possible funders for his many international programs under the Tufts flag. The venue was particularly interesting, as he was invited to host a major reception at the Kim Koo Museum in the Namsan region of Seoul. It is a beautiful facility and honors one of Korea's foremost "freedom fighters." In fact, he was in consideration for the presidency of the Republic after the war until an assassin's bullet took his life. His brother and granddaughter represent his legacy in Seoul, and Mrs. Kim Mee, his granddaughter and I have become quite good friends. She sent her son to Tufts University, and he served in the Korean Air Force. So, former Air Force personnel had a good time comparing notes and generations at several meetings. We seek to have her talk to our students, but something always seems to intervene. Such persons are quite busy as she is Director of the Kim Koo Museum and, of course, has her own fundraising to attend to. Mitchie and I enjoyed the evening even though Kim Koo comes across as an entirely different person in Japanese history books. As an aside, one of the things we feel we have been able to do is to bridge that gap that sometimes is seen between Japan and Korea. Respect for those who served their own country has to underlay many relations in East Asia—as happens to me and colleagues who were not exactly happy to see me several decades ago when I was serving in Vietnam or when I was with SAC or in the Pentagon.

By the 20th of January, we were deep into the mock visit. The two-man team of Randy Boxx and Jerry Trapnell arrived and began putting us all through the hoops. We started at 0800 hours with myself and the Executive Vice Dean Pat Leonard meeting with Randy and Jerry for breakfast and questions. You know, everyone needs to do this kind of meeting once or twice in their lives, but looking back maybe that is why my hair is so white and so scarce at this point. No, that was General McKee and the *Pueblo* Incident, on second thought, General Philpot and the Cuban Missile Crisis, but I digress.

Randy and Jerry finished up by Wednesday the 22nd at 1300 and departed for their hotel in Seoul where they finished writing their report. The out brief that they provided gave us quite a bit of hope that in March when the real folks would arrive, we might be ready. I make it sound like we were hanging on by our fingernails, but remember my professional field was international relations. I had learned quite a bit about a business school since 2007, but it still was not in my comfort zone. Pat Leonard, on the other hand, was an old pro—almost as old as me—but his life had been in professional business education. We had worked together so long that when I coughed when a detailed question came screaming at me, he was right in with the right response. As I often say, it is a team that gets things done, and this was a good example.

On that Wednesday afternoon, the 22nd, I sent a "Dear Colleagues" note to all the faculty saying that in the out brief we had heard things said about our program that mothers usually say about their children. Also, such terms as "best practice," and "benchmark." I gave special thanks to the AACSB Mock Task Force, but really everyone in the school.

By the 1st of February, we had received an important letter from AACSB saying that we could go on with the official team visit as planned. Our "pre-visit letter" had been accepted by the Chair of the

Initial Accreditation Committee, and final plans for a March visit could continue.

The letter coming when it did and the general progress being made toward AACSB accreditation came at a particularly important time in the life of Woosong University. The foundation behind the school was coming up on its 60th Anniversary. In light of this development and the passing of Sassy, our daughter's Golden Retriever back in Atlanta, I wrote an article for our local newspaper titled: "A Moment of Transition." It covered the death of Sassy and the touching final moments involving a young Golden Retriever added to the family to give company to Sassy in her final months. It also talked about the Woosong Foundation and how its impact first, on the youth of South Korea, and now on the youth of Asia was a transition probably never foreseen by the founder Dr. Kim Jung-woo.

An exciting letter from Saudi Arabian colleagues also arrived in early February, and it let me know that they wished me to be an informal advisor to their own AACSB accreditation process. Having not visited that nation since the early 1980s when I was still deep into my military career, and knowing these colleagues well from meetings held by AACSB, I was delighted and awaited further news.

By mid-March, former U.S. Congressman, the Honorable Donald Manzullo, the President and CEO of the Korea Economic Institute of America, located in Washington, D.C., sent a note that he was planning to visit Korea and would be available for a visit to SolBridge probably in April really only two weeks away. I was delighted as I do sit on the Advisory Board for that organization and am a great believer in the many products they publish and make available to scholars for no charge. (Later, when he did come to SolBridge, he gave a special lecture in our 4th-floor auditorium.)

While two weeks was not far away, of much more immediacy was the visit by the Peer Review Team. The day had finally come to scream "All hands on deck!" Of course, an Air Force guy probably should not use that expression, but I do not know of anything more appropriate for the moments that were immediately ahead. It has the same meaning of "incoming!" when mortar fire was being received on base in Vietnam—I never received artillery fire, but even more appropriate then. The official visit headed by the Dean of the Turner College of Business of Columbus State University, Dr. Linda Hadley, arrived with her two team members, Dr. R.C. Natarajan, and Dr. Robert F. Scherer and we went into full alert status.

The team, of course, was all business. Each person had their own area of expertise and met with appropriate faculty, students, staff, and even some of our members on the Corporate Advisory Council. Everyone knew of their presence and an air of high intensity was so real, it could almost be cut and served. One room was set aside for their deliberations and review of the extensive records used to back up our narrative. We had to be ready to prove everything that had gone on record about our school, our claimed accomplishments, and especially anything we said about our students and the course work they had or were taking to complete their degree. The reviewers were especially interested in the role of the faculty in the governance of the school as well as the interaction between students, faculty, staff and one another. Even what kind of extracurricular activities we offered to students and whether or not they helped prepare our graduates for the competitive work environment awaiting.

We constantly brought up the theme of "Soft skills" which we believe contribute especially to successful graduates in the 21st Century and the challenges of rapid technological change, and of course, our special focus on learning the lessons Asia has to give in the modern business and economic development world. We stressed the theme that we taught the elements of business, both undergraduate and graduate, but added a distinctively Asian flavor, and did so in a very diverse environment, with only 30% of our students Korean and only 20% of our faculty. We acknowledged that we were young, but on a fast-paced stage in search of innovation and creativity, being young was not necessarily bad, but exciting and rewarding. Requiring all Korean undergrads to take three years of Chinese and all international students to take three of either Korean or Japanese added to the uniqueness of our school.

At the final meeting held just before their departure for Seoul, the Team Leader, Dr. Hadley, informally gave us the great news that their report, as the AACSB Peer Review Team, would be positive, but that there was still a formal review process that remained. Only days later, on the 3rd of May, we did receive a note from the Senior Manager of Accreditation Services that the all-important Initial Accreditation Committee had met and "concurred with the team's accreditation recommendation." You can imagine we were all ecstatic. A few days later, on May 9, we received the official notice of accreditation, and our joy could be shared with others in the education community.

And just like that, we were an AACSB accredited institution.

However, a dark, funereal cloud had descended over the Korean peninsula, and any joy and jubilation we might have felt were muted. Just a few weeks earlier of the announcement, tragedy had struck the country on April 16 when a ferry, the *Sewol*, on a voyage from Incheon to Jeju capsized off the tip of South Korea in waters known for their extremely strong currents. Some 443 passengers, 33 crew members and 2,142 tons of cargo were aboard. In a final count, 304 individuals died, most of whom being students from Danwon High School on a school trip to Jeju. Those who survived largely ignored the announcement to stay in their rooms and jumped into the cold sea to await rescue.

The story was one of deceit and illegal procedures from the moment the ship had been redesigned and underwent modifications that altered its handling and led to the disaster. It was authorized to carry 987 tons of cargo in its new configuration, but at the time of capsizing, was carrying 2,142 tons, which later was determined as the cause of the accident. However, the real story of this tragedy was the students and teachers who had stayed onboard waiting to be rescued. Accounts of students waiting in cabins and sending text messages and videos of the tragedy unfolding gripped the nation as time quickly ran out to rescue them.

So while we were thrilled at being accepted by AACSB as one of the five percent of the world's business schools accredited by them, practically all in South Korea were observing an unofficial period of mourning in light of *Sewol*. Toasts at meetings were withheld, as was the consumption of alcoholic beverages. School trips and other extracurricular functions were scrubbed or postponed. Even at SolBridge, our annual Culture Day Festival which has been held in early May was postponed until autumn. The nation was in a very somber mood, and eventually, this attitude took on an increasingly critical opinion of President Park Geun-hye who had performed somewhat erratically during the disaster that increasingly found disfavor with the population. It was one of the items that finally ended her political career, and brought President Moon Jae-in to office.

Actually, in a very thoughtful gesture, the President of AACSB, John J. Fernandes, sent us a letter about the *Sewol* sinking which was appreciated by all. It showed that this was a disaster the world as a whole had observed and sent their regrets.

Shortly after the good news of accreditation, our SolBridge Debate Society Team that was engaged in the 2014 China Debate Open literally won it. It was the first time a Korean team had won and captured the title in China. We were on a roll. Again, I would like to take time out in this narrative to emphasize how important debate has been at SolBridge. Under the guidance and tutelage of Joshua Park, our SolBridge Debate Society has made inroads all across the peninsula and Asia. Even when its members did not win a competition, the name of SolBridge continued to earn a reputation as a formidable powerhouse for debate. In many ways, our debate team has also put SolBridge on the map. (I always like to say, it is my football team, as in America, a university president usually has the football team to carry the school's banner. Here in Asia we do just fine with debate.)

However, footballs (to continue the theme) can bounce in unexpected ways and in June, I received a request that I never expected in my life to come. A high fashion magazine titled *HEREN* asked if I would be a model for a feature in their magazine called "Dress Your Age." Of course, I was given the over 60s role and told to come to Seoul with all sorts of clothing to serve as alternatives. Mitchie and I went after spending considerable time choosing clothes that I would consider appropriate. Really, it was not easy.

Upon arriving at the studio, I was shown a rack of coats and trousers and our quite charming producer scanned the lot and grabbed one coat and one pair of pants and pointed to the changing stall. I soon found out that Slim Fit contains a four-letter word: slim. What an effort, and no belt. Actually, the belt would have only hidden what was happening around my waist. I did get the pants on—without turning blue—and noticed they were about 4 inches too long. I then put on the jacket, and the sleeves were two inches too long making it look like a Chinese Mandarin's outfit—though I might be slightly overstating the case, but you get the general idea and overall impression that I was about to make.

Emerging from the stall, I was met with enthusiastic smiles and words far beyond my Korean vocabulary. I took that as a good sign.

Quick work was done with my trousers—the overlap folded inward so as not to show and coat sleeves turned up like they were supposed to be that way. Then came the shoes—they were so pointed they could be registered as a dangerous weapon—and it was off to the next room and the photo shoot. It was a rather painless ordeal, something that has become part of my job description with all the promo work I have done for SolBridge and Woosong. Actually, about two months later, the magazine came out and was positioned in all the hair stylists, beauty shops, and high end cafes and airports, etc. Well there in the middle—almost a centerfold—I stood representing all those over 60s males who still thought they were 30. The pictures actually looked good, but the memories of how they felt while wearing them made me wonder about all the female models throughout the world and the outfits they wear. (And all those clothes we brought with us from Daejeon never made it. Obviously what I held in high esteem did not make the cut. We learn every day.)

Sometime later I was talking to the individual that made that happen, and he let me know the jacket I wore was $700 and the shoes a similar price. Now, you know I lived the simple life of a military officer for 28 years, and dressing decisions were made for me and easily followed. Options in those days were long sleeves, perhaps short sleeves, but really not much more. Thus, I never spent much on clothes. You can imagine I was very happy not to know that I was wearing a $700 jacket, let alone the shoes. Well, it was a great opportunity to see how the other side lives for one afternoon on the 23rd of June.

While the *HEREN* came out in July, that month was also the moment for two spectacular developments. On July 2 we received news that our grant proposal for the Ministry of Education's CK-1 Project had been accepted. CK stood for Creative Korea, and our proposal set out in detail what we would do with one million per year. Well, we got it, and in the process were given the award for the best globalization program in Korea. That was music to our ears, and we were really indebted to one of our new Korean professors for "bird-dogging" this project and getting the spectacular results.

Professor Kim Jin-sung had come to us from Korea University after 18 years there, and the first project we had given him was the CK-1 Proposal. Well, after it won, this Ph.D. in Economics from the

University of Kansas looked mighty fine. I had been operating as Acting Dean for more than a year, and wheels were set in motion to end that additional duty, and soon I was able to send a note to the faculty announcing that one of their colleagues would be the new Dean. I ended the note with "I will drop the Acting Dean title and replace it with a smile." Welcome aboard Dean Kim; was I ever so happy to see him.

The good things July brought just would not stop. By mid-month my colleague Assistant Professor Nakamura Toraaki and I were in Yangon, Myanmar on a business trip to pay a courtesy call on the Ministry of Education, discuss opportunities with Yangon Institute of Economics, and generally see the lay of the land regarding this "hermit kingdom" that was slowly coming out of the shadows of suppressive military rule. To be specific, we saw the Shwedagon Pagoda on the first day, met with the economics faculty on the second, as well as read a great book about General Aung San, flew to the new capital and met the Deputy Minister of Economics on the third. On the fourth, we visited the Martyr's Mausoleum—for tragedies in 1947 and 1983—and saw the Independence Monument in downtown Yangon. The visit was all too short, and the education aspects still need to materialize. It was essential to see this country of great promise, but having been very aware of what happened during the Ne Win regime, I understand the distance that is still to go.[37]

In August, one of our colleagues, Bob Graff, who has lived in South Korea for over 20 years, and in fact has Korean citizenship, received some news that was certainly unsettling. Years ago, he and his wife had built a house on a mountain that overlooked the sea near Kangnung on the East Sea. The Olympic Committee charged with choosing the locations for the various winter competitions decided that the ski jump site should be placed exactly where our professor had his house. I should let him tell the story, but in short, there were many negotiating sessions regarding fair compensation for all the village folk

---

[37] One specific memory stands out. I was in Tokyo at the old Sanno Hotel on a Sunday morning enjoying a leisurely breakfast not long after the March 1962 coup that brought Ne Win to power. Reading the *Japan Times* I came across an article about a Burmese fugitive who had been captured by their police. The article relayed the news that so and so had been captured, would be tried next Thursday, and executed the following Saturday. Besides almost spilling coffee over my Sunday church outfit, I suddenly realized the nature of the Ne Win Regime. It became the "Burmese Way to Socialism" as I recall.

impacted. In the end, our economics professor accepted a new location, built a new building that would house a coffee shop on the ground floor and his living quarters on the second. I have not seen it, but all who have indicate it was a great swap. So, not only did he get a new vantage point from which to observe the Olympics, he could do so selling coffee and pastries. To me that sounded almost irresistible; a place to retire and a retirement income at the same time. So, some of the unintended consequences of Olympic construction can be extremely beneficial.

And if you just so happen to find yourself in Kangnung one day and spot a sign featuring a smiling man, you know you have just found Uncle Bob's Coffee House. Stop in and have your favorite kind of java or tea. You won't regret it.

Besides going to Myanmar this summer brought another pleasant opportunity. Our Japanese language professor, Nakamura Toraaki, needed us to visit one of our partner schools, but while in Tokyo we also visited the Minister for Education and Olympic Games, the Honorable Shimomura Hakubun. After giving a lecture on my favorite subject—the need for a Limited Nuclear Weapons' Free Zone for Northeast Asia—we made an appointment to visit the minister as he had received an honorary doctorate from Woosong only two years previously. Of course, one of the main topics I wished to discuss was the fact that SolBridge had received AACSB accreditation this past April and was now one of 13 such business schools in South Korea. We discussed that fact that at that time Japan had only three schools so accredited.

As September neared an end, we had a stirring Platinum Lecture by Ms. Amy Jackson who was head of the American Chamber of Commerce in Korea. She had a very interesting career in business before taking the post with Korea AMCHAM, and her outgoing personality and speaking skills were just what we needed at SolBridge that had now reached 820 students in size and was increasingly becoming more female than male in nature. Certainly, we have enough men to put before our students in Korea, but successful businesswomen of the stature of Amy are hard to find. She made a great impact on the audience as she talked about her way up the ladder in business and the challenges she faced. "Well done!," was the verdict and when we had lunch with students after the talk, the buzz was still evident. It was great to see a large group of students surround the speaker at the conclusion of the talk—and they were all women.

On the first of October, the Woosong Foundation that supports Woosong University marked its 60th Anniversary, and a large gathering was invited to celebrate with us. One of the many events put on to celebrate multiculturalism was a mass wedding (actually 16 couples) of multicultural couples who lived in the area surrounding our university. Having the new brides bow to their mothers-in-law in unison was quite a site; several of the couples were invited to the microphone to recount their individual stories about their marriages. Happily, I was not called upon to marry these happy couples, but as you know, during my tenure in South Korea, I have been at the altar on many occasions. (To tell you the truth, I quite enjoy marrying young people in love and treasure these opportunities. That will be over when we return to the States.)

In the middle of October, I met General Bernard Champoux, the 8th Army Commander at a function in Seoul and informed him of the unbelievable performance by General John D. Johnson when he had come to SolBridge in 2011. I mentioned, "Even our students from the PRC were ready to sign up." He responded like I had spilled hot coffee all over his dress uniform, but I could sense that his interest was piqued. "Of course, you can come to SolBridge," was my response. I was so thrilled as our military leaders in South Korea are always impressive and dedicated to the mission of defending Korea and U.S. interests here and in Asia. When I can get them to address our students, we not only get a great speech, but a very positive image for all our students.

November 2014 was a month I remember as typical of the rewarding activities that a university president has. First was my participation in the 2014 Daejeon Global Innovation Forum, held in the Daejeon Convention Center from November 12-14; the second was a trip to the Academy of Korean Studies in Seongnam-si, Gyeonggi-do on the 18th of November, and the last was the Woosong University ROTC Festival held on the 21st of November at Woosong.

In the Global Innovation Forum I had the happy responsibility to take part in the University Presidents' Forum looking at the issue of university and business collaboration in creating regional strategic industries that could help South Korea advance new "profit centers" that could aid materially in the development of university/industry alliances that would ultimately show major gains in Korea's GDP. Many of the presidents outlined areas in their particular regions that could benefit from greater university-industry integration. I was no exception as I highlighted our Railroad Transportation College and the possibilities of joining in the worldwide boom in railroad developments. I did mention the need to help create new land transportation infrastructure for developing states or upgrading current stock, much interest is found in the spread of high-speed rail. With over 580 major rail projects in the world today, I stressed the need for Korea's rail industry to actively seek a major piece of this development pie.

This forum gave me an opportunity to share with the audience the personal role that the Daedok Valley played in my coming to Daejeon. As I was negotiating with Woosong University, I happened to come across an article in a Japanese journal that compared the Korean experience with innovation centers (i.e., Daedok) and that of Japan (i.e., Tsukuba Science City in Japan.) The article made a point of the concentration of Ph.D.'s in science and technical fields and the fact that Daedok seemed to outperform Japan's Tsukuba by a significant margin. I read this account and found myself drawn to the active intellectual life of Daejeon. The audience seemed interested, but I knew when to stop.

My second major involvement in the Innovation Forum was my role as moderator for a panel considering "Fostering Innovation Capabilities of Higher Education Institutions and Research Institutes." Distinguished members on this panel included Dr. Bjong Wolf Yeigh the Chancellor of the University of Washington Bothell Campus who gave us a keynote speech; Dr. Flavia Schlegel, Assistant Secretary General for Natural Sciences from UNESCO; The Honorable El Tayeb Mustafa, President of Future University, the Sudan; Dr. Eberhard Becker, Former President of TU Dortmund University in Germany; Dr. Malcolm Parry OBE, Director of Surrey Research Park in the United Kingdom; and Dr. Herbert Chen, COO of Tsinghua University's Science Park in Beijing, China. Now I do not intend to recount each speech presented by the panel; my point here is to demonstrate to you the kind of individuals coming to Daejeon. It was impressive by any world standard.

The next remarkable event that took place in November was my journey to the Academy of Korean Studies in Seongnam-si, Gyeonggi-do. I was met and briefed by its President, Dr. Lee Bae-yong former President of Ewha University and long-time advocate of the study of history as one of the basic foundations for ensuring a successful future. In this case, Korean history. In the first instance, I must say the campus of this Academy in itself is reason enough for a visit; however, upon receiving a briefing and tour from President Lee, the unique role this Academy plays ensuring that "academic learning will lay the theoretical basis for a country with mature values whose cultural prestige matches its industrial development" is clearly evident.

The faculty has approximately 60 renowned scholars on many aspects of Korean culture and history. The facility also holds some fantastic collections of original Korean texts known as the Jangseogak Archives of 81,946 books. In addition, the Academy has published the 28-volume of the *Encyclopedia of Korean Culture*. I am only touching the top of this exceptional institution that also has a graduate teaching/research role. Since its establishment in 1978, it has performed a multitude of scholastic roles to ensure that Korean history is represented to the world in the professional way the academic history of Korea demands.

The final comments on November relate to the new ROTC Detachment that we began in 2012. On the 21st of November, we hosted the 2nd ROTC Festival involving examples of the unique talents held by our male and female cadets. The highlight was an introduction and a ring ceremony for the 23 graduating cadets who will join in defense of the nation in 2015. I wanted to share with you the fact that these remarkably dedicated cadets and their officer and civilian instructors were able this year to place first in the rankings of all Korean University Detachments. A big salute from the old Colonel who was himself an ROTC grad, albeit Air Force ROTC.

December ended this very eventful year with graduation ceremonies for SolBridge and Woosong International students, our annual end of the year dinner that involved all faculty and their families, which increasingly included a growing number of children of all levels of activity and noise. It really became a fun session as attempts at serious talk were easily overpowered by the background of animated discussions and children crying.

Mitchie and I departed for Atlanta on the 21st arrived that same morning in Atlanta giving us all day Sunday to hit the malls and those stores we have come to depend on at Christmas time in Atlanta. As has been the case the past couple of years when we have gone home for the holidays, it was also a time for us to catch our breath after another busy year in South Korea. And of course, a time for us to be thankful for the good work that we have done.

* * *

Dear readers, at this point, I will bring this detailed accounting of my life to a conclusion. Looking back on the full story that I have relayed to you, I realize that the most important story, that of the love I have for my wife Mitchie, and the interaction between us, has only appeared on occasion and not nearly to the degree that would be correct if you received a full accounting of my life. To our marriage, I owe, not only two wonderful children who have seen our love for each other but thanks for a caring advisor who has kept me on course for over 60 years. Through all the turbulence of a 28-year Air Force career, three years as Director of the Institute for National Strategic Studies, the almost 20 years of an academic and policy entrepreneur, and finally these 13 or more as leader of a Korean university, she has been there a seasoned, intelligent and loving partner. As we have journeyed through life together, she has been my guiding light. She is what completes me. Perhaps, that is the subject for my next book.

TWENTY-FIVE

Postscript

When I sat down and started to pen my memoirs a few years ago, I had intended to stop at the end of 2014, the year that saw SolBridge gaining AACSB accreditation. To me, that was a good place to end—a fitting ending as it were to all that I have accomplished since coming to Korea in 2007, which includes not only the work I have done with the limited nuclear weapons' free zone in Northeast Asia but also all that I have achieved at Woosong and SolBridge. However, the five years since the close of 2014 were also very important years in my life, as well as the life of the university. Therefore, I wish to include the four years not covered in the main narrative. Not to say a few words here would be a missed opportunity to talk about some of the exciting things which have happened and the impact they have had on my life, Woosong, and SolBridge. Perhaps, by the time my memoirs are published, a post-postscript will be in order.

2015

One thing is for certain when you are the president or chancellor of a school, nothing ever runs on autopilot. Even though we gained AASCB accreditation the previous year, there was no time for us to rest on our laurels. No sooner had the reality sunk in that we were indeed an AACSB accredited school than we started thinking about the next accreditation period.

The year also was marked by several exciting trips to places I had not been for a while or not at all as well as some esteemed visitors to SolBridge. For example, I visited a university in Saudi Arabia to advise them on AACSB accreditation, and in mid-June went to Ulaanbaatar to discuss future options with Ministry of Education official, energize our contacts there and visit a giant statue of Genghis Khan which I can claim to have a part in planning its construction.

In May we hosted General Bernard Champoux, Commander of the 8th Army, Chief of Staff for the United Nations Forces, as well as Commander of ROK-US Combined Forces Command for a lecture at SolBridge. By the time I got out all of his titles, it was time to go to lunch. This was the second time for SolBridge to invite the 8th Army Commander to SolBridge for one of our special lectures. And like the last time, when General Johnson spoke in 2011, Champoux did not disappoint. The students loved him.

Travel in September involved a trip to London and Bath, United Kingdom, to discuss collaboration with several British institutions. Mitchie joined me on that trip as it became an opportunity to show her some of the locations of my memories of school in London in 1950. It was hard to find Sutton Place and the old Paddington Technical College High School even with a seasoned London taxi driver. Perhaps he had other missions that day, but one certainly did not include finding the location of my high school that I had not visited in over fifty years. Rest assured, those memories have found a special place earlier in this narrative. On a more pleasant note, we did visit the East India Club which held fond memories for both of us and of course the house in Hampstead where I had spent a year in 1950. I am happy to say it has weathered quite nicely, perhaps better than I have, and it still commands a second look if you admire British architecture of the 1930s. I have been told not to ask the price of homes in that area of London, it approximates those in similar New York City locales.

Also in November that year, I visited Macau to lecture on "Transforming Higher Education Institutions: A Balanced Development," for the University Presidents' Forum of 2015. It is always fun to address such groups, but how the reaction turns out is always a toss of the dice. (Oh, not the phrase to use when in Macao!)

This particular group, to be specific, did include quite a few university presidents. Perhaps their research phase is over, and they are deep into implementation. In a sense "Don't confuse me with the facts" might be appropriate here. I enjoyed making the presentation, but the emphasis was not on the discussion, just presentation.

On a more personal and festive note, rounding out the year in early December I made a batch of Christmas puddings to give to faculty and staff, as I was certain that no one had eaten this marvel of English cuisine correctly. And I have to say, they were quite delicious. It marked the first and last time in South Korea that I attempted something of that scope in the kitchen.

2016

Early in 2016, we received word that we had won one of the coveted prizes of the AACSB Innovations that Inspire Awards. It was an award that sought to identify those innovations being done by the world's business schools that really make a statement in society. We won for the great work done by our SolBridge Debate Society (SDS) working with a local school system to introduce debating to not just privileged students, but everyone. Asked by the City of Osan to help, Professor Joshua Park and his team worked with the teachers of the secondary schools of Osan and integrated debate into their curriculum and then supplied members of the SDS to help train the teachers in debating. Approximately twenty individual schools were involved. However, even more importantly, it turned to address those in the schools who really wanted to be elsewhere and were known as "troublemakers." Upon being asked if they would be interested in debate, many said "Yes." It was remarkable, but it is with these children that "Inspire" happened. All of a sudden, students who normally spent all their time playing video games turned to books and became energized debaters. The story is all positive, and they not only began debating but began to win and, in order to win had to be prepared and had to study. A great story of how students can take their skills learned in college and impacts their younger cousins possibly changing lives. I had to go to an AACSB meeting and accept the award in April and did so with unbounded joy.

The year was also marked by a very useful MOU between SolBridge and the Korea Development Institute (KDI), one of the oldest governmental institutions charged with the development of Korea and setting goals for various economic endeavors. With KDI besides receiving a visiting faculty member, we co-hosted an International Student Workshop in May. It was a great opportunity to showcase some of our better students in a very competitive event. Also in May, we received the Dean of the School of Business from Carleton University in Ottawa, Canada. After he saw our operation, facilities and faculty, several great agreements were made where our students would spend their last year at Carleton receive both degrees and a job. That was a great advantage for those interested in working abroad. In October, we began our first Early Childhood Education International Symposium. Speaking to that group allowed me to stress the vital importance of a positive early childhood introduction to formal education. I stressed the point that as they succeed, so do we, only several decades later.

We had a very special visitor to SolBridge in May when U.S. Ambassador Mark Lippert spoke to the student body. He spoke several months after he had been attacked by a deranged individual—a very serious attack that he bravely dealt with, leaving him with injuries to his face and hand which required hospitalization. He gave an inspiring speech and then took questions—even posing for a "selfie" with students which soon went viral on the U.S. Embassy's Twitter page. One thing I have to say about our Platinum Lectures and Special Lectures is that they provide our students windows on business and the world. I'm very proud of these lectures and the people we have invited to speak at SolBridge. The Ambassador represented the United States at the highest level of professionalism imaginable. Our hats off, and constant good wishes as he enters his new life and career after diplomatic service.

Lunch followed at Woosong's Solpine Restaurant and the chance to showcase some of the culinary expertise of our Culinary Arts Department which included Cincinnati-style chili, which as you can imagine, was very near and dear to this Cincinnati Kid.

2017

With the increased importance of small and medium businesses not only in South Korea but across the world, entrepreneurship always important became even more so. SolBridge moved toward adding a specialization in entrepreneurship and began the search for a university partner that could be a partner for collaboration in that field. We all knew that there is one school that has become the center for the study of entrepreneurship, and that is Babson University. The Dean and I traveled to Boston to discuss this matter with their president and other involved officials. By the end of January, we had entered into a collaborative agreement and began sending selected students there for their short term programs, especially in the summer.

In early March, Woosong had a naming ceremony for the new Endicott College of International Studies. I had been pressing for greater offerings of liberal arts and social science courses, and one late December night our Chairman called to say the Foundation had finally agreed, and a new college would be added to Woosong, and it would be named after me. You can expect I was surprised and pleased. The naming day had guests from all over Asia and Georgia Tech as well. Our daughter Charlene came to represent the "clan" from Atlanta, and the old Colonel had to be brought down to earth gently after that.

Later that same month I was invited to give two speeches to two universities in Nanjing, China. It was a great opportunity to express our thanks to schools that had sent students to SolBridge and Woosong for several years. Having prepared the talks and arrived in China, I was informed that rather than being a speaking tour, it would be a listening tour. The Chinese Government took exception to the deployment of THAAD, the Theater High Altitude Air Defense System, in South Korea by the U.S. and was going to rescind the invitations to speak, and call on other representatives of foreign universities. It was just a matter that I represented a Korean university, and I happened to be an American.

All during the year, I was able to hear the construction noise that came from just beyond my office in the Woosong Headquarters. As the Endicott Building progressed, I took pictures and guests (male) to see and record the progress of this very special architecture from the best vantage point available, the third floor restroom directly above the site. Needless to say, some awkward moments did arise.

2018

Early in the year, I was invited to I-Shou University in Taiwan, where we have a robust relationship and some abiding friendships. Not my first time to visit Taiwan or I-Shou, this time I was asked to join in a ceremony for the new president's inauguration. Of course, it was a delight to be part of such an important moment, but when the ceremony actually began, I was in for one of the most enjoyable ceremonies I have ever seen. There were probably 40 presidents from other universities, and the audience of perhaps 200 was full of close friends of either the incoming or outgoing president.

As the outgoing president said his goodbyes, you could see he was genuinely happy to be going. In fact, his final words were actually sung in a strong and delightful voice. As he handed the seal of office to his successor, the reaction of the audience was overwhelmingly joyous and most spontaneous. May I say that his talk was interspersed with many jokes and the audience, for the most part, was practically rolling in the aisles.

When the new president took over, it was just like the old radio program "Can You Top This," where one joke followed another as two speakers tried to outdo the other. So it was. When it was all over, I had tears from laughter, which is all the more surprising because the exchange between the two speakers was all in Chinese—a language I don't speak. You must believe me I would go back in a heartbeat.

The ICAM Conference for AACSB in 2018 was in Hawaii, and this was just too good to miss. As you may recall, Mitchie and I spent our first years of married life in Honolulu living either in Manoa Valley or Radford Terrace a Navy Housing Area near Hickam Air Force Base. Our trip back to Hawaii (our first since we had left) became our second honeymoon. After meetings at the conference were out of the way, we saw old neighbors, old places, Tripler Army Hospital where Mitchie had given birth, and the Hickam Air Force Officers' Club—still grand but almost deserted. It wasn't one of those "never go back moments" that some people might feel when revisiting haunts from their past as we really enjoyed seeing old friends who we had met almost 60 years ago. While it might have seemed that life had "stood still" for my wife and I as we "journeyed back" in time as it were, it was a most pleasant experience for us. Who says you can't go back "home" again?

In May we received several visitors from the Air Force Academy in Colorado for an inspection visit to see if Woosong could host several U.S. Air Force Cadets for language training in the summer. They seemed to like what they saw, and during the summer 2019 term, the first group of four to five cadets arrived.

In early June, our son, John II, arrived to join with us for the opening of the Endicott building which was now finished and awaiting a formal opening. We had that ceremony on the 5th of June, and much to Mitchie's and my pleasure John could represent the "clan" for the event. It was a bright and rather hot day, and all the speeches took place in the open air central plaza surrounded by the building itself. Our special university guest was from Pittsburg State University in Pittsburg, Kansas, where my father received his teaching degree many years ago. As part of the ceremony, we signed an MOU between Endicott College and Pittsburg State and are now working to send our first students.

August brought with it the news that we as a university had been selected as a "Self-Autonomous University" by the Ministry of Education, thus making the cut as a top university of South Korea. A comprehensive review was done by the Ministry at all universities in response to the critical demographic situation that came with a national birth rate of 1.02. In real terms that meant that with an overall ability to take in 650,000 freshmen and women every March, only 400,000-450,000 would be showing up in 2020. To reduce this overcapacity, the Ministry examined all universities declaring the best to be Self-Autonomous, 86 to be "weak" and an additional 38 to be eliminated by 2021. We might have breathed a collective sigh of relief having made the cut as it were, but as is the case with our AACSB accreditation, there is no time to rest on our laurels. There is much work to be done to ensure that we continue to live up to the expectations we have created for ourselves and for the students who pass through our doors.

Not long after that good news, actually in October, we received additional good news from the Ministry granting Woosong approximately 9 million dollars to spend on coordinating and improving IT and Software programs throughout the university. Some 28 universities had competed in the competition, and five had won; Woosong was said to have completed the best proposal, and we received the designation as possessing a "Software College." It was another demonstration of our professional staff in action, for which I am continually grateful. Working with great people who have a common goal can be one of the most rewarding functions in life. Thanks again, Woosong!

Throughout this narrative, I have been praising the work of our SolBridge Debate Society and have mentioned some of their specific achievements. However, permit me to give you their status as 2018 came close to ending. I think you could say we are almost the Ohio State of Korean debating—or would that be Michigan? No! No! No!!!

I think this is as good a place as any, to show exactly what I mean by our activity and success in debate this past year through November (2018).

Summary of key accomplishments by SolBridge Debate Society:

1. 2018 China BP Debating Championships (October, Beijing): Champions (Team) and Overall Best Speaker (Individual). This is an annual international tournament in the British Parliamentary (BP) debating style hosted in Beijing that features around 300 participants from all over the world. Our students were Champions of this event for the second straight year (following our first Championship at the event last year).

2. 2018 Asian BP Debating Championships (October, Hanoi): Semi-finalists (Team) and 3rd Best Speaker (Individual). This is the most prestigious British Parliamentary debating tournament in Asia, with over 200 participants, representing the Asian region before the Worlds. SolBridge is the first team from Northeast Asia to have advanced to the elimination rounds for the third straight year, with this year's accomplishment being our best performance yet. The 3rd Best Individual Speaker Award is also the highest for a Northeast Asian institution to receive in the history of the tournament.

3. 2018 KIDA (Korea Intervarsity Debating Association) Open (August, Seoul): Champions (Team) and 2nd Best Speaker (Individual).

This is the annual international tournament hosted by Korean universities' English debating body, featuring teams from all across Asia. SolBridge students won this competition for the second year in a row.

4. 2018 Beijing Debate Challenge (April, Beijing): Champions (Team) and 2nd Best Speaker (Individual). This is the annual international tournament hosted in Beijing, featuring over 250 participants, with teams and judges from all over the world. Two of our teams were featured in the Grand Final (four teams participate in each round in the BP format), with one of the winning the Championship.

5. 2018 Pan-Pacific Debating Championships (February, Honolulu): Champions (Team) and 2nd Best Speaker (Individual). This is an annual international tournament hosted by Hawaii Pacific University, featuring teams from the United States, Asia, and the Americas. Our students were the first Asian team to win these Championships.

6. 2018 World Universities Debating Championships (January, Mexico City): ESL Semi-finalists. SolBridge was the only team from South Korea to advance to the elimination rounds at Worlds, advancing to the ESL Semi-final rounds.

2019

It was my original intention to stop the narration of my life with the accounts of 2018, but as we progressed with the final edit also did time; so, permit me to add some events and thoughts about 2019, as it was a most important year for me and both SolBridge and Woosong that it is appropriate to close it off in September 2019.

Woosong University had its Annual Grand Opening Ceremony on the 3rd of January, and as always it was a very meaningful event. Two weeks after the opening I went to the ROTC Winter Encampment to cheer up our kids who at that moment were being exposed to some very cold winter activities in mountains about an hour and a half northeast of Daejeon. The facilities are extremely pleasant, if you stay in the dorms, but that is not what it is about—it is all about experiencing winter weather and dealing with it as a part of being in the military.

By the end of the month we were saying good bye to our Dean, Jerman Rose who had been with us two years and a half years, and had done the heavy lifting on the 19th of January welcoming the AACSB Continuous Improvement Review Team who gave us an informal re-accreditation wink as they returned to the States. It was on the 8th of March that we received the formal documentations—at that time we had to settle with thanking him by e-mail.

In mid-February I was so fortunate to receive an Honorary Doctorate in Political Science from Dankook University, a much larger university than ours with almost 30,000 students. Its President, Chang Ho-sung became aware of the almost three decades I had been working on the security situation in Northeast Asia, and was determined to recognize it. He did so in a magnificent ceremony on the 21st of February that Mitchie and I will always remember. There was a very good turnout from Woosong as well that was much appreciated.

In early March I had the opportunity to join the Board of Advisors of the ROK Army TRADOC, or Training and Doctrine Command. After clearing that invitation by the U.S. Air Force, I participated in a major conference where the ROK strategies for dealing with the 4th Industrial Revolution were discussed. It was a fascinating chance to interact with young generals who were on the same wave length as our leaders in the US Futures' Command. It was clear that the ROK Army is seeking ways to create an environment for innovation and creativity—definitely needed in dealing with the challenges of AI, Big Data and the Cloud.

On the 27th of March Woosong University was invited to sign an MOU with the University College of Leuven-limburg, Belgium to facilitate exchange of students and faculty between our two schools. But this time it was different: the King of the Belgians and his wife were visiting Korea to encourage trade and cultural exchanges and our MOU signing ceremony was to be graced by His Majesty's presence. It was somewhat less than expected, but I did get to interact with the Rector of the university and see the King. However, with about 200 participants and a bum leg, I was not up to a football or rugby maneuver to get near the King.

April and especially mid-April was as busy as I could take. My leg, having injured it coming down some steps in March was still not one hundred percent back to normal; in fact, more like thirty percent. But my wife and I traveled to Scotland to take part in the annual ICAM meeting of AACSB. I really could barely walk, but we gave it the old college try. If you see any pictures from that time you will notice I am leaning heavily on Mitchie for support—please, I was not inebriated.

While it was important to go to Scotland, it was even more important to be back at Woosong by the 17th to welcome the Ministry of Education University Evaluation Team that was here to re-accredit or not our university. After a very tough introduction by the evaluation team leader, saying more or less that they were on a mission to weed out marginal universities, we all did our best to show the inspectors the heart of our university. In the end, we received a wonderful out-briefing and a grand congratulation from the Team Leader and his colleagues. Nice way to loose five pounds in a hurry.

By the 3rd of June we had a visit from four US Air Force Academy Cadets who were here to study the Korean language and experience Korea's history and culture. As you might recall, I taught at the Air Force Academy for seven years and it had sent me to the Fletcher School to earn my Ph.D. We welcomed them and took them to visit the tomb of General Kyebeak a hero of the Paekche Kingdom of 660. It was a test run, to see if cadets could come every year for such an orientation into Korea. At this time I know they enjoyed the visit and learned a lot of Korean, but I cannot say if it will be an annual affair.

June and July turned out to be much more active than they should be with a trip to Uzbekistan to discuss a Woosong offshore campus, taking part in the annual U.S. Independence Day Gala in Seoul, and presenting a paper at the 2nd Hanseatic League Conference held at Incheon National University. As a result, Woosong did join the 2nd Hanseatic League of Universities which of course has its historic base in the Baltic—not the East Sea. It made my heart run a little faster that day.

Presidents from the recently selected universities as Software Focused Universities had their first conference in July, and the middle of July found me at the Bastille Day Celebration at the French Embassy where we were able to meet one of Korea's giants of commerce who agreed to come to SolBridge in 2020 to give a Platinum Lecture. I assessed that visit to Seoul as time well spent. However, one of the most meaningful ceremonies I have attended—anywhere—took place on the 19th of July on the plaza in front of the Daejeon Railroad Station. Here the Mayor of Dong-gu, Korean and American generals and one university president (me) with other invited individuals met to mark the 69th anniversary of the death of Train engineer Kim Jae-hyun. I will never forget that moment as Engineer Kim had given his life in an attempt to rescue General William Dean, Commander of the 24th Infantry Division who was desperately trying to slow down the North Korean invasion of South Korea in the Battle of Daejeon.

He drove a train with 31 American Special Forces aboard that attempted to rescue General Dean. He was killed along with 30 of the 31 Americans. Two other Korean train engineers were also involved—one seriously wounded and the youngest the engineer who drove the train home to safety. It was a magnificent ceremony with the son of Engineer Kim taking part. It was a most meaningful example of the meaning of the Korean-American Special Relationship.

The last week of July and the first week August were spent in Marietta on home leave. As often happens all the plans we had were overturned by a visit to my cardiologist. Since the first thing we did was attend the graduation of our grandson, John Charles Endicott, from Kennesaw State University we were able to accomplish the most important item on our schedule. The next day I visited my heart doctor and, unexpectedly, I spent the next several days in the hospital where he and his associates put a new stent in and gave me another 10,000 mile warranty. Thanks Dr. McKee I guess I really needed that! Our planned visit to see my sister, Alice, in Kentucky had to be postponed, but we did get to celebrate with family my birthday and our 60th wedding anniversary before returning to Korea.

I think I can say we are as up-to-date as possible and let you know of two September events that mean a lot to me. On the 4th of the month, I received notice that I had been selected as a 2019 Albert Nelson Marquis Lifetime Achievement Awardee—the organization that publishes Who's Who in America and Who's Who in the World, and other related publications. That was really unexpected, but most appreciated.

Then finally for this book on the 6th of September we officially announced to Woosong and the SolBridge Faculty, that the new Dean Dr. Hamid Bouchikhi had officially taken over the helm for SolBridge and I could delete "Acting Dean" from my signature bloc. As you might expect I was most delighted to share that news with my SolBridge colleagues.

I will now absolutely put a period to this narrative and thank you my dear readers for staying the course. Now I can say, "Okay Mitchie I am coming to lunch."

TWENTY-SIX

Lessons Learned

I have written quite a bit at this point, and you have been so dedicated to read what I have recorded, but I think I would be remiss if I did not sum up this account with what I did learn and what might be useful for any young person reading my story. I am so thrilled that the number of lessons is only eight. If it turned out ten, you know the wags out there would be saying that old Endicott is turning out his own "Ten Commandments." Well, please consider what I have added below, as I certainly am not the first to sum up a life of service in like manner. Let me first list my "Eight Recommendations" and then say a bit about each.

Endicott's "Eight Recommendations" from Lessons Learned

- Follow your heart
- Study languages whenever given the chance
- Work on your "soft skills"
- Constantly seek new challenges
- Travel, travel, travel
- Take care of your health
- Keep an ethical code
- Place your family first

Follow your heart

By all means, pick a career that is something you really love to do. I believe there is nothing worse than following the money trail and finding at the end, there is no satisfaction, no feeling that you personally made a difference while on this earth. Of course, it is up to you, but doing something you like will probably increase your time on the planet, and you also will enjoy it while here.

Study languages whenever given the chance

In my career, I studied German (middle school and high school – except for the ninth grade when I studied French in London), Russian (four years at Ohio State as an undergraduate), Japanese (getting married in 1959 to my Japanese sweetheart made it a life-long affair and I am still a student), Vietnamese (the Air Force gave me the choice of intensive Vietnamese before going to Vietnam in 1965, and it made for a most meaningful year in difficult times), and now at 83 I am a student of Korean as my wife, and I begin our 13th year in Korea.

Thus, I studied English, my mother tongue, German, French, Russian, Japanese, Vietnamese, and Korean. Now, you notice how I cleverly did not say how many languages I mastered, only studied. As an American, unfortunately, we do not have much opportunity to keep our proficiency up, and the languages become rusty and very difficult to use. However, when we study languages, we also often study culture, history, religion, and traditions that make the various languages unique and actually the windows into the world.

So, what I am suggesting is take the opportunities that present themselves to learn new languages, but also use these moments to learn what goes with the language, especially history. Good luck, and may you be exposed to so many interesting voices.

Work on your "Soft Skills"

As we enter the era of the 4th Industrial Revolution, one of the most useful skills you will encounter is what we call "soft skills." These really relate to how you interact with other individuals. Do you work well in a team? Can you lead a team when it seems you are the best to do so, and can you step back and let others lead when you seem out of your element? Can you give a presentation in another language other than your own? What about two? Do you feel comfortable working with individuals of diverse cultural backgrounds, and can you get the most out of them? It is all about your ability to be flexible and operate in conditions that are changing and demanding. Can you handle pressure without blowing the pressure valve? These are not easy skills, but those who master them are going to be in a better situation than those who do not.

Constantly seek new challenges

This is a rather difficult lesson, as well. Sometimes the boss will ask for someone to take on a task that does not seem too closely related to the business at hand. However, later on, someone in the back of the room will say, "Is there anyone who has done whatever, or gone, wherever?" Well, it just so happens that you can be the one who answers. Then off to a new adventure. There is another reason to take new challenges; you may end up enjoying this new twist even more than the one you chose before. Take it if it fits.

Believe me, when I served in the Air Force opportunities often came up. Studying the Vietnamese language was one of those things that was basically an add on, but gave me further depth as an Asian specialist. Not only was I heavily into Northeast Asia, but as a result of training prior to going to Vietnam and then one year on the scene, I could offer aspects of Southeast Asia to my portfolio.

Travel, travel, travel

This lesson follows closely the "seek new challenges" lesson. I have never ceased to learn something from a trip, however so short, that I have had to make. Of course, my first travel overseas was with my father and mother when he was a Fulbright Exchange Teacher in London from 1950-1951. But, you have to be an "active" traveler. If you go to Tokyo, for example, check in to your hotel and turn on HBO, where is the Tokyo-related knowledge? Take the available on and off bus tours. If you have the time, take a bus tour that takes you all around the city you are visiting—then branch out and select those cites that really are historically significant. That also means grab a guide book or history book about the place and when you return home, voila! not only can you spell this new town, you can say something intelligently about it as well. Does that sound like fun? Well, it doesn't get any better.

My wife and had a strategy about travel. Since all my overseas assignments in the Air Force were in Asia or at Asia's footstep, we decided to take our overseas vacations in Europe, so we would get to know the great cities of Europe one by one or vacation by vacation. We used the method described above and tried to make every vacation an educational one. For example, one summer we wanted to go to Portugal, but we had no knowledge of it whatsoever. So we went to a language school in Atlanta and explained we needed at least "survival Portuguese" for our upcoming trip. No problem—well actually lots of problems as it was not an easy language—but for six weeks we prepared, learning the language and history. It was one of the most delightful vacations ever, and we learned a lot. We still have to visit Porto, however, what could I possibly do to get ready?

Take care of your health

This is a vital lesson, as it determines just how long you can enjoy the career that you have chosen. I cannot say that I mastered this lesson, but I did learn a lot. Throughout my twenty-eight years in the Air Force, I kept in good physical shape as the Air Force had these annual tests to make sure you were not falling out of shape as the years progressed. Basically, I jogged about three miles a day (Monday thru Friday), played as much tennis as I could, and watched my weight. However, my family has a history of circulation and heart issues, and my time came when I was 62 some twelve years after retiring from the Service.

Seems that my vascular system had become seriously clogged by cholesterol and both carotid arteries had to be cleaned as well as three areas around my heart. February, March and April 1998 became months to remember as both carotids were operated on in February and March and a triple bypass was done in April. At this time, it has been 21 years since the operations, and all have been pretty good since. My best friend Dr. Robert Marmer who had gone to school with me from kindergarten through Ohio State was the doctor who realized I had a major problem. So, pick your best friends well. I owe my life to him, and whenever we return to Atlanta for home leave, we get together for sure.

Thus, take care of your health, but remember you can only do so much. DNA has set a course, and as modern medicine begins to mess with DNA, we may have an increased chance to even affect DNA proscribed futures. The best advice I can give is to not smoke and drink alcohol in moderation. For my younger readers, please no binge drinking.

Keep an ethical code

I am not going to recommend any particular religion in commenting about this lesson, but each religion of the world has an ethical code, and my recommendation is to follow it. At many points in one's career offers are made that seem too good to pass up. Our prisons are filled with disappointed folks who tried to take a short cut to fortune. If you are doing what you like to do, you don't need a fortune anyway. Wonderful lives can be ruined by accepting bribes either money or "personal" services. Skip them all and go "steady as she goes" toward retirement and fulfilled life.

Place your family first

This is not easy, and sometimes it comes with an impact on your career. My own example came in 1977 when we as a family were at the U.S. Air Force Academy in Colorado Springs, Colorado. I was working hard in the Political Science Department and had written several books on Northeast Asia and U.S. defense policy. I became particularly active in that field and was asked by the Pentagon Office of ISA (International Security Affairs), to become the "Desk Officer" for Japan. That basically was an offer to be the principal advisor to the Secretary of Defense regarding our affairs with Japan. It was a post that I had prepared for all my career and would have been a real chance to be involved in the policy arena involving Japan. Great! Well, maybe not so great.

I found out when I took that news home over the evening dinner table that one member of the family was not impressed at all—our daughter, Charlene. She was coming up on her senior year in high school and wished to be able to graduate with her friends that she had made since we returned to the Academy from the Fletcher School in the winter of 1973. We basically had a family caucus and decided – as a family—that dad would pass this one up. We all would wait a year and see what was offered then. In the meantime, we would choose a college for Charlene, and that could be factored in as we made the next career move—heading toward the Pentagon.

Well, the folks at ISA were not happy and responded: "don't expect a second offer." Well, no second offer came, but the world did not end. I was assigned to the Pentagon in the War Plans and Mobilization Office and learned some great lessons in the vital importance of logistics and logistics on time. Then it was a tour as the Director of the Office of International Affairs in the Plans Directorate which led to a special relationship with the Secretary of the Air Force, Dr. Hans Mark. Well, a chance to work closely with a brilliant physicist and eventual Deputy Director of NASA was a rewarding assignment. It led to the Associate Dean's position in the National War College, then the Director of Research for the National Defense University, and ultimately the Director of the Institute for National Strategic Studies serving the Secretary of Defense and the Chairman of the Joint Chiefs of Staff. Well, that was okay, and that job led to being recruited by Georgia Tech and ultimately my presidency in Korea. Thanks, Charlene!

And while on the subject of family, there's one more thing that I would like to add here, which in many ways, is related to the years I have spent at SolBridge—and that would be diversity. As I reflect on the experiences that both our children had as they grew up, and I should say Mitchie in her own right, diversity does not come easily. When it does it has a degree of friction like my Headmaster in London knew how to deal with. "Don't mess with the Yank or you'll have me to deal with!" However, the greatness of diversity—the benefits of diversity—deliver unexpected dividends every day. I like to say that diversity is the key to innovation and is the handmaiden of creativity. Basically, it has become the SolBridge brand, a brand that I am most proud to stand behind.

Everyone will develop their own lessons over a lifetime, but if you start out with mine, they will serve as a guide for the first years. Build upon them. Make them your own. They should serve you well on your journey through life.

ACKNOWLEDGMENTS

As I have indicated many times in this account, my marriage to Miss Mitsuyo Kobayashi was one of if not the most wonderful moments of my life, and each day the impact of this union is replayed. Thus, may I acknowledge that I would certainly not be the same person I am today without her influence, guidance, and love. I also need to reiterate the impact of my mother and my sister. Mom sent me off to school every day with the spelling words of the day ringing in my ears. She also taught me the finer arts of eating and enjoying dinner conversations with guests from afar. My sister was, as I said before, "my older brother" and saw that my early troubles with bronchitis did not interfere with my ability to enjoy school. She was always there when I needed advice and help, and her younger brother could have been more considerate when winning the annual Thanksgiving football game with Elder meant so much to her. She cleared the path I walked in so many ways—in school and in life.

Professionally, I owe so much to so many. The many teachers I refer to in the text are only a few who stand out: Miss Slutz at Western Hills, my high school counselor, Mrs. Dorothy Heninger, and the Headmaster at Paddington Technical College High School, Mr. John A. Hullett , who oversaw the transformation of the Yank and knew all the time what he was doing. I would also like to thank my advisor at Ohio State, the great academic, Dr. Harold Zink, who was pushing me all the time to think beyond the norm. And a special shout out to my colleagues in the Ohio State Stadium Dorm where 22 fellows in one big room learned to live together and celebrate differences of race, religion and national origin—are all part of my story.

John E. Endicott

My colleagues in the Air Force and Army—even though for many years they thought they had a Lt. Fuzz on their hands—General Richard Lawrence who bet on an Air Force Ph.D. to run his Institute for National Strategic Studies and Colonel Fred Keiley who ran the National Defense University Press and coached the National War College baseball team.

Serving in the military, especially in a time of war, creates bonds between men (and women) unlike no other time in one's life. Of those "special" people in my life, many of whom have already departed this mortal coil, there are two, who I can never forget: My Army roommate in Nha Trang who did not survive the war in Vietnam and my roommate in Saigon who took to the air early one day not waiting for me, as we had planned, and did not come back.

Colonels Eagle and Beagle who led us through the Cuban Missile Crisis, and Dr. Hans Mark who led the Air Force as Secretary and bonded with a young Colonel—I owe them all debts that cannot be repaid. My friends at the Fletcher School of Law and Diplomacy especially, Dr. Allan B. Cole, my advisor, and Ambassador Hisahiko Okasaki who made possible the research program in Japan as I wrote my dissertation provide memories to now individuals out of reach.

Our lives are touched by so many people, and there are some who open new doors of opportunity. One such person was the President of Georgia Tech, Dr. Pat Crecine who called me to his university to help "internationalize" the institution giving me the chance to begin the Center for International Strategy, Technology, and Policy. And of course, that paved the way for me to come up with the idea of a regional limited nuclear weapons' free zone for peace in Northeast Asia. And a special thanks here for his colleague and at that time Head of the School of Social Sciences at Tech, Dan Papp who led the way through the maze of university politics, as well as our mutual friend Bob Kennedy—plus many more in the 18 years at Georgia Tech. They all made a difference and helped craft the writer who now tries to inadequately thank them.

I must also recognize the many officers, scholars, diplomats and peace activists who became part of the movement to realize a Limited Nuclear Weapons' Free Zone for Northeast Asia: such names as William Clark, John Kelly, Richard Freytag, Generals Shikata, Bunin, Bolaytko, Kim, Lee, Choi, and Admiral Pendley plus Michel Desclaud,

341

Markku Heiskanen, Ravdan Bold, and Dr. Yan from Beijing. All must be honored as many can no longer be thanked. They all worked together in the interest of regional peace and helped earn two Nobel Peace Prize nominations for our work.

Then I must acknowledge those here in South Korea who had faith to hire a Japan specialist with a Japanese wife to lead his university, Dr. Kim Sung-kyung, Chairman of the Board of Woosong Education Foundation. He is closely followed by Dr. Jung Sang-jik, who became my friend and advisor as we together built SolBridge International School of Business into an institution accredited by AACSB with students from 55 nations. Then that cold December night when Dr. Kim called to say the Foundation had agreed on adding a college of Liberal Arts and Social Sciences and naming it Endicott College of International Studies. How do you acknowledge such a debt? These are only the few that I can remember who did so much along the way.

My wife and I treasure many of these names as mutual friends as 2019 marks the 60th anniversary of our wedding. And, of course, our children, Charlene and John II who played and still play that role of human bonding that is essential to any life well lived. Their children, Alexander, Kayleigh, and Nick from our daughter and Jack (actually John Charles) from our son. Their spouses, Greg and Virginia, we are indebted to for providing the right match for our children for a happy and rewarding life—what more can we hope for?

I apologize for only mentioning those above, there have been so many more, but my 83 years have had some impact, and I beg they understand there are limitations as we remember the past. Thank you all. Let me not forget, the editor of this book and my colleague at SolBridge, Jeffrey Miller. Both of us are former Air Force types and speak a very special language, which I hope you saw in this volume.

Special thanks to President Chang Ho-sung from Dankook University and his efforts to award me the Honorary Doctorate in Political Science in February 2019, for the work done to make Northeast Asia a more safe, secure and prosperous region. Such degrees are the way academics recognize their peers; it is the highest honor one academic can receive from another, and for this honor may I publicly thank and his faculty. A similar debt is owed to our friends at the University of Toulouse; a sincere thank-you is more than warranted.

Of course, the work for regional and international peace is never-ending. One of the reasons I undertook the writing of this book is to insure those following learn from our mistakes and ultimately do a better job. With that in mind, good luck to all our readers; when you do make mistakes, let them be new ones. Remember, "perfect is the enemy of the good."

APPENDIX

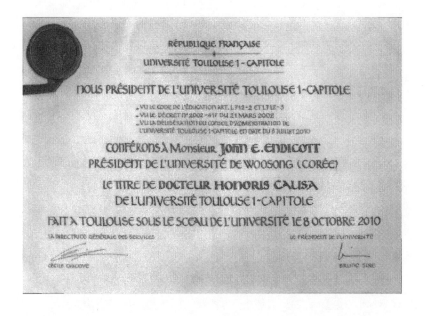

Honorary Degree from Toulouse University

John E. Endicott

명박 제 118호

학 위 기

국적 : 미국

존 엔디컷

1936년 8월 9일생

이 분은 '동북아시아 제한적 비핵지대화' 운동을
통해 세계 평화 증진에 지대한 공헌을 하였기에
본 대학교 대학원위원회의 심의를 거쳐
명예정치학박사 학위를 수여하고자 이에 추천함.

대학원장 정치학박사 안 순 철

위의 추천에 의하여 명예정치학박사 학위를 수여함.

2019년 2월 21일

단국대학교 총장 공학박사 장 호 성

학위번호 : 단국대2018(명박)제3호

Honorary Degree from Dankook University

Dankook University

Upon the recommendation of
the Awarding Committee of the Graduate School
hereby confers on

John C. Endicott

the honorary degree of

Ph. D. in Political Science

with all the honors, rights, and privileges thereto pertaining,
in recognition of his contribution to the enhancement of
world peace through the movement for Limited Nuclear
Weapons-Free Zone in Northeast Asia.

Given at Yongin, Republic of Korea
on the twenty-first day of February, 2019

Sooncheol An, Ph.D.
Dean of the Graduate School

Hosung Chang, Ph.D.
President of Dankook University

Honorary Degree from Dankook University

PLATINUM/SPECIAL LECTURES

One of the pillars of SolBridge has been the school's Platinum/Special Lecture series which brings leaders from business, economics, politics, and education to talk about issues important in today's ever-changing business world.

4/23/2010   Dae-whan Chang, Chairman, *Maeil Economic Daily*: "2010 Super Momentum."

5/10/2010   Tae-young Chung, CEO, Hyundai Card: "The Rule of Game for Finance.

6/7/2010   Suk Kim, President & CEO, Samsung Asset Management: "Samsung's DNA."

9/6/2010   Ahmed Subaey, CEO, S-Oil: "A Successful Global Leader in Making."

10/7/2010   Michael Byung-nam Lee, President, LG Academy: "Markets & Minds."

11/11/2010   Shin-bae Kim, Vice Chairman & CEO, SK C&C: "How to Lead a Fast, Flat, & Smarty World."

3/17/2011   Peter K. Kwak, GM, Nike Sports Korea: "What Makes Nike a Leading Global Brand."

5/3/2011   Chin-wook Cho, Chairman & CEO, BASF Company, Ltd: "My Life, My Career, My Work."

9/6/2011   Sang-chul Lee, CEO, LG U+: "The Opportunities and Challenges of the New ICT Era."

9/22/2011   John D. Johnson, Lieutenant General, Commanding General, Eighth Army: "Leadership for the Future: The Strategic Importance of Korea and the Strength of the Alliance."

10/5/2011   Charm Lee, CEO & President, Korean Tourism Organization: "Korea Tourism Industry."

10/24/2011   Hae-dong Kim, Chairman, HQ of Braun Asia/Pacific: "Destiny: A Result of Judgment or Luck."

11/8/2011   John Walker, Chairman, Macquarie Group of Companies, Korea: "The Macquarie Story."

3/15/2012   Khee-Hong Song, Managing Partner, Deloitte Consulting Korea: "World of Consulting, Its Attraction, and Preparation to be a Consultant."

4/17/2012   Haeng-hee Lee, President & General Manager, Corning Korea: "Leader vs. Leadership."

6/7/2012   Jong-shik Kim, CEO, Tata-Daewoo: "Sustainability of the Tata Group."

6/8/2012   Chong W. Kim, Dean, College of Business, Marshall University: "How to Improve Interpersonal and Organizational Communication."

9/4/2012   Herman Kaess, President, Robert Bosch Korea, Ltd: "From Technology Pioneer to Successful Global Player by Unique Leadership."

5/8/2013   Min-Soon Song, Member of the National Assembly of South Korea & Member of the Foreign Affairs, Trade, and Unification Committee: "Politics of East Asia Including the United States."

5/15/2013   Leslie Bassett, Deputy Chief of Mission, US Embassy: "View from the Embassy."

9/10/2013   Kil-Choo Moon, President, Korea Institute of Science and Technology (KIST): "Time to Share Our Experience."

10/16/2012 Jie-Ae Sohn, CEO, Arirang TV: "The Road to Becoming a Global Leader."

4/10/2014   Donald A. Manzullo, President & CEO, Korean Economic Institute of America: "Reflections on Twenty Years in Congress and US-Korea Relations."

5/15/2014   William "Trey" Freeman, Managing Director/President, AIG Global Real Estate Corporation/AIG Korean Real Estate Development, YH: "Real Estate Development and IFC Seoul."

9/25/2014   Amy Jackson, President, American Chamber of Commerce in Korea (AMCHAM Korea): "Doing Business in Korea."

10/16/2014 Howard Thomas, Dean, Lee Kong Chiang School of Business, Singapore Management University (SMU): "Pathways, Patterns, and Options: My Journey."

10/21/2014 E. Edmund Kim, Professor, Radiological Sciences, University of California at Irvine, USA: "Health & Faith: Can We Conquer a Cancer?"

10/28/2014 Dong-hoon Choi, Adviser, Environmental Energy Service (EES) Korea: "Banker's Trust Company: Its Success & Failure."

3/30/2015   Hee-jung Ahn, Governor, South Chungcheong Province, Republic of Korea: "Powerful 21C: New Ideas & Talents."

4/9/2015   Andrew Dalgleish, Minister-Counsellor & Deputy Head of Mission, British Embassy, Seoul: "The History of the United Kingdom's Relationship with the European Union."

4/29/2015   Seung-Soo Han, Former Prime Minister, Republic of Korea; United Nations: "Air and Water: Are They Free Goods?"

5/20/2015   Bernard "Bernie" Champoux, Lieutenant General, Commanding General, Eighth United States Army: "The Eighth Army: An Enduring Commitment to Stability and Prosperity in the Asia-Pacific Region."

10/8/2015   Xianqin "Lisa" Wallace, Director, Revenue Management and Alliances, Delta Cargo, Delta Airlines: "Logistics: Creating a Global Competitive Advantage."

10/12/2015 David A. Horne, Emeritus Professor of Marketing, College of Business Administration, California State University Long Beach, USA: "Strategy: Your Choice or Theirs."

11/10/2015 Christopher K. Wood, Representative Director & General Manager, Estee Lauder Companies, Korea: "Business Without Borders."

11/16/2015 Frank Schaefers, President, Robert Bosch Korea Ltd: "Leadership in a Time of Change."

12/01/2015 Kun-Mo Chung, 12th and 15th Former Minster, Science and Technology, Republic of Korea: "Nation

John E. Endicott

Building Through Science & Technology: Korean Experience and Vision for the 21st Century."

9/12/2016   Se Young Ahn, Chairman, National Research Council for Economics, Humanities, and Social Sciences: "Asian Miracle Korea: From Rags to Riches."

10/13/2016   Joelle Hivonnet, Deputy Head of Delegation, Minister Counsellor, EU Delegation to the Republic of Korea: "The EU and the Republic of Korea Addressing Global Challenges Together."

11/01/2016   Dan LeClair, Executive Vice President and Chief Strategy and Innovation Officer, AACSB International: "Why Business Education Matters."

11/08/2016   Gita Wijawan, Entrepreneur, Vice President at Goldman Sachs, 2001/President Director at JP Morgan, 2004/Minster of Trade of Indonesia, 2011: "Entrepreneurship in a Changing World."

11/16/2016   Myung-sook Kwan, President, Intel Korea: "Inventing the Future."

3/21/2017   William B. Gartner, Professor, California Lutheran University and Copenhagen Business School: "What do Entrepreneurs do? An Overview of 35 Years of Research on Entrepreneurial Behavior."

4/25/2017   Byung K, Yi, Executive VP & CTO, Interdigital Communication Incorporated: "Fourth Generation Industrial Revolutions: Enabled by the 5th Wireless Communication."

5/16/2017   Woong Park, CEO, Eastspring Asset Management Korea: "Success, Successful Career, and Successful Investment."

5/18/2017   Marc Knapper, Charge d' Affaires, Embassy of the United States of America, Seoul: "Economic Partnership's Key Role in the U.S.—Republic of Korea Alliance."

5/25/2017   Na Kyung Won, Chairperson, Low Birthrate and Aging Society Special Committee, National Assembly, South Korea: "Together We Can!"

9/14/2017   Iain Jamieson, Visa Country Manager, Visa Country Manager for Korea and Mongolia: "Succeeding in Life & Business as a Global Nomad."

3/27/2018   Donald Kirk, Journalist and Author: Covering Asia at War and Peace."

HISTORY OF THE LNWFZ-NEA

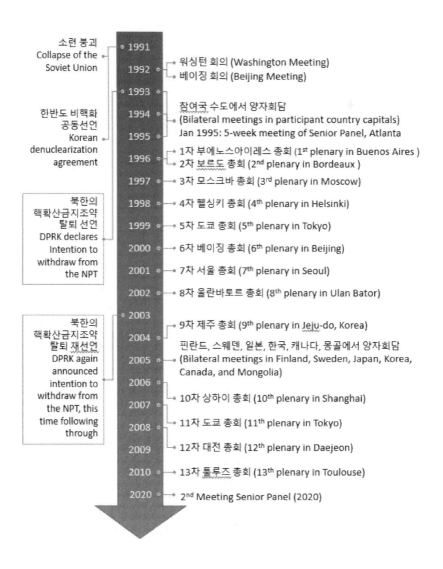

소련 붕괴
Collapse of the
Soviet Union

1991

1992 → 워싱턴 회의 (Washington Meeting)
베이징 회의 (Beijing Meeting)

1993

한반도 비핵화
공동선언
Korean
denuclearization
agreement

1994 참여국 수도에서 양자회담
(Bilateral meetings in participant country capitals)
Jan 1995: 5-week meeting of Senior Panel, Atlanta

1995

1996 → 1차 부에노스아이레스 총회 (1st plenary in Buenos Aires)
2차 보르도 총회 (2nd plenary in Bordeaux)

1997 → 3차 모스크바 총회 (3rd plenary in Moscow)

북한의
핵확산금지조약
탈퇴 선언
DPRK declares
Intention to
withdraw from
the NPT

1998 → 4차 헬싱키 총회 (4th plenary in Helsinki)

1999 → 5차 도쿄 총회 (5th plenary in Tokyo)

2000 → 6차 베이징 총회 (6th plenary in Beijing)

2001 → 7차 서울 총회 (7th plenary in Seoul)

2002 → 8차 울란바토르 총회 (8th plenary in Ulan Bator)

2003

북한의
핵확산금지조약
탈퇴 재선언
DPRK again
announced
intention to
withdraw from
the NPT, this
time following
through

2004 9차 제주 총회 (9th plenary in Jeju-do, Korea)

핀란드, 스웨덴, 일본, 한국, 캐나다, 몽골에서 양자회담
(Bilateral meetings in Finland, Sweden, Japan, Korea,
Canada, and Mongolia)

2005

2006

2007 → 10차 상하이 총회 (10th plenary in Shanghai)

2008 → 11차 도쿄 총회 (11th plenary in Tokyo)

2009 → 12차 대전 총회 (12th plenary in Daejeon)

2010 → 13차 툴루즈 총회 (13th plenary in Toulouse)

2020 → 2nd Meeting Senior Panel (2020)

Keynote Address
International Seminar
Arms Race and Nuclear Developments in South Asia
By
Professor John E. Endicott
South Asia and the Second Nuclear Age
21 April 2004

Conference Organized by the Islamabad Policy Research
Institute
In Collaboration with The Hanns Seidel Foundation
South Asia and the Second Nuclear Age
Islamabad, Pakistan

It was with great pleasure and humility that I accepted the invitation to take part in this vital seminar that is featuring specialists from Pakistan, India, and other involved states. As many in this audience know, I have now spent some 45 years of my professional life involved in the study of Asian affairs—and almost that long participating in the debates, both inside and outside of government, regarding the employment and then the control of nuclear weapons.

It is also my great pleasure to return to Islamabad after more than twenty years. In 1982 as Associate Dean of the National War College in Washington, D.C., and as a Colonel in the Air Force, I led a two-week trip of a dozen senior military and government civilian students to Pakistan and India. On that occasion, we had the opportunity to visit Karachi, Islamabad, Peshawar, Lahore, New Delhi, Mumbai, and Agra. It was only a glimpse into this remarkable region, but it signaled a very real moment in the development of all of us who took part.

John E. Endicott

It was during that trip that I met Dr. Imtiaz Bokhari, now Vice President of IPRI. May I recognize publicly our decades-long friendship developed as we jointly tried to understand the official policies of our respective governments. Also in the audience is Major General Nawaz Chaudry, also a dear friend, who as a Brigadier and Military Attaché participated in the very first class of international military officers to attend the U.S. National Defense University.

To all gathered here, I reiterate the great honor I feel in having this opportunity to take part in this meeting. To all here from South Asia, especially Pakistan and India, I want to thank you for individually accepting the challenge to work for peace in South Asia. For all my colleagues not from South Asia, I gratefully join you in sharing our experiences with our friends from the vast sub-continent. During my brief time with you, I hope to share some of my personal experiences as a nuclear weapons targeting officer in the U.S. Air Force; comment about Paul Bracken's work on the 2nd Nuclear Age; describe briefly what we have been doing in Northeast Asia to create a new regional security infrastructure; and suggest some ideas for organizing for this 2nd Nuclear Age. In this final respect, I hope to have general comments and some specific to the situation in South Asia.

Not that many years ago, it really seems almost like yesterday, my boss, an Air Force two-star, came into our room in the underground of SAC Headquarters and looked around with some authority. All was ready. He turned to us and said, as best I can remember, "We have some time, why don't you call your loved one and say goodbye. But don't let on why you are calling!" My wife can still remember that call. Call it a woman's intuition, but we both remember that day as clear as a bell.

I was an Air Force Captain working in the underground planning bunker of the Joint Strategic Target Planning Staff, the group responsible for the Single Integrated Operations Plan for the U.S. military—the nuclear war plan, and it was October 1962. The world stood on the brink of the first nuclear exchange in history. SAC was sealed; aircraft were on airborne alert; all "hanger queens" aircraft that were in for repairs but still flyable were brought to operational status; headquarters based qualified flight crews were relieved of administrative duties and assigned targets; and the great military establishment with SIOP responsibilities be they Air Force or Navy

355

stood as one giant bow, pulled back to the point of release—the detent point in French—waiting for the command to fire.

Fortunately, the command did not come. The airborne alert was reduced, and all eventually returned to normal—perhaps DEFCON Five. In the aftermath, we learned that President Kennedy was pleased with the response of his military, but that General Lemay was not. We also learned from later exchanges between senior Russian and American participants how well prepared Soviet forces on Cuba were. We indeed dodged a bullet, or to continue with the metaphor, an arrow that would have eliminated most of western civilization as we know it.

Paul Bracken, in his book *Fire in the East: The Rise of Asian Military Power and the Second Nuclear Age*, notes that we have indeed entered the Second Nuclear Age.[38] The first lasted from 1947 to 1991. But it was the period 1947-1967 that was the most dangerous. Certainly, I would agree. He argues that deterrence did work during this early stage, but it was marked by some very close calls—Berlin, Panmunjom, Taiwan, Beirut, and Cuba. Ultimately, after the Cuban Missile Crisis, both sides realized the magnitude of an error and began the steady process toward developing the restraining infrastructures that made the period from 1968 to 1991 so much more predictable.

Certainly, the number of nuclear weapons reached much higher levels in the latter part of the First Nuclear Age. Vertical proliferation reached astounding levels with 125,000 warheads and more coming on the scene just from the U.S. and the Soviet Union. (The U.S. produced approximately 70,000 and the USSR 55,000.) But because of the arms control and eventual arms reductions efforts, the relationships between especially the U.S. and the Soviet Union were stable. Possibly, India and Pakistan have just passed their most unstable period. Perhaps, with the inevitable impact of cricket diplomacy, and the results of the current bilateral dialogs, a growing infrastructure of restraints will evolve into a mature deterrent system that will reflect stability and the prospects for enhanced confidence-building measures.

(By the way, when I speak of cricket, may I explain that I spent my freshman year of high school in England in 1950. There, I was the

---

[38] Paul Bracken, *Fire in the East: The Rise of Asian Military Power and the Second Nuclear Age* (New York, N.Y.: Harper Collins Publishers, 1999).

wicketkeeper for Faraday House, one of the four houses in my school. I'm one of the few Americans who actually knows what a silly short leg is.)

Bracken's thesis in his book stresses that the non-proliferation regime that was put in place in 1968 was remarkably successful. Most experts believed we would have 25 proliferators by the 1970s. He notes that the first "outlaw bomb" was the Indian test in 1974, that is unless you count the Israeli capability which he puts as being realized in 1969. While these did occur along with South Africa, it was the May 1998 events that he marks as actually ending the First Nuclear Age. The nuclear age marked by a competition between two superpowers was replaced by a nuclear age which "seemed to emerge out of a hodgepodge of unrelated regional issues."[39] Please hold this thought, as I wish to return to it later in my presentation.

Other characteristics of this 2nd Nuclear Age were identified as: an era less Eurocentric in nature; more nationalistic—in fact, reflecting "national insecurities that are not comprehensible to outsiders whose security is not endangered"[40] with very intense almost hysterical nationalism being involved. He sees a kind of nuclear deterrence existing where decisions are made involving rage and religious hatreds negating the western experience. He contends Nuclear warfare during the First Nuclear Age, between the U.S. and USSR was approached with a certain "detachment and rationality."

(May I disagree somewhat here. I would agree that among professionals, there was no hate, no invective toward our Soviet adversaries. We, as professionals, were going to do our job. Later, several years after the fall of the Soviet Union in one of our meetings with active and retired military officers from Northeast Asia, a Russian general noted that there now existed hatred toward the U.S. among his troops. This may have moderated to some extent in recent years after 9/11, but is still open to question. But, if Bracken is trying to imply that there was no invective, no hate during the U.S.-Soviet competition, I would like to remind him of John Foster Dulles, Senator Joseph McCarthy and the members of the John Birch Society. One of the most unforgettable examples of this kind of disruptive rhetoric was

---

[39] Ibid., p. 110.
[40] Ibid., p. 111.

Dulles' 1952 *Life* magazine article entitled "A Policy of Boldness." In this scathing criticism of the Soviet Union, Dulles writes about the moral law that exists in the world that sets out clearly right and wrong. "This law has been trampled by the Soviet rulers, and for that violation, they can and should be made to pay."[41])

Bracken opines, however, that the western model is certainly less than satisfactory as we chart a new course into a 21st Century non-proliferation regime. To complicate matters further, his last common characteristic for new nuclear weapon states focuses on their relative poverty.

All this introductory data on Paul Bracken's work is to set the stage and to indicate my general agreement. I do agree that we have entered a 2nd Nuclear Age and I stated that in a June 1998 speech which marked my recovery from a triple bypass operation. Quoting Rebecca Johnson of Disarmament Diplomacy, I noted: "Rather than berate India and Pakistan, the Permanent Five need to work collectively to remove the basis for insecurity in South Asia, but as we know, this is also part of the problem. Regional conflict resolution needs to be initiated, as well as bilateral agreements for insuring stability, coupled with an overhaul of the entire worldwide non-proliferation regime."

I firmly believe that our answers to a new regime for the 2nd Nuclear Age must be based on responsible and able regional groupings—associations that can address regional security issues with a familiarity and commitment unmatched by globally oriented institutions. To make my case clear, permit me to draw on the experiences we have had in Northeast Asia as we have tried to realize a Limited Nuclear Weapons' Free Zone for that region. When I speak of "we" in this case, I refer to the Center for International Strategy, Technology, and Policy which I founded in 1990 at Georgia Tech after 31 years in government—28 in the Air Force and three as a senior civilian directing the Institute for National Strategic Studies in Washington, D.C.

---

[41] Townsend Hoopes, *The Devil and John Foster Dulles* (Boston, Mass.: Little, Brown and Company, 1973), p. 127. The *Life* magazine article appeared 19 May 1952 on pages 146-157.

When the DPRK and ROK governments agreed to a non-aggression pact and to denuclearize the peninsula in 1991, as a Northeast Asian specialist, I applauded the progress but believed that such a bilateral agreement must be buttressed by a regional agreement involving all the neighboring states. I believed the best vehicle to get such reinforcement would be through a nuclear weapons-free zone that would have a secretariat, an inspection structure, and an agency for dealing with the questions that would inevitably arise and need rapid attention.

I came up with a simple initial design that was a circle 1200nm in radius centered on the DMZ in Korea. My first thoughts were to ban all nuclear weapons activity from the area but took pains to insure the Russians could maintain their nuclear bastion in the Sea of Okhotsk. I took fewer pains to moderate the impact on China's deployed resources and paid for that later. In February 1992, I traveled to Washington, where the concept was vetted among 24 top members of the Executive Department—remember I am a retired Colonel and want to keep my retirement. After a vigorous four-hour exchange, I was given the go-ahead that basically recognized that perhaps there was an opening window of opportunity and if Endicott wanted to make a fool of himself, he would not be prevented.

The first presentation to an international body was at a conference we co-sponsored in Beijing the next month—March of 1992. Seventy-five participants from all the states of NEA including North and South Korea, Mongolia, China, Japan, Canada, Hong Kong, Russia, and the U.S. heard the presentation, and all but one country were positively excited. The one delegation unhappy with the idea was that of the PRC. I had stepped on 60% of their deployed assets, and it was not a pretty scene. Discouraged but not undaunted, we followed that meeting with a trilateral in Atlanta the next March between unofficial representatives from China, Japan, and the U.S. To my astonishment the Chinese delegation presented a common and united front—this time in favor of "positive consideration" of the concept. A week later, my joy soon gave way to a realization that the DPRK was about to leave the NPT. No one in NEA wanted a North Korea with nuclear arms, including China.

The next few years were filled with trips to all the capitals of the states of NEA, and discussions with Ministries of Defense and Foreign

Affairs. That is, except for the DPRK, I kept in touch with them through their officials at the United Nations. In January 1995, I called together five general-level officers to work on a basic draft agreement. A General from the ROK, a Lt. General from Japan, Major Generals from Russia and China and myself made up the invited Senior Panel. We met for five difficult weeks that were marked by almost as much disagreement as agreement. However, what finally emerged was a consensus document that called for a limited nuclear weapons-free zone in NEA. A total ban in the area was unrealistic, and this group of seasoned pragmatists agreed that the perfect is the enemy of the good (an old Russian saying). Only tactical weapons would be banned; the area included in the ban would have to include some American territory and not so much Chinese. The heart of the agreement was the establishment of a regional agency charged with inspectorate duties as well as overall administrative responsibilities. The concept was an endorsement of starting small, so at least a beginning could be made. As a group, we took our final product to Washington, D.C., New York, Boston, and San Francisco and collectively, as a team, briefed the arms control community and other interested parties.

Once that was accomplished, we began to expand the number and type of participants to include retired diplomats, scientists, academics, and peace activists. This ever-increasing group met first in Buenos Aires, then Bordeaux, and over the next seven years in Moscow, Helsinki, Beijing, Tokyo, Seoul, and Ulaanbaatar for plenary meetings and Shanghai and Vancouver for planning sessions. At each meeting, some new development or refinement was added to the formulation that represented the maturation of the idea and reflected the growing willingness by all parties to improve the product.

It went forward in the face of determined opposition by the U.S. arms control community that doggedly opposed any multilateral treatment of the issue with so many verification problems. The issue was to be solved in a bilateral context and in terms of a dogma that was not subject to review. Some other sectors of the U.S. government, however, appreciated what we were attempting and we went forward. By the Helsinki meeting, we had incorporated official observers into the meetings, so all ideas—good and bad—got back to the respective governments. Mongolia was added to our talks as they had much to provide with their past experience and present nuclear-free status.

While we can not claim victory yet, we can point to the on-going six-party talks and see many of the items we struggled over in our almost ten-year process of keeping an idea alive. We all would prefer to see Mongolia join in the talks as it has distinct ties to North Korea its government and its people. The endorsement of a nuclear-free peninsula; the need for an on-going security forum; and ultimately the need to resolve the issue regionally and not bilaterally have been embraced. However, it was the joint development or formulation of a concept from the very beginning to its present state that we take the greatest pride. The appreciation of each member's particular security situation was fundamental to the progress that was made. It is clear that it is with the full participation of the states of the region involved when meaningful progress can be made.

With a draft, treaty agreed to by participants at our Ulaan Baatar meeting in 2002, the members of the LNWFZ-NEA look forward to our next plenary meeting to be held in Cheju-do, ROK this coming summer. There we will review the progress made by the Track I Six-Party Talks and consider the question of the need of a continuing Track II effort in the face of such massive official involvement. Whatever the results of our meeting in Cheju-do, the lesson to me from the experiences that span more than the past decade point to a new non-proliferation regime that is based on regional sub-systems, not a global infrastructure driven by central concerns often out of touch with the security realities of specific regional interests. In this sense, I believe you can already tell where I am heading. It is time to create a non-proliferation system for the 2nd Nuclear Age that addresses specifically the needs of the regional hot spots of the world.

Ultimately, states will resort to nuclear weapons when their own security interests cannot be met by alliances and global reassurances. Until we address such fundamental security concerns, how can we expect to stem the tide of proliferation? When college students can find weapons design information on the web it seems imperative we move beyond the temporary expedient of trying to stop the flow of technology, in fact, trying to stop the flow of science itself. This is, to put it very clearly, a vain endeavor.

Recently, the U.S. government announced a program of new measures to counter the threat of weapons of mass destruction. In fact, President George W. Bush introduced this initiative on February 11,

2004, in a speech at the National Defense University—my old stamping ground[42]. It was, in a sense, part of the new pragmatism that has been evinced by the U.S. since the events of 9/11. All here in this room, recall the startling reversal of U.S. policy after that fateful day. Sanctions placed on both Pakistan and India in 1998 were lifted by a nation sadly made aware of the complexities of our new age.

In the February address, President Bush outlined seven steps to "strengthen the world's efforts to stop the spread of deadly weapons."[43] The President called for expanding the Proliferation Security Initiative to encompass law enforcement; strengthen laws for international control; expand Nunn-Lugar-type support for former Soviet states; banning enrichment and reprocessing functions from states not now possessing them; making the Additional Protocol for inspection mandatory to import equipment for civilian nuclear programs, create a special IAEA committee to stress safeguards and verification, and finally preventing countries under investigation for violation of non-proliferation obligations from serving on the IAEA Board of Governors. I applaud this interest in addressing some of the symptoms of our disease but would prefer we begin to address the causes themselves.

Indeed, some of the above recommendations seem to significantly impinge on the specific guarantees of Article IV of the NPT, especially paragraph 2 of that article that loosely states that all parties will facilitate the "fullest possible exchange of equipment, materials and scientific and technological information for the peaceful uses of nuclear energy." I would prefer an acknowledgment of the 2005 NPT Review Conference, and the need to address such issues in the forum precisely for such modifications to treaty obligations.

Thus, we have come to a realization that the current system is need of some repair—indeed overhaul—what might be used to address the extreme variances we face in today's international security system? Can we look at regional nuclear-free zones? Why should we

---

[42] President George W. Bush, "Remarks by the President on Weapons of Mass Destruction Proliferation," Fort Lesley J. McNair—National Defense University, Washington, D.C., 11 February 2004. http//www.whitehouse.gov/news/release/2004/02/20040211-4.html

[43] Ibid., pp. 5-6.

call them nuclear-free zones when they probably will not be? Should we look again at Article VII which states: "Nothing in this Treaty affects the right of any group of States to conclude regional treaties to assure the total absence of nuclear weapons in their respective territories." Are we not caught in the perfect is the enemy of the good dilemma again. Why should we be calling for the total absence of nuclear weapons when weapons already exist, and the formation of regional security organizations could ultimately lead to a total absence and regional understanding.

These regional organizations could function as joint command centers for the exchange of critical information at the time of high crisis or tensions among member states. They could also serve as valuable points of information exchange about NGOs operating within the area, but not sanctioned by any official body. As far as South Asia is concerned, the sharing of correct information is crucial, and the mistaken interpretation of available data almost led to an outbreak of hostilities in 1987 between Pakistan and India. What was an exercise, almost became an operation.

You can see where I am going. The regional institutions created should have ongoing responsibilities. They should not be debating societies that meet quarterly but should be preferred assignments for the best military personnel in the region. They should be in operation 24 hours a day and possess the best communications equipment available. Ultimately those assigned to these centers would represent their countries, but at the same time would begin to function as a team.

The new organization for the 2nd Nuclear Age should have no outliers. The regime should be universal in scope allowing all the existing nuclear-free zones to interact with IAEA and the Security Council. From where I sit, it should include additional regional organizations: Northeast Asia, South Asia, and the Middle East. Just as in the experience of the international community, the League of Nations gave way to the United Nations, and in our own experience the Articles of Confederation gave way to the Constitution, the NPT needs to be fashioned anew to meet the requirements of a new day and a new age. The Permanent Five collectively must recognize that the world did not stand still after July 1968. The fundamental requirement of a successful international security system is the need to adjust to change—to face realities—even though they may not be pleasant.

There certainly are more than five nuclear powers in the world today. The need for plentiful peaceful nuclear power in the years ahead will become painfully clear as we progress deeper into the 21st Century.

The NPT, as one of the successful instruments of the Cold War, now needs to be modified to reflect our changed international environment. Of course, while we are at it, let's not forget Article VI and the commitment to nuclear disarmament. The Permanent Five need to invite all nuclear powers to review just where we are in the principal normative goal of the entire Treaty. Let us take on the overhaul of the non-proliferation system with a resolve of immediacy which it deserves. Perhaps after the NPT, let's get serious about the UN Security Council—failure to adjust to changed realities cost the world dearly in the 20th Century. Let us not fail to meet this exciting challenge for a future nearly nuclear weapons-free.

In the few moments remaining, permit me to make an observation about the situation as it specifically relates to South Asia. In the last several months, we have seen encouraging progress in a meaningful dialog between the leaders of India and Pakistan. In fact, our meeting here over the last two days is only the latest manifestation of a regional rapprochement that has the world at last paying attention to this incredibly important area. At the same time developments in the modernization of the arms of both states have also occurred. We have seen the testing of the Shaheen 2 and the Prithvi missiles, and we have observed the granting of "Non-NATO" status to Pakistan in the past month[44]. As a one time military person, I can understand the desire for the latest and best technology possible by both military services, and the need for testing in the open; I can also see the need to aid especially the forces of a nation so committed to the campaign against the al-Qaeda network so entrenched in neighboring Afghanistan.

The concern we all have with offensive capabilities is the need for adequate, no permit me to say, accurate information on the state of both militaries. I recall when the events of May 1998 were fresh on everyone's minds, Senator Sam Nunn, the person after whom our school is named, fearing that misinformation, disinformation, or incorrect information on the status of the Indian or Pakistani forces could lead to an unintended disaster, recommended that Russia and

---

[44] "U.S. to give Pakistan easier access to arms," *The Japan Times*, 19 March 2004, p. 4.

the U.S. provide real-time data derived from our space resources to both states. In that same vein, I would like to draw your attention to the Phalcon airborne warning and control system that recently was sold to India by Israel[45]. Mounted in the Russian made IL-76 medium-range transport aircraft this system reportedly can simultaneously track up to 60 targets over a 700-800-km circle—supporting defensive and offensive operations.

Is it possible to begin discussions that would consider inviting Pakistani participation onboard airborne Phalcon systems, or Pakistani involvement in the ground-based processing of Phalcon-derived data? Adopting some variant of this idea could demonstrate an unparalleled degree of transparency and guarantee in the least, that hostilities would not be based on mistaken interpretations of partial intelligence. It would also seem appropriate in this kind of venture to seek funding support from Nunn-Lugar-like set-asides for regional security-based groupings. These are just the thoughts of an outsider. I am sure the defense communities of India and Pakistan will come up with better and more feasible answers to the challenges of living side-by-side in the 2nd Nuclear Age. Just let me say it has been an honor to share these thoughts with you, and participate in this important occasion. It is my greatest hope to see the United States as your partner for peace in South Asia. Thank you for this opportunity to address this body.

---

[45] "India, Israel ink the Phalcon deal," *rediff.com*, 5 March 2004.
http://ushome.rediff.com/news/2004/mar/05phal.htm

OTHER WORKS BY THE AUTHOR

Authored Books:

Japan's Nuclear Option: Political, Technical, and Strategic Factors,
New York, Praeger Publishers, 1975.

Co-authored Books:

The Politics of East Asia: China, Japan, Korea, with William R. Heaton,
Westview Press, 1978.
U.S. Foreign Policy: History, Process, and Policy, with Daniel S. Papp and
Loch Johnson, Pearson Publishers, 2005.
Regional Security Policy, with Patrick Garrity and Richard Goetze,
Institute of Higher Defense Studies, National Defense university,
1991.

Co-edited and Contributed to:

American Defense Policy, 4th Edition, with Roy Stafford, The Johns
Hopkins University Press, 1977.

In addition, I have written many articles in American and Korean
scholarly publications, as well as monthly contributions to Korean
news publications since 2007.

RECOMMENDED READING

Cold War

Beschloss, Michaek R. *The Crisis Year: Kennedy and Khrushchev, 1960-1963*. New York: Harper Collins, 1991.

Caro, Robert A. *The Years of Lyndon Johnson*. Vol. 2, *Means of Ascent*. New York: Alfred A. Knopf, 1990.

———. *The Years of Lyndon Johnson*. Vol. 4, *The Passage of Power*. New York: Alfred A. Knopf, 2012.

Chace, James. *Acheson: The Secretary of State Who Created the Modern World*. New York: Simon and Schuster, 1998.

Cheevers, Jack. *Act of War: Lyndon Johnson, North Korea, and the Capture of the Spy Ship Pueblo*. New York: Penguin, 2014.

Dobbs, Michael. *One Minute to Midnight: Kennedy, Khrushchev, and Castro on the Brink of Nuclear War*. New York: Alfred A. Knopf, 2008.

Gaddis, John Lewis. *The Cold War: A New History*. London: Penguin, 2005.

———. *We Now Know: Rethinking Cold War History*. New York: Oxford University Press, 1997.

Harbutt, Fraser J. *The Cold War Era*. London: John Wiley and Sons, 2002.

Lerner, Mitchell B. *The Pueblo Incident: A Spy Ship and the Failure of American Foreign Policy*. Lawrence, KS: University Press of Kansas, 2002.

Mobley, Richard A., *Flashpoint North Korea: The Pueblo and EC-121 Crises*. Annapolis: Naval Institute Press, 2003.

Smith, Jean Edward. *Eisenhower in War and Peace*. New York: Random House, 2013.

Stern, Sheldon. *The Cuban Missile Crisis in American Memory: Myths versus Reality*. Palo Alto, CA: Stanford University Press, 2012.

Thomas, Daniel C. *The Helsinki Effect: International Norms, Human Rights, and the Demise of Communism*. Princeton: Princeton University Press, 2001.

Northeast Asia

Armstrong, Charles, Gilbert Rozman, Samuel Kim, and Stephen Kotkin (eds.). *Korea at the Center: Dynamics of Regionalism in Northeast Asia*. New York: M. E. Sharpe, 2006.
Calder, Kent E., and Min Ye. *The Making of Northeast Asia*. Stanford: Stanford University Press, 2010.
Chen, Jian. *Mao's China and the Cold War*. Chapel Hill: University of North Carolina Press, 2001.
Cho, Lee Jae (ed.). *A Vision for Economic Cooperation in East Asia: China, Japan, and Korea*. Seoul: Korea Development Institute, 2004.
Chung, Jae-ho. *Between Ally and Partner: Korea-China Relations and the United States*. New York: Columbia University Press, 2006.
Cohen, Warren I. *East Asia at the Center: Four Thousand Years of Engagement with the World*. New York: Columbia University Press, 2001.
Ebrey, Patricia Buckley, Anne Walthall, and James B. Palais. *East Asia: A Cultural, Social, and Political History*. Boston: Houghton Mifflin, 2006.
Garver, John W. *The Sino-American Alliance: Nationalist China and America's Cold War Strategy in Asia*. Armonk, NY: M.E. Sharpe, 1997.
Miller, John H. *Modern East Asia: An Introductory History*. Armonk, NY: Me. E. Sharpe, 2008.

North Korea

Armstrong, Charles. *The North Korean Revolution, 1945-1950*. Ithaca, NY: Cornell University Press, 2004.
Cha, Victor. *The Impossible State: North Korea, Past and Future*. New York: Harper Collins, 2013.
Harden, Blaine. *Escape from Camp 14: One Man's Remarkable Odyssey from North Korea to Freedom in the West*. New York. Viking Penguin, 2012.
Ishikawa, Masaji. *A River in Darkness: One Man's Escape from North Korea*. Seattle, WA: Amazon Crossing, 2017.
Martin, Bradley. *Under the Loving Care of the Fatherly Leader: North Korea and the Kim Dynasty*. New York: St. Martin's, 2006.

John E. Endicott

Myers, B.R. *The Cleanest Race: How North Koreans See Themselves and Why It Matters*. New York: Melville House, 2010.

Tudor, Daniel and James Pearson. *North Korea Confidential: Private Markets, Fashion Trends, Prison Camps, Dissenters and Defectors*. Rutland VT: Tuttle Publishing, 2015.

Nuclear Weapons

Anderson, Martin, and Annelise Anderson. *Reagan's Secret War: The Untold Story of His Fight to Save the World from Nuclear Disaster*. New York: Crown Publishers, 2009.

Bird, Kai and Martin J. Sherwin. *American Prometheus: The Triumph and Tragedy of J. Robert Oppenheimer*. New York: Vintage Books, 2006.

Bernstein, Jeremy. *Plutonium: A History of the World's Most Dangerous Element*. Washington DC: Joseph Henry Press, 2007.

Bundy, McGeorge. *Danger and Survival: Choices About the Bomb in the First Fifty Years*. New York: Random House, 1988.

Cirincione, Joseph. *Bomb Scare: The History & Future of Nuclear Weapons*. New York: Columbia University Press, 2007.

Freedman, Lawrence. *The Evolution of Nuclear Strategy*. New York: Palgrave Macmillan, 2003.

Iklé, Fred Charles. *The Social Impact of Bomb Destruction*. Norman OK: University of Oklahoma Press, 1958.

Moore, Richard. *Nuclear Illusion, Nuclear Reality: Britain, the United States, and Nuclear Weapons, 1958-64*. New York: Palgrave Macmillan, 2010.

Rhodes, Richard. *The Making of the Atomic Bomb*. New York: Simon and Schuster, 1986.

———. *The Dark Sun: The Making of the Hydrogen Bomb*. New York: Simon and Schuster, 1995.

Rosenbaum, Ron. *How the End Begins: The Road to a Nuclear World War III*. New York: Simon and Schuster, 2011.

Schlosser, Eric. *Command and Control: Nuclear Weapons, the Damascus Accident, and the Illusion of Safety*. New York: Penguin Books, 2013.

Shambroom, Paul. *Face to Face with the Bomb: Nuclear Reality after the Cold War*. Baltimore, MD: Johns Hopkins University Press. 2003.

Sokolski, Henry D., ed. *Getting MAD: Nuclear Mutual Assured Destruction, Its origins and Practice*. Carlisle, PA: Strategic Studies Institute, U.S. Army War College, 2004.

South Korea

Bracht, Mary Lynn. *White Chrysanthemum*. London: Penguin, 2018.

Brazinsky, Gregg. *Nation Building in South Korea: Koreans, Americans, and the Making of a Democracy*. Chapel Hill: The University of North Carolina Press, 2007.

Breen, Michael. *The New Koreans: The Story of a Nation*. New York, St. Martin's Press, 2017.

Clifford, Mark L. *Troubled Tiger: Businessmen, Bureaucrats, and Generals in South Korea*. Armonk, NY: M.E. Sharpe, 1993.

Fehrenbach, T.R. *This Kind of War*. Washington, DC: Potomac Books, 2001.

Gleysteen Jr., William H. *Massive Entanglement, Marginal Influence: Carter and Korea in Crisis*. Washington, DC: Brookings Institution Press, 1999.

Gregg, Donald. *Pot Shards: Fragments of a Life Lived in the CIA, the White House, and the Two Koreas*. Washington, DC: New Academia Publishing, 2014.

Halberstam, David. *The Coldest Winter: America and the Korean War*. New York: Hyperion, 2007.

Hastings, Max. *The Korean War*. New York: Simon & Schuster, 1988.

Kirk, Donald. *Korea Betrayed: Kim Dae Jung and Sunshine*. New York: Palgrave Macmillan, 2009.

———. *The Korean Crisis: Unraveling the Miracle in the IMF Era*. New York: Palgrave Macmillan, 2000.

———. *Korean Dynasty: Hyundai and Chung Ju Yung*. London: Routledge, 1995.

Lee, Min Jin. *Pachinko*. New York: Hachette Book Group, 2017.

Miller, Jeffrey. *War Remains*. Daejeon: Rockwell Road Books, 2010.

Nahm, Andrew C. *Korea: Tradition and Transformation*. Seoul: Hollym, 1988.

Oberdorfer, Don and Robert Carlin. *The Two Koreas: A Contemporary History*. New York: Basic Books, 2013.

SaKong, Il, and Young-sun Koh (eds.). *The Korean Economy: Six Decades of Growth and Development*. Seoul: Korea Development Institute, 2010.

Stueck, William. *The Korean War: An International History*. Princeton, Princeton University Press, 1995.

———. *Rethinking the Korean War: A New Diplomatic and Military History*. Princeton: Princeton University Press, 2002.

John E. Endicott

Wickham, John. *Korea on the Brink: From the "12/12 Incident" to the Kwangju Uprising, 1979-1980.* Washington DC: National Defense University Press, 1999.
Winchester, Simon, *Korea: A Walk Through the Land of Miracles.* New York: Harper Perennial, 2005.
Young, James V. Eye on Korea: *An Insider Account of Korean American Relations.* College Station, TX: Texas A&M University Press, 2003.

Vietnam War

Goodwin, Doris Kearns. *Lyndon Johnson and the American Dream.* New York: St. Martin's Griffin, 1991.
Goscha, Christopher. *Vietnam: A New History.* New York: Basic Books, 2016.
Halberstam, David. *The Best and the Brightest.* New York, Random House, 1969.
Karnow, Stanley. *Vietnam: A History.* New York: Viking, 1983.
Oberdorfer, Don. *Tet! The Turning Point in the Vietnam War.* Baltimore: John Hopkins University Press, 2001.
Sheehan, Neil, *A Bright Shining Lie: John Paul Vann and America in Vietnam.* New York: Random House, 1988.

Index

(SDS)
SolHeim Guest House, 214
Toward a "Neighborhood Asia",
    193, 194
Songdo, 164
Sorge, Richard, 138, 150
South Korea, 6, 17, 18, 23, 52, 67,
    73, 75, 87, 91, 114-115, 119, 121,
    125, 140-141, 146-148, 153, 163-
    164, 166-167, 169-172, 174, 175,
    176, 179, 181, 186, 190-191, 195,
    198-199, 201, 205, 209, 210-212,
    215-216, 221, 223-224, 226, 228,
    230, 233-234, 236-237, 240, 242-
    244, 246, 255-257, 268, 276-278,
    283-284, 288, 290-293, 295-296,
    298, 301, 304, 306, 309, 311, 314-
    317, 319, 320, 322, 324, 326, 328,
    342
Sputnik, 275
St. Paul's Cathedral, 21
St. Petersburg, 272
St. William Avenue, 15, 17
St. William Catholic Church, 10
Strategic Air Command (SAC), 53,
    54, 57, 58, 71, 113, 184, 260, 263,
    265-268, 296, 308
Strategic Defense Initiative, 96, 291
Sun Joun-yung, 259, 262
Sun Tzu, 35, 75
Surrey Research Park, 317
Tachikawa, Japan, 44, 69
Taepodong 1 Missile, 134
Taepyongdong, 174, 242
Taft, Robert A., 17, 31, 294
Taft, William Howard, 13
Takachi, Tomonari, 287
Tan Son Nhut Air Base, 66
Tang Dynasty, 167
Tata Services, 202
Teachers' Day, 242

Terasaki, Osamu, 197
Thailand, 257
The 1996 Olympics, 108, 135
The Atlanta Journal-Constitution, 153
The *Bordeaux Protocol*, 125, 126
*The Fog of War: Eleven Lessons from the
    Life of Robert S. McNamara*, 92
The Godfather, 163
The Helsinki Process, 128
The Making of Northeast Asia, 235
The McKinsey Study, 289, 291
The Ozaki Foundation, 220
The Patriot, 92
Theater High Altitude Air Defense
    System (THAAD), 324
Thomas, Lowell, 7, 13, 17
Tiger Division, 67
Tokugawa *Bakufu*, 45
Tokyo, 15, 45, 46, 48, 49, 51, 71, 72,
    76, 113, 129, 130, 164, 170, 172,
    173, 174, 187, 212, 220, 235, 256,
    263, 287, 296, 299, 302, 303, 315,
    335, 360
Tokyo Union Church, 46, 50
Toulouse, 229, 246, 299
Training and Doctrine Command
    (TRADOC), 329
Transforming Higher Education
    Institutions: A Balanced
    Development, 322
Trapnell, Jerry, 302, 306, 308
Treaty of Reconciliation and
    Nonaggression, 114
Treaty of Tlatelolco, 124, 297
Tsinghua University, 180, 317
Tsukuba Science City, 317
Tsushima, 224
Tuft's University, 307
Turkey, 56
Turner College of Business, 301, 309
24th Infantry Division, 331

ABOUT THE EDITOR

Jeffrey Miller has spent three decades in Asia as a university lecturer, writer, and journalist. Originally from LaSalle, Illinois, he relocated to South Korea in 1990 where he nurtured a love for spicy Korean food, Buddhist temples, and East Asian History.

Currently an Assistant Professor of English and History at SolBridge International School of Business, he is the author of ten books including *War Remains a Korean War Novel, Ice Cream Headache, The Panama Affair,* and *Bureau 39.*

Made in the USA
Middletown, DE
20 February 2021